"Tim Keel writes with the eye of ᵢ .... tor, the mind of a philosopher, aᵢ .... ₒᵢ a visionary. His intuitions will inspire your own, and his voice will add so much to the conversation about what is emerging in our lives, churches, and world."

Brian McLaren, author/speaker (brianmclaren.net)

"Tim Keel has written a fascinating and engaging book that will quickly become both a starting point and a standard bearer for thinking about leadership in the emerging church. In addition to reimagining the nature of leadership, it also offers an implicit and enticing portrait of the type of community that will be formed in response to the vision and values described in these pages. In other words, if we follow the direction set forth in this volume, things will start to look different in the church. For many of us, that's a reason to hope that this book is widely read."

John R. Franke, professor of theology, Biblical Seminary

"Deeply personal and human in its approach, *Intuitive Leadership* both charms the mind and informs the heart. The result is a wise and gentle tracing of the contours of postmodernism that is as healing as it is liberating."

Phyllis Tickle, contributing editor in religion, *Publishers Weekly*

"Erudite, eloquent, and engaging, Tim Keel's *Intuitive Leadership* is a landmark in pastoral ministry, for he brings together the multiple streams of emerging church, postmodernity, media theory, biblical interpretation, church planting, cultural studies, and holistic, missional life. This book is destined to be a church leadership classic."

Tony Jones, national coordinator of Emergent Village; author, *The New Christians: Dispatches from the Emergent Frontier*

emersion

Emergent Village resources for communities of faith

An Emergent Manifesto of Hope
edited by Doug Pagitt and Tony Jones

Organic Community
Joseph R. Myers

Signs of Emergence
Kester Brewin

Justice in the Burbs
Will and Lisa Samson

Intuitive Leadership
Tim Keel

Losing My Religion
Samir Selmanovic (September 2008)

www.emersionbooks.com

intuitive
Leadership

EMBRACING A PARADIGM OF NARRATIVE, METAPHOR, AND CHAOS

TIM KEEL

BakerBooks
Grand Rapids, Michigan

Published by Baker Books
a division of Baker Publishing Group
P.O. Box 6287, Grand Rapids, MI 49516-6287
www.bakerbooks.com

Printed in the United States of America

Library of Congress Cataloging-in-Publication Data
Keel, Tim, 1968–
    Intuitive leadership : embracing a paradigm of narrative, metaphor, and chaos / Tim Keel.
        p.   cm.
    Includes bibliographical references.
    ISBN 10: 0-8010-6813-4 (pbk.)
    ISBN 978-0-8010-6813-3 (pbk.)
    1. Christian leadership. 2. Storytelling—Religious aspects—Christianity. 3. Leadership—Religious aspects—Christianity. I. Title.
    BV652.1.K425 2007
    253—dc22   2007023976

ēmersion is a partnership between Baker Books and Emergent Village, a growing, generative friendship among missional Christians seeking to love our world in the Spirit of Jesus Christ. The ēmersion line is intended for professional and lay leaders like you who are meeting the challenges of a changing culture with vision and hope for the future. These books will encourage you and your community to live into God's kingdom here and now.

Intuitive Leadership is a unique book in the field of leadership. Tim Keel puts forth a call to leaders that if answered will allow the church of the future to continue with the vibrancy of Christianity's best days. What Tim asks for is just what is needed, that we find the core of our leadership in new places: in our creativity, in our imagination, and most importantly in our story.

Because the world has changed and the outcomes needed in ministry have changed, so must our leadership. What is suggested in this book will prove to be a seminal contribution not only to the field of leadership but to the lives of leaders everywhere.

Intuitive Leadership is a most important contribution not only to the ēmersion line but also to the lives of those who are called to lead in any situation.

Emergent Village resources for communities of faith

 ēmersion

To the two most beautiful brides I know:
His, and mine

Contents

Section 2: Engaging Context

Section 3: Embracing Possibility

Foreword

Intuitive Leadership is a wonderful book written for all those travelers in God's kingdom trying to make sense of a mixed-up world and a crazy time for the church.

A few days ago, on a warm, sunny west coast afternoon I sat outside a coffee shop with a young pastor listening to his story and the underlying frustrations shaping his life just now. Each week I get emails from leaders just like this friend. He has a strong sense of vocation. God has called him into leadership. He's doing this within a particular kind of congregation but feels stuck and frustrated. His sense is that something is not right about the congregation or his leadership, but he doesn't have the language to give words to his experience. Like many other church leaders he's been to conferences and listened to leaders from the other side of the world talk about church and change. But deep inside he's frustrated! He's bright enough to know that a lot of what he hears at these events doesn't land in the social reality of his context. He wants to discover friends and mentors with whom he can partner in this confusing time of transition. This young leader was making the same kinds of comments and asking the same kinds of questions I hear from many other leaders: "People in my church don't get it! It's like going upstream against the current! It's such hard work! What do I do?"

Tim's book is like a guide to these leaders. It doesn't provide a program or even a set of simple principles that, if properly applied, lead to all the answers. In these pages you will engage with the story of one leader's journey as he engages those questions I keep hearing leaders asking all over North America. It's a book that begins and lives in story; Tim invites you into the narratives of his own journey with a host of people in the midst of which he is continually discovering the ways God is at work forming his life and that of the community that has come into being in Kansas City.

One thing Tim would want to communicate to my young pastor friend is the importance of being willing to listen to and enter the questions and stories shaping his own life just now. My experience is that such leaders have similar narratives to the one Tim unfolds about himself. Under the surface these leaders are asking similar questions, but somehow they don't know how to give themselves permission to own and give voice to these narratives and questions. What I find compelling about this book is the way story invites response *in story*. The default search for solutions and answers is so strong among us because we have not yet been invited into the God-given space of naming our own story and questions. This is the location and raw material for our own imaginative engagement with God's life. There is little permission given to leaders to attend to the narratives going on inside themselves.

What is beguiling about this book is the way Tim invites us to track with him by reflecting back on our own narratives. He begins by confessing his love of reading, and I am immediately drawn back to my own boyhood. I am living in the midst of a painful and conflicted family watching my older siblings leaving home because it's all too much to bear. I'm too young to understand what's going on but see myself withdrawing in order to survive. Then, around nine or ten, I discover libraries and books. They plunge me into this amazing world of words and imagination. I read about the great explorers of the sixteenth and seventeenth centuries; I live into stories about amazing adventures in a world I had never imagined existed as a little boy confined to an inner-city neighborhood. Tim's narrative connects me to my own. I'm drawn into his journey and in so doing recognize he's not trying to fill space by talking about books. He's describing a journey about inquisitiveness, about the willingness to be dissatisfied and ask questions even when you don't understand their implication for life at the time. Books become one place where the imagination is fed. For you it may be something other than books; it may be a person or a specific experience or a place. But it's the story of one's own formation in a specific place, among a particular people at the certain time that becomes the fertile soil within which our imaginations are formed. In the midst of that imagination lie our own God-given questions that must be addressed. But first they need permission to be given voice. Tim's book offers that.

Tim's narrative has also taken me on a journey of asking questions without settling for or accepting quick answers or formulas that might have taken away the anxiety or supplied the security of a needed paycheck. On that journey I was making connections. I saw myself in the hard work, the pain of not just accepting what is but being ready to risk paths that weren't clear or laid out. Tim knows this is no easy road. It's filled with painful moments of being misheard (and judged as arrogant) and of mishearing. As Tim will say in these pages the places and times where God's presence and life are experienced most generatively are very often in the midst of our discontentment and questioning. It is important to say this because for those young leaders I know who are restless and struggling with their vocations, Tim's narrative of his journey says something incredibly important: only with a willingness and courage to live into the questions and confusions of one's time in life is it possible to discern the emergent shape of God's work. Tim is telling us that whatever else he's doing in this book it is about the hard, restless work of discerning the ways of God in a time of huge discontinuities.

There is a good deal of storytelling in this book about the changing shapes and contexts of our complex world, too. You will engage stories of how modernity developed, the shifting movement to a postmodern context, the transitioning from a purely "word"-based culture to one far more sensual, somatic, and earthed. These are the ways Tim frames his own understanding of the changes and shifts that make this such a different world in which to form communities of God's kingdom. Again, it is not so important to decide whether one agrees with the precise ways Tim has mapped this narrative history of cultural, intellectual, and experiential shifts. That is to miss the point. Tim is continuing to invite us to journey with him as he risks asking questions and, out loud as it were, shares with us how he's shaped his own imagination about what is happening. So you don't get a "this is what's going on and this is what you now do to deal with it" kind of book. What you have is a book that invites you to risk a similar journey out of your own story, questions, and mapping of the world. This is a huge gift!

Throughout *Intuitive Leadership* you will be continually rooted in a place and among a people. The theology of the incarnation is an overarching subtext. Tim continually earths its narratives in real people and ordinary places. He's saying to us: "You can't work these issues out in the abstract! There are no universal principles or six values that get at the questions of Christian identity and leadership in our time." Our narratives and the formation of our communities can only emerge from a willingness to live into risky local experiments with ordinary people. He's right! Jacob's Well is not a community from which you can abstract principles and manufacture them somewhere else. It has been birthed from narratives and practices that have slowly formed in Tim and Mimi and hundreds of other folk who have been willing to voice questions, experiment, fail, experiment again, learn about place and stillness, and be open to hearing God among one another.

I would say to my young friends raising questions about their anxieties and frustrations with the churches they know: Read Tim's book. Let it invite you to connect with your stories, the markers along the road that have been shaping you so far. Let it permit you to give voice to your questions and then let's talk. Let's see how these narratives and the metaphors shaping your life might provide all kinds of clues for the risky ways in which God is calling you to embrace the chaos of our time with hope and expectation. Thanks, Tim! You resisted an answer book and in so doing invited others to embrace the radical hope of God's future.

Alan J. Roxburgh
vice president, Allelon Canada;
mentor/instructor for Fuller Theological Seminary's
Missional Leadership Cohort DMin program;

Acknowledgments

In many ways *Intuitive Leadership* chronicles *my* story. However, it is not my story alone. My story plays out in the context of a larger story expressed and embodied through a broad and diverse community of people. Thank goodness for that. To me, the best stories are always the ones populated with compelling characters, especially when they are doing interesting things in unusual circumstances. This broader story that I am a part of is one littered with an embarrassing wealth of fascinating and generous characters. Certainly the nature and circumstances of the time in which we live are unusual. Whether or not we are doing interesting things remains to be seen. Regardless, the people with whom I am sharing life have made the living and telling of this story not only possible, but much more interesting than it otherwise would have been. While most of these people do not make it into the narrative explicitly, they are the cast of characters whose presence is implicit throughout. Therefore let me acknowledge and express my deep gratitude to them.

To the people of Jacob's Well: I am profoundly grateful and humbled to follow Jesus alongside you. Thank you for sharing yourselves with me, each other, God, and the world we are invited to love and serve for the sake of Christ. I hope in writing this story I have caught some sense of the life we are exploring and sharing here together. You make it possible.

To the staff of Jacob's Well: I love serving alongside you. Thank you for your creativity and commitment and willingness to trust and risk. Also, a hearty thanks for tolerating me through the writing this book. Though this cast has changed over time, Mike and Laura Crawford, Shayne and Suzanne Wessel, Mike and Vicki King, Ginger and Mike Broyles, Leslie and JT Tenjack, Philip and Christine Lesniewski, Beth Mercer, Mimi Keel, Kelli and Ted Arrandale, Moe Didde, and Charity and Pete Marrone have made Jacob's Well more than a place of work. It has become the best sort of beautiful, messy home—one filled with life and chaos and laughter and music.

To the elders of Jacob's Well: Ashley Cleveland, Don and Lori Chaffer, Ed and Ansie Marquette, Tim and Alisa Roth, Mike and Vicki King, and Paul Dewees—I could not do it without you. You have my deepest respect, love, and gratitude. Thanks for telling me to write.

When the Jacob's Well story began there were a few people who were there in ways so important that I cannot begin to describe them; you trusted my gut before I did. Matt and Mikelan Coleman, Ruthie Harrison, Jeff and Andrea Onnen, Paul Dewees, Laura Lesniewski, and Philip Lesniewski all deserve (and have) my deepest thanks and love.

I joined another fascinating cast of characters early on in my journey. This group developed an integral and life-giving friendship without which I would not have survived. Together we have discovered language and ideas that have given permission and shape to the previously hidden, intuitive longings and impulses explored and expressed in this book. We have struggled together for almost a decade. From this corporate struggle the generative friendship that is Emergent Village was birthed. Let me specifically acknowledge the impact that my friends Doug Pagitt, Chris Seay, Jason Clark, Tony Jones, Brian McLaren, Rudy Carrasco, Karen Ward, Ivy Beckwith, Tim Conder, and

Joe Myers have had on me. You all are wonderful traveling companions.

I am grateful for my friendship with Don Chaffer and the way he has helped me to discover and tease out the threads of this narrative and has himself been woven into the tapestry that is our shared life.

In the same way the friendship and guidance of Fr. Adam Ryan (OSB) has been an unexpected yet integral gift who has enriched my life beyond measure. Alan Roxburgh has likewise been a great gift.

I have a big family. I am grateful for and love you all, especially my mom, Pam Strausbaugh, my dad, Ron Keel, and my brother Mark. The story started with you. You each have blessed and shaped me. Thanks.

To the people at Baker: thank you for your help in bringing to the surface what has been stewing in my soul, especially my editor Chad Allen.

Finally to my wife, Mimi, and our children Mabry, Annie, and Blaise: you are the best, most beautiful story I know. Words fail . . .

Introduction

My book opens with a simple confession: I love books. As you will soon discover, I am a sucker for words printed on a page, particularly if they are there in service to a halfway decent story. When I have a free moment I go to bookstores and browse shelves, touching books, reading jacket sleeves, evaluating design, even smelling them. It's been that way since I was a kid.

As I have aged, the subject matter of the books I read has undergone an understandable shift. I still love a good science fiction novel, and I have always had a weakness for Tolkien, to be sure. But now you are just as likely to find me hovering in the history section, around shelves stocked with books on philosophy or technological innovation, or the contextual analysis and cultural studies section. Who needs fantasy and science fiction these days? Our world is bizarre enough. In fact, in a culture changing as rapidly and dramatically as ours, there are always fascinating new books available on all of these seemingly inexhaustible topics. Even so, none seem to be thriving in the way that contextual analysis and cultural studies are.

I am sure that you have seen at least some example of this phenomenon. Wherever we turn we can find historians, futurists, theologians, cultural analysts, physicists, editorialists, economists, semioticians, environmentalists, anthropologists, and sociologists to describe our cultural location and the flux in which we exist. These books sit atop bestseller lists and on the tables we pass when we enter local booksellers' stores—or perhaps more true to our time, their thumbnail images pop up when we open the Amazon.com webpage.

We are flooded with analysis that seeks to make sense of the tidal wave of change that has swept over the world in the last several years. Some of the analysis is cautionary and alarmist, warning of dire consequences facing us individually and collectively if we do not change our ways. Some of it is optimistic, holding visions of a chastened but nevertheless idealized utopian future secured though technology, human ingenuity, and willpower. And some of it is simply journalism, setting forth cautious and researched observations made from a particular angle that provide unique vantage points from which to survey broader issues affecting our cultural situation.

If we highlight only the writing coming out of those particular disciplines, we miss what is being expressed in and from the creative world. Response from the world of fine, graphic, and performing arts as well as the work of filmmakers, musicians, novelists, and poets has likewise been prolific, and while the creative world has given us less of an analysis of exactly *what* is happening, the arts have provided an expression for what it *feels* like to live in this quickly evolving world. In fact, some of the first intimations that reality as we have known it was fracturing came from the world of the imagination expressed in the cubist paintings of Picasso and Braque and the discordant, atonal compositions of modern composers at the turn of the last century. They have their contemporary equivalents, to be sure.

The book you hold in your hands is an example of the former genre of materials that describe, within the world of theology and faith, the ways in which our world is changing and how some people and communities and leaders are responding in ways different from what has come before. Of course theology and faith and leadership are not practiced in a vacuum but in the same context of the larger network of issues and forces that so many of the books I describe are aimed at marking. As a result, *Intuitive Leadership* and other books in this genre are being written by people like myself who have sought (and continue to seek) to live life, express faith, and revitalize or birth new Christian communities in fresh and organic ways—as a response to God, our broader communities, and this emerging cultural context in which we are living. To do so we have become students of our world, including our individual places in it, in addition to being students of our Scriptures, theology, and church history.

This and other lines of books and resources come out of a particular cultural phenomenon within Christianity that is being labeled the "emerging church." These nascent communities see themselves emerging from and into a world that is in transition (and will be for a very long time). While we do not know yet where or who we are fully, we nonetheless are increasingly able to say where and who we are not and what we are beginning to be.

At the most basic level within emerging churches, we recognize that the contexts and frameworks in which we have lived our lives and practiced our faith and expressed leadership are unalterably changed. Those within emerging church circles are not simply seeking to discover new techniques or methods proven in other places to grow megachurches, nor are we looking to retreat into a gloriously reimagined past. We want to engage where we are in creative and redemptive ways. In order to do this we are asking questions more fundamental than many of those asked by others likewise trying to engage the culture on Christ's behalf.

For those of us lumped into this category of *emerging*, we know that we have experienced a shift in our cultural location, and we want to respond with integrity as natives of this new world, not as people trying to *reach* it. The growing tide of relationships, communities, networks, and materials now available function to both name the change, mark some of its characteristics, and propose new understandings, frameworks, relational categories, and postures for engaging our way forward. The variety and diversity of responses to these realities function to illustrate the dynamic nature of the change we are undergoing.

I know such statements may strike some as inflated, if not grandiose. That is understandable. Change is the one constant, and the poet/philosopher of Ecclesiastes reminds us that in fact, there is nothing new under the sun. I don't deny this for a second. But does that automatically mean there are *no* times of unique change or upheaval when the broad frameworks and conceptual categories for how we understand our world and location in it should not be questioned? Is there really *nothing* different about this age? Do we suffer from some kind of age-related, era-centric hubris? Is it the case that this age is like every other that has preceded it? Is the phenomenon of the emerging church and the environment to which it is responding (a world in massive transition) overstated? I am tempted to liken those who think so to the proverbial ostrich with head neck-deep in sand—they respond to change by pretending there is nothing happening at all. In their insistence that all is as it has always been, they quickly make themselves irrelevant and are soon heard from no more. Time will ultimately be the judge.

But there is merit in questioning exactly what *is* happening: it needs to be allowed that the fact that our world and culture are experiencing transition does not mean that all people are experiencing that transition in the same way or on the same timeline. The transition we are experiencing is a staggered one: in some quarters the dynamics of the emerging world have been in effect for so long that for many there is little sense of a transition at all—this brave new world is all that is known. For others, the world and the way in which they live has ostensibly undergone very little change. In the same way as those native to the emerging world, life in some cloistered quarters is as it has always been.

For most of us the reality is somewhere in-between. We lean more or less to one or the other end of the continuum, so there can never be a description or a solution that is one-size-fits-all. That aim itself is an example of modernity's hubris at work, which I will seek not only to deconstruct but also to move beyond into something that is hopefully more humble and more rooted in local context.

The truth is that one of the marks of this world to which we belong is that it is multifaceted, and characteristics that appear to be mutually exclusive in reality overlap all the time and defy any kind of easy categorization. Therefore any observation I make about the nature of life in the world around us must be made with humility and with the recognition that I describe a semblance of reality for only a small segment of people, in fact maybe only for myself. But that is where the broader community of which I am a part comes in.

We, the community of Jacob's Well Church, the broader community of the emerging church in general, and many of us connected to Emergent Village in particular, are seeking to live life in common. We are in the process of responding to the lived context of our lives. Additionally, and critically, we have sought to abide creatively and faithfully within the lived narratives of our Scriptures and our history as a church through time. As we have done so, others have come alongside and found meaning and hope in our journey and in the many different ways it is being expressed. They have asked us to tell them our stories (but more often we have been asked to describe our "model"). So we have begun telling stories about the world in which we live and why, for increasing numbers of people, the world no longer makes sense in the same way it once did.

Telling these stories has begun to create meaning and new ways of understanding and living out our lives and our faith as disciples of Jesus Christ. Telling these stories has connected us to larger groups of people and communities for whom meaning has been functionally lost beyond the repetitive and increasingly meaningless maintenance of behaviors that are often no more than going through the motions. And for better or for worse, people are paying attention. Our little tribe has begun to increase. It is out of this context that I seek to tell a kind of story about the world in which we find ourselves and what leadership might begin to look like in such a world.

It is beyond the scope of this book to chronicle all the ways in which our world is undergoing change. Certainly among all the categories and genres of materials I list above, one can find ample evidence of the many ways in which the environment of the early twenty-first century is unique. To live in the world today and not be aware of the radical transition of our context is to be either hopelessly out of touch, dangerously naive, or willfully stubborn. My guess is that most readers of this book are none of these. But that doesn't mean you automatically agree with me—or other people in the emerging church for that matter (nor are the people in the emerging church the only ones articulating these things). There is a good chance you are aware of what is happening around us. You pay attention, read the analysis, and debate the meaning of it all.

Many for whom the emerging church is a concern have a sense that perhaps we have misread the culture, probably the Scriptures, our mandate as the church, or some combination of all of these things. These are valid concerns. I hope this book addresses some of these issues. I also hope that those who are concerned about or critical of the emerging church will find this book to reflect a humble posture and a passionate desire for the church to faithfully represent Christ in the world.

But a great many more have recently discovered a strange group of words on the walls of their homes, churches, denominations, and seminaries: *mene, mene, tekel, parsin*. They have been read and received. Now they must be interpreted in a way that provokes transformation. I confess that it is to this latter group that my book is primarily aimed. *Intuitive Leadership* lays out a story, a contextual understanding, and a paradigm for leadership that I hope will be useful to these brothers and sisters, for theirs is my tribe too.

Whichever your tribe or whatever your starting point let me clarify at the outset something of the nature of this book, specifically what this book is not. This book is not a manual—a book of explicit instructions for operating a device or some other such machine. Manuals (leadership or otherwise) tell you at the beginning what you are going to learn and then provide the basic data to get you there in a step-by-step manner. Much of what is written in the genre of leadership could be classified within the framework of a manual. Such an approach toward leadership does have an implicit whiff of logic. If nothing else leaders are generally pragmatic, results-oriented creatures. Manuals are pragmatic guides that guarantee results—if you will simply do what they say. But therein lies the problem of leadership in a postmodern world: we need something beyond pragmatism. How can we be sure of the results we seek when who and where we are and what we are trying to do is no longer as obvious as it once might have been? In this context a manual is not only unhelpful, it is deceptive and dangerous.

Because leaders are being faced with profoundly different issues, circumstances, and contexts than what has come before, the ways in which we approach leadership must likewise be adjusted from previous approaches. In *Intuitive Leadership* I invite you to join me on a journey of exploration—the same journey that I undertook when all the paradigms for leadership and maps of the territory I found myself in proved to be, if not deceptively drawn, at least so out-of-date they were dangerous to myself and others. It is the journey that I believe every leader must undergo in one way or another if they want to engage God, themselves, and the world they are a part of.

I have divided this exploration into three parts as a sort of map that charts the trajectory of this journey. The first section is "Entering Story"; in it we will explore the ways in which story is at the heart of God's activity in the world. The second section, "Engaging Context," explores three interconnected spheres that are critical for recognizing and responding to God's activity in and around us: our context, our theology, our systems and structures. Finally, in "Embracing Possibility" I chart a different way of understanding oneself and one's role and approach as a leader.

For some this approach may be confusing at first. As readers we often approach books in specific genres with an unstated but implicit contract: this is a book on leadership, therefore I can expect these fill-in-the-blank outcomes delivered in this predetermined format. My hope in writing this is that you would instead be surprised and filled with hope by what you find along this journey. My hope is that you would be willing to set aside some of your assumptions about what leadership is in order to discover something new about God, yourself, and the world you are a part of. In fact as you journey with me I pray that you recognize something of your own journey. I hope you find a point of departure that sets you off on your own path of exploration for the sake of God, the gospel, and the world that God has invited us to serve.

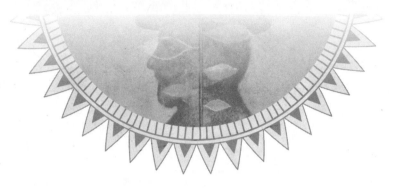

ENTERING STORY

In the Beginning

rediscovering the power of story

Now the earth was formless and empty, darkness was over the surface of the deep, and the Spirit of God was hovering over the waters. And God said, "Let there be light," and there was light.

Genesis 1:2–3

People want to see and hear stories and experience their own stories in the context of larger, maybe more dramatic, more explicit, or more intense ones. . . . I am sure we all want to hear stories, from the moment we are born to the moment we die. Stories connect our little lives with the world around us and help us discover who we are. The Bible is a storybook, and the Gospels are four stories about the birth, death, and resurrection of Jesus, who himself was one of the greatest storytellers.[1]

Henri Nouwen, *Sabbatical Journey*

A "Storied" Life

I love to read, and not just a little bit. In fact, my wife might say I *live* to read. When she gets tired of it she tells me she is a book widow. I know it's true. I am not as bad as I used to be; I have learned to moderate it. But sometimes it can't be helped. It's in my DNA.

I discovered this passion for reading toward the end of elementary school. In about fifth grade I began to simply disappear into books. But the reading was secondary to something else, a means rather than an end. It became a portal into another world: the world of story. What I know now is that I came to love a good story—wherever I could find one. I still do.

In the years before books became constant companions, my favorite thing to do was to run home from school in time to catch the 3:45 p.m. afternoon movie on channel 5. Story time. I watched a lot of movies. I don't really remember any one movie. Well, actually there was this freaked-out one called *Bad Ronald* that still haunts me at night, but I've mostly blocked that out. What I do remember, however, were five consecutive days of "themed" movies. Halloween was always "Monster Week," with classic Boris Karloff and Vincent Price movies, viewed in the safety of my living room during the daylight hours. Other themes included the *Planet of the Apes* week, John Wayne week, Doris Day week, Godzilla week, Three Stooges week, World War II week—you get the picture. I never cared one whit for cheesy made-for-television after-school movies. I wanted *real* stuff.

It was a passion I shared with my mom. I could almost always count on her to plop down on the floor beside me with some popcorn and a deck of cards. We would watch television, play gin rummy, and munch. Of course, she was constantly popping up and down, making dinner. Her timing was miraculous, though. Somehow dinner always coincided with the conclusion of whatever we were watching. I was lucky. Some kids are forced to abandon the stories they have become engrossed with before they reach resolution—that is, if they want to eat. I never had to decide. I had a coconspirator, another story lover.

As I came to discover books, I learned a coconspirator was a good thing to have. Every time my mom hit the bookstore, and it was often, I came away with something for myself. I mean, how can you buy books for yourself and refuse your kid standing right there next to you begging for books to read? She didn't. She might grouse at me at bit, but she really didn't care.

So I began to consume books. Almost any book would do, which is still true. I have been shaped my whole life by stories. It wasn't just my mom, though, nor do I owe it all to after-school movies. It began long before that.

My dad's side of the family is a clan of story*tellers*. I grew up in the midst of a complicated oral tradition, intricate systems of giving nicknames, and other such tribal practices. I later discovered that my dad's family had their own language. "Carni-tongue," they called it—a secretive way of talking that had developed among carnival workers to communicate when the situation demanded secrecy. Apparently somewhere in my past is a carnival heritage complete with Pidgin English. I know—it's the nuttiest thing I ever heard too. But as a child it was glorious (and it still is). Holidays were communal story times. Uncles, aunts, cousins, grandparents, and even great-grandparents gathered to reconnect and celebrate. Of course, food was everywhere, and as we ate, somewhere in the midst of the meal someone would push back from the table and start to talk. It usually began with some kind of good-natured argument or long-held controversy once again being played out. Sometimes I would ask them to retell a favorite story. They didn't take much prompting.

My dad came from a family with four kids, three of whom were boys. So the stories almost always involved something gross, some story of revenge, a practical joke, or the legend of a neighborhood kook. Each person weighed in and made his or her own contribution to the tale. If some detail from the tradition was omitted, someone else could be counted on to pick it up, even one of us young ones. It was always the same stories over and over, but somehow that didn't matter.

Other times Grandpa would begin to talk. In my early years he used to scare me a bit. He didn't seem to know what to do with little kids. Now I understand why. He had grown up during the Great Depression and had been sent to live with an uncle when his own family couldn't keep him. And the way I heard it with my young ears, that didn't seem like a good place to be. I remember hearing him tell stories of being knocked from his chair for leaving food on his plate, and somehow back then I knew I was being addressed for refusing to finish off a plate of vegetables. All the hilarity would leave the room, at least for me. But he was ultimately a very gentle man, deeply tender and proud of us all. I would listen to him bluster and sit still until it passed, or maybe I would slide out of my chair and go play with my brother or my cousins. But anytime someone began to laugh or to share, I stopped what I was doing and went back to the table to listen.

So I grew up listening to stories and reading. I believe that shapes a person. I have become a listener and an observer of life, because if we are attentive we discover stories playing out around us, everywhere, all the time. We all have them. They may be explicit, but many times they are not. We are constantly awash in stories whether we recognize it or not: secret stories, family stories, neighborhood stories, religious stories, political stories, cultural stories, stories that say there are no stories.

More than that, we are story-generating people. We are not passive observers of others and their goings-on. I am constantly *living* out stories, a player in unfolding narratives, some dramatic, most mundane, but nevertheless real. I can't escape this simple reality, but even if I could, why would I want to?

Stories shape and create identity. For individuals, for families, for communities, and for peoples. For better or for worse. We live. We participate. We generate. We listen. And somehow I have become not just an observer or a listener. I've become a teller.

A "Storied" Faith

So stories shape and create identity—and not just for individuals. They shape identity for families, communities, and cultures. We are awash in stories, and when they are good and well told, they can locate us in the world even when that world feels chaotic and without purpose. Throughout history people have told stories and been shaped by them, and in doing so they have discovered and constructed ways of understanding who they are and what is happening in the world around them.

The Bible is filled with stories that locate people in place and time, too, though we may not be used to seeing it that way. They are the same kinds of stories I describe above: secret stories, family stories, neighborhood stories, religious stories, political stories, cultural stories, stories that say there are no stories. And somehow these seemingly disparate stories are placed within the scope of God's story even though they are often not the kinds of things we expect to find in "Holy" Scriptures: stories filled with murder, adultery, war, betrayal, assassination, but also love, sacrifice, friendship, transcendence, and the craziest people you could ever imagine.

Actually, for some, these people and their stories may be easier to imagine than we first suppose. In fact, sometimes when I read these biblical stories, the people I find there staring back remind me an awful lot of myself, my friends, and my family. These characters play out on the pages of Scripture with their own nicknames, languages, and oral traditions. There is no way around it. Stories are a vital part of the spiritual genetic code of God's people. It's in *our* DNA.

In the Scriptures we discover the story of a deity who interacts with human beings in history. He reveals himself with the mysterious name Yahweh—"I am that I am." At the beginning of the story this character Yahweh calls a clan of people into a relationship with himself through Abraham. We quickly learn that it is not just any relationship, however. Yahweh calls them to a specific kind of relationship called a covenant. This covenant binds God and this clan one to each other eternally. It is Yahweh's purpose to shape a people out of Abraham and his family and lead them to a new land that he promises will one day be their own. Abraham is also told that he and his people will be blessed—but not for their own sake. They will be blessed with purpose: the clan of Abraham and later the nation of Israel, which develops out of his clan, will be an instrument of blessing to the surrounding tribes and nations. They are not only to live and embody the story of Yahweh, they are called to be a nation of priests to the world, storytellers who describe the account of their own interaction with their God as a means of inviting others into this kind of covenant relationship.

So the plot develops and time passes. This small and seemingly insignificant people grow into a nation called Israel, translated "he who wrestles with God." And wrestle they do—with God and with others they are called to bless. The land they were promised turns out to be contested soil in a geographic hot zone surrounded by a succession of powerful empires. Everybody wants the land on which they live. How they relate to those around them tests their character and reveals the nature of the faith they have in the God to whom they have been bound in covenant.

What a dramatic and compelling story. And this story continually unfolds in new and surprising ways: constantly moving forward in time and space while at the same time consistently reaching backward into the memory of what God had done before. The Scriptures are filled with stories of God acting in the lives of common people, and they rehearse over and over how God acts and intervenes to make, protect, shape, and preserve this people.

The Torah tells the stories of the formation of this people and the laws that would govern them in covenant faithfulness. The histories tell the unfolding story of this people living in the land under a progression of leaders (patriarchs, judges, and kings) in relation to the surrounding kings and kingdoms. Their songs (Psalms) are a collection of Israel's greatest themes and motifs, sung frequently as prayers to remind them of God's faithful presence and guidance. But these songs are true to human experience, and so they also tell stories of apparent abandonment, loss, and grief.

As these people live out their stories, they live in relation to neighbors in surrounding lands who have different stories about the gods, who is favored, and who ought to inhabit this particular parcel of earth. The Jews are constantly tempted to listen to these other stories—different versions of reality that undermine their identity and dissolve the unity and purpose of this covenant people. It is into situations like these that God sends prophets to warn the Jews, to retell the story, to remind and rearticulate to them God's historical and present activity for their sake. Sometimes these reminders come by way of a simple retelling of the ancient stories that all Jews knew well. And sometimes they come in the ragged and frustrated prophetic voices of men filled with anger and fear raging at stubborn people who seem more inclined to forget than to remember.

In fact, if we start really paying attention, we begin noticing that particular words appear and reappear throughout the story. Specifically the Hebrew word *zakar*. "Remember! Don't forget." Over and over and over again. Don't forget what? Don't forget the stories, the identity that flows from these stories, and the God at the genesis of the stories. Does it occur to you that the stakes are very high for something as simple as a story? Isn't one story as good as the next?

The stunning insight throughout all *these* stories is that Yahweh, the creator and sustainer of the universe, has tied himself to *this* particular people in *this* particular place at *this* particular time. This is the scandal of revelation and particularity. The Scriptures revisit this again and again, stretching from the pages of the first covenant with Abraham into the pages of the second covenant and into the particularity of the incarnation of Jesus Christ. In the world we inhabit today, we are scandalized by the story of particularity. We like a universal God, not a particular one.

A Bible Story?

It has been my experience that most people don't see the Scriptures as a collection of stories about God and his people in creation. The Bible is supposed to be something else entirely. If the Bible is God's Word, then certainly it has to be more than a book of stories. Doesn't it? It is almost as if we believe stories are for children. And ironically, we often dismiss children from our worship services to let *them* be told stories in their Sunday school classrooms. Meanwhile, we adults deal with the more "meaty" aspects of faith. We go to the Scriptures in search of certainty. We go to the Scriptures systematically, seeking to extract principles from them. If the stories are acknowledged at all, it is as if we are embarrassed by them, by their particularity, their earthiness. So we mine them for universal truths that instead can be applied to anyone or everyone. We explain them. We domesticate them. We apologize for them. We neuter them. We ignore them. What a tragedy.

The Bible as encyclopedia of topical religious information? Check. The Bible as blueprint for how to make life work? Check. The Bible as a book of answers, especially for refuting those with whom we disagree? Check. The Bible as supporting material for systematic theology? Check. The Bible as the story about the confusing presence of a personal deity engaging bizarrely unpredictable people in astounding *and* mundane ways over a long period of time? Can I get back to you on that?

Do you think I am being unfair or overstating my case? Maybe so. But consider my story, particularly my religious story.

I have a pretty mixed pedigree when it comes to my church background. I started my journey as a child in a Methodist church, went through adolescence in a Southern Baptist church (while at the same time attending a youth group attached to a local Episcopal church), and became a disciple of Jesus with the help of a group of people planting an Evangelical Presbyterian Church in the mid-80s. In college I interned in a PCUSA church (Presbyterian Church United States of America) during the summer. I also attended Friday night worship gatherings at an independent, charismatic church in Kansas City that was briefly affiliated with the Vineyard. After college I worked as a youth pastor in a seeker church modeled after Willow Creek. Later, I received my master of divinity from a conservative Baptist seminary. While I was in seminary in the mid-90s, I worked with an innovative pastor planting a Gen X church, which was only secondarily Southern Baptist. My sixty-year-old father recently completed seminary and was ordained into the Episcopalian priesthood. Additionally, my three children attend a Catholic parish school just blocks from our home. Personally, I receive spiritual direction and friendship from a wonderfully passionate and godly Benedictine monk. Deeply suffused throughout my faith journey has been a strong parachurch influence as well: Young Life, K-Life, Kanakuk Christian Sports Camps, and Icthus Christian Fellowship, to name a few. So I suppose I have more than a mixed pedigree. I am a full-on mutt.

Perhaps this kind of diverse background is unique, but maybe not. It is certainly a product of a number of cultural influences, one of which was simply being an American at the end of the twentieth century. However, reflecting on my ecclesiological journey, I see how deeply and widely different streams of the Christian tradition have influenced me. At the time of this writing I'm nearing the end of my fourth decade of life and have been in ministry for more than half that time. I have seen or experienced firsthand a lot of what the church has to offer. When I make observations about how we approach the Bible, I know I am painting with a broad brushstroke, but I don't believe I am distorting what is out there, nor am I hostile. I write from the inside, as a person who loves the church and has given his life to serving God by serving God's people.

We are confused about the Bible and what we find there. We are also confused about how it ought to shape how we live and interact in and with the world around us. At least part of the reason for this is that we have been inhabiting a very confusing story about the nature of reality, and this story has come to shape how we see the Scriptures, our faith, and our lives.

Our Missing Stories

I began this book by describing my passion for stories and how deeply I can lose myself in a good tale. The irony is that somehow my passion for story never got connected to the Bible, even though I was a Christian who read the Bible—a lot. Do you see the irony in this? Theologian Stanley Hauerwas has said that this itself is the story of modernity: "The story we have is that we should have no story except the story we chose when they said we had no story. And we call that freedom."[2] We don't know our story. We don't think we have a story. And that is a story in itself. In particular, it is the story of the modern, Western world.

What do I mean by that? Or perhaps more importantly, what is our cultural story or stories? How have those stories shaped the way we approach the Scriptures or even how we live or perceive the world?

To begin a story we have to admit that we are a part of history—that we do in fact inhabit a specific time and place in the world. Exactly where we are and what is the nature of this specific time and place is the subject of a lot of debate, especially for Christians right now. To be sure, there is no shortage of authors and speakers who are telling the story of modernity and postmodernity and what their implications might or might not be. All of these are stories about how as a culture we have interpreted and lived in the world based on what we have believed reality is.

Without going into a great deal of detail, and since we are using a broad brush, let me say a few things about the story that I believe has been shaping us for a long while. I will have to simplify things considerably, but I want to sketch out a rough idea of the story we have inherited and now animate. We will go into greater depth later.

Several hundred years ago, people in the West began to live into a new story. The story we began to tell ourselves was that there was no story. Rather, that the world we inhabit is a world that can be adequately understood, explained, and reckoned without any connection to the past. Moreover, the world is a place that can be reckoned with most accurately by abandoning memory in favor of the future, progress, and what we can observe with our senses. We traded *zakar* for amnesia.

In the 1500s and 1600s religious wars tore Europe apart. While it was an incredibly complex time for a number of reasons, an enormous part of the struggle was the issue of knowledge and how people arrive at knowing. In philosophical terms, this is called *epistemology*. Until the intellectual revolution of the Enlightenment, knowledge was primarily conveyed through tradition, mysticism, or personal revelation. What is more, it was held in the hands of a select few. As a result, life during that time was often unstable and lived at the mercy of people who believed they were acting in accordance with the will of God. Not surprisingly, many people, and more significantly kings and religious leaders (sometimes one and the same), had differing ideas about God's will. The unfortunate and obvious problem with this is that when kings disagree about the nature and scope of God's will, it usually results in more than theological parlor talk. Wars are waged. In addition, when people are convinced they are acting out God's will in opposition to heretics (people who disagree with us as we listen to God), they become capable of the most extraordinarily inhuman behavior—in other words, Europe of the 1500s and 1600s.

These religious wars ultimately birthed the Enlightenment, the Age of Reason, and what has come to be called modernity. All of these periods reflect an attempt to find knowledge and truth objectively—that is, outside the realm of mere personal revelation and previous cultural tradition. That which was universal was to be preferred over that which was provisional. Miroslav Volf describes this dynamic in his book *Exclusion and Embrace*: "Especially in the seventeenth century, Christians were not inclined at all to be provisional. They fought one another bitterly over the beliefs they claimed were directly revealed by God. Partly against the backdrop of Christian inability to settle differences in peace by appeal to God, Enlightenment thinkers argued that the only impartial court of appeal is *reason*, freed from the ballast of tradition."[3] Central to this quest was the belief in a world that was comprehensible to the human senses. By observing the world using the faculties of reason people could arrive at a series of undeniable and axiomatic "truths," truths available to anyone, independent of one's starting point or tradition.

René Descartes is the patron saint of the Enlightenment; he is rightly famous for his words *"Cogito ergo sum"*—"I think, therefore I am." In that statement he located the rational, cognitive self as the starting point of reality, and reality became that thing that was accessed by thinking. From that simple starting point, Descartes and many, many others developed systems of knowledge based on deduction, looking to the universe as a rational, orderly, and comprehensible place. In this way, people believed that laws that can be deduced from observation shape reality. Even more, when humanity submits to these laws, progress results. I imagine it was an intoxicating time to be human. We gained much. We turned our newfound eyes outward and discovered a universe awaiting our dissection, resolving tension and illuminating ambiguity. We demolished mystery and marginalized and domesticated imagination. We revolutionized our thinking by breaking it down and systematizing it. And nothing was beyond our scope. Including God. Including the Bible.

Modernity's story is the one we are struggling to live in today. We are independent, autonomous knowers, objectively encountering and engaging the world rationally as we progress toward a good future and away from a past clouded by ignorance and superstition. Or that is the story anyway.

Now a quick disclaimer about the preceding paragraphs: in order to locate us historically I have grossly oversimplified very complex and nuanced historical, philosophical, and theological history. I said I was going to paint with broad brushstrokes, but over four hundred years of history in a couple of paragraphs! In writing so broadly I am surely obscuring as much as I am revealing. Admittedly so. This kind of reductionism is one of the tools modernity has bequeathed me, and I apply it here liberally. Nevertheless, I don't believe I have misrepresented in my brevity what others have taken more time and words to explicate. Such historical, philosophical, and theological exploration is beyond the scope of what I am seeking to do here. In writing this I am assuming that my reader is at least moderately conversant or sympathetic with these kinds of assumptions. In chapter 5 I will explain further why this particular story about where we have been culturally is important in birthing something new and vital for the culture that is emerging.

So in many ways we jettisoned story (and much else) as a way of understanding reality in favor of a certain kind of rational knowing, and while these two are not mutually exclusive, they seem to have become so. When our confidence in God's revelation diminished, we replaced it with increasing confidence in our own ability to discover truth using our minds. Surprisingly (or maybe not so much so), just like those premodern kings before us, the more certain we became in our knowledge, the more justified we felt in dominating those who disagreed, whether they were native peoples, the environment, or the dissenting voices among us (and there are many). Ultimately it was World War II, and really all of the bloody twentieth century, that shook the West out of its progress-induced stupor. Nothing could have been more sobering to a Western world convinced of its own superiority and notions of human growth and evolution than to look in a mirror and see a reflection of the 1500s and 1600s. The only differences were that progress had allowed us to become far more efficient and prodigious in killing, and the source of our authority for doing so had moved from God's revelation to the cold logic of reason. We grew uglier, all the while believing we were more beautiful than ever. Sobering indeed.

An Unfolding Story

We continue telling stories about reality; it is impossible not to. But we now live in a world with competing stories. Modernity and its children once had a hegemonic hold on our view of reality and how to access it, but it has been knocked from its throne. In the West, postmodernism is an alternate story that is being told in the wake of modernity's sweeping and mythical narrative. Around the world there are others. We truly live in a liminal, or transitional, time.

While it is true that life and reality in our time is chaotic, confusing, and disruptive (even as much so as in the 1500s and 1600s), it is my personal belief that it is a time of new life, new realities, and new opportunities. For better or for worse the church in the West bought modernity's claims. We were baptized in its story (even though it said it did not have one) and accepted its categories and definitions. But somewhere along the way we also began to believe that the ways in which we accessed knowledge about God or Jesus or the Spirit or Christianity were those things themselves. We mistook our contingent knowledge of God for God, trading the worship of God for images fashioned in our own likeness in what Peter Rollins, echoing Jean-Luc Marion, has named conceptual idolatry: "any system of thought which the individual takes to be a visible rendering of God."[4] Thus, our faith became domesticated, made in our own image, deprived of its wildness. In our pursuit of the systematic, rational, objective, and universal, we lost the particular, intuitive, imaginative, poetic, and creative. I am afraid we lost the ability to discern and follow the Spirit of God, especially as he leads us in places unfamiliar and unknown to our domesticated faith.

We no longer live in the world of modernity. Oh, it's still out there, but not in the same way. We are indebted to it and wary of it, and well we should be. It's our story. But the story is moving on. The world is changing. Reality is in flux. Unfortunately, it seems as though the church is in denial, and if not outright denial, then confusion that leads, on one hand, to often ill-conceived reaction and, on the other, to inactivity verging on paralysis. Christians, the people of Jesus, seem gripped by fear. How counter to the life of Jesus. We know something is going on around us, but we're not sure what it is, how we should feel about it, and what, if anything, we should do. But we have been called to freedom and courage. We are called to story. To remember. To live. To tell.

I opened this chapter quoting from Genesis 1, the story of creation, the start of life. We are told that the Spirit of God hovers over the chaos (in Hebrew, *tohu vabohu*, "formless and void") and from that chaos calls forth light and life. I believe in that story. I am living in it. And it is that story that I want to tell in this book. It is a story about living in tension, not trying to resolve it. It is a story about learning to access a kind of knowing and being that moves us beyond our minds and reunites us to our hearts and our souls and our bodies. It is a story that frees us from a radical individualism and reconnects to our communities. And it is a story about learning to respond to God and lead from those places. It is not a new story. It is not the only story. But it is a story for our time.

And the truth is in the telling. . . .

A Way in the Wilderness

journeying toward a new story

We shall not cease from exploration
And the end of all our exploring
Will be to arrive where we started
And know the place for the first time.[1]

T. S. Eliot, "Little Gidding"
(No. 4 of *Four Quartets*)

The Cost of New Life

I am not a gardener, nor do I have a green thumb. It's not that I kill things . . . per se. I just don't have whatever it is that causes a person to see life—the green variety—flourish under their care. My one success is a piece of bamboo that I have in my office. Fortunately, it doesn't require much.

My wife is skilled as a gardener, however. So are both our mothers. I am fortunate to be surrounded by women who create environments that pulse with beauty and life. Most of *my* life related to nature has been spent either playing out in it or keeping it trimmed to the appropriate length. In fact, reflecting on my family just a bit more causes me to see that in my experience, Mother Nature more often than not has bequeathed her gifts of growing to women in our brood, and we menfolk are kept around to operate the machinery that keeps the growth in check. Not always, of course. But I have to say that if it weren't for my wife, I would be mowing dirt and crab grass.

Have you ever tried to grow anything? It takes patience. Maybe women, who allow a fetus to gestate inside their own bodies for nine months, have a head start when it comes to understanding something of the organic nature of growth. At the same time, growth must sometimes come as the result of profound struggle, through strength, perseverance, and the will to generate something new. For example, have you ever had to scrape your yard clean and start from scratch? When I was a young boy I remember my mom and dad rounding up all the neighborhood kids to tear out a disastrous yard in order to start over. All day long kids pulled grass, broke up and tilled ground, smashed hard clods into soil that could receive seed. It was hard, dirty work. As payment at the end of the day, we were all thrown into the back of the station wagon and driven for ice-cream sundaes (served in upside-down miniature plastic baseball helmets) at the local Dairy Queen. Maybe that experience explains my aversion to yard work. It is not easy to grow something new. Most of us no longer live in agricultural contexts, and so the rhythm of life and the skills it takes to grow something out of the ground is as foreign to us as Sanskrit.

The process of growth is brutal. Have you ever noticed that? Take my example of grass. When you want to grow grass, what do you do? First, you must break up the soil. You then throw out some seed and rake it in so the roots have a chance to grab hold of the earth. Your work isn't over. Every day you must soak the soil with water: early in the morning, afternoon, late in the day—days, even weeks, all the while hoping for the sun to bake the same soil while you wait. *Break. Throw. Rake. Grab.*

Soak. Bake. These are some tough words, words that describe a battle. It's primal and recalls God's words to Adam:

> Cursed is the ground because of you;
>> through painful toil you will eat of it
>> all the days of your life.
> It will produce thorns and thistles for you,
>> and you will eat the plants of the field.
> By the sweat of your brow
>> you will eat your food
> until you return to the ground,
>> since from it you were taken;
> for dust you are
>> and to dust you will return.

Genesis 3:17–19

No kidding!

But in the midst of all the labor and fighting something happens. One morning you step outside and what do you know? The thinnest carpet of pure green begins working its way up from beneath the earth. All that breaking and raking and so on gives birth to something new. It is wondrous.

I use that metaphor because in many ways that is how I understand my story thus far. Metaphors of growth and birth, of creating and nurturing life are incredibly evocative to me. Sometimes people think anything worth having ought to come easily—"If God is for us, who can be against us?" and all that. When we believe we are working for God it can be worse—"I am doing thus and such for God, therefore I know it (or 'I') will succeed." God's economy, which is that of creation and that of the soul, dictates otherwise. Take the apostle Paul, for example. Paul employs this agricultural metaphor for growth when he reminds the people of Galatia that they should not allow themselves to be deceived, that "God cannot be mocked. People reap what they sow. Those who sow to please their sinful nature, from that nature will reap destruction; those who sow to please the Spirit, from the Spirit will reap eternal life. Let us not become weary in doing good, for at the proper time we will reap a harvest if we do not give up" (Gal. 6:7–9).

Paul speaks from experience. Following Christ became a daily lesson in suffering and surrender—but even so, to read Paul is not to read a litany of complaints leveled at a God who has not lived up to his end of the bargain. Rather one sees, even feels, Paul's joy and the presence of Christ in the midst of his suffering. Christ has crafted a soul through a laborious process. All Paul's subsequent work and struggle on Christ's behalf stems from the way he has been shaped through his own suffering. In the Gospels Jesus talks of the seed of the gospel falling into the soil of a human being's life: body, soul, mind—it is from here that fruitfulness occurs or does not occur. Fruitfulness involves struggle, a reality that Jesus illustrates when he declares that "unless a kernel of wheat falls to the ground and dies, it remains only a single seed. But if it dies, it produces many seeds" (John 12:24). John Howard Yoder observes a similar pattern of redemptive struggle: "The people who bear crosses are working with the grain of the universe."[2]

When a person decides to embark on a journey, he or she begins an undertaking whose destination and outcome is often as unpredictable as it is unseen. In fact, not only do we often not know where we are going, we do not know who we will become or whether we will even recognize ourselves at the end of our paths. The hobbit Bilbo Baggins says as much to his young nephew Frodo at the beginning of the Lord of the Rings saga: "It's a dangerous business, Frodo, going out your door. You step onto the road, and if you don't keep your feet, there's no knowing where you might be swept off to."[3]

So it has been for me. These metaphors—growth, birth, journey—tell and help me to understand my story: where I have come from, where I am, and where I might go. They predict possibility and the cost associated with realizing it.

My journey has been a strange one; I never anticipated the life that I am living. *Break. Throw. Rake. Grab. Soak. Bake.* These verbs are a few that describe the activity in my body, heart, mind, and soul. So it is for people who claim and are claimed by the Messiah Jesus, who at the end of his life uses the metaphor of broken bread and spilled wine to approximate his vocation: *Take. Break. Give.* Following Christ and seeking to be faithful to him has hijacked my life in a way that I could never have anticipated. That part of being faithful to Christ has led me to participate in the growing of a church *plant*—well, the irony is not lost on me of the brown thumb.

Meeting Jesus in His People

It wasn't a given that I would become first a follower of Jesus and later a pastor who would start a church just miles from where I grew up. People who knew me in high school are regularly surprised—shocked really—to see what has become of me. I look back at them and nod in agreement.

I began to follow Christ during my senior year in high school. It was a tumultuous time in my life for many different reasons. During middle school I began engaging in some fairly self-destructive behaviors, and by the time I was getting close to graduating from high school, my life was out of control. I regularly abused drugs and alcohol, engaged in sexual experimentation, and got in fights. I have told the story of my mom and dad and the families that gave shape to my life and identity, and I have explained how families created in me a love for stories. However, like so many other kids growing up in the 1970s and 1980s, my story came to include divorce. My senior year of high school was the year my family formally dissolved. Divorce fractures reality for kids no matter what their age. Looking back at that time I see that it was an incredibly painful time for everyone, each of us coping in our own ways the best we knew how. I believe that much of the self-destructive behavior I chose was an adolescent coping mechanism for a painful and confusing environment. Some of it was just plain stupid regardless of the environment.

In the midst of that time I began to date a girl one year my senior, a girl named Melissa, known as Mimi to her close friends and family. In some ways we were very much alike. Mimi and I both grew up in middle-class, suburban homes. We went to the same public school. We both worked part-time jobs throughout high school and participated recreationally in athletics. Like me, she was a child of divorce. Neither of us could have been more lost had we tried. We both came from families where addictions were present and active at times in family members. However, the environment and her reactions to it were different from mine in some significant ways. Where I was self-destructive and reactionary, she worked hard to make things better for herself and others. Where I saw the dissolution of my family at a time when I could reckon with its impact, her parents divorced when she was only eight months old. She never knew another way of being family, and while they had their difficulties, her family figured out ways to be mostly amicable. Our religious background also differed significantly.

In the last chapter I described my religious pedigree: I can't really remember a time in my life when I was not aware of God's presence in my life or when I wasn't involved in a faith community of some sort. Even so, its impact on me in high school was nominal—if that. Mimi's church attendance corresponded to the times when she stayed with her grandparents, semiregularly accompanying them to a small, aging Presbyterian community struggling along in St. Louis. While I had a head full of religious information and experience, she had very little understanding of spiritual things and virtually no knowledge of the Bible whatsoever. When she told me, shortly after we began dating, that she had recently become a follower of Jesus, I was not pleased. Not by a long shot. I was reading

Camus, Kafka, and Sartre. I listened to depressive, cynical, and often atheistic music while I drove around smoking cigarettes, being melancholy, and thinking it was cool. When I saw buses unloading kids for the Saturday night programs at a local parachurch youth ministry, I would scream epithetically out my window, "Jesus freaks!"

I spent hours trying to talk Mimi out of her stupid decision. At the time, most of the people who were helping to nurture her newfound faith were trying to talk her out of dating me, and with good cause too. I knew way more than she did about Christianity, and I used my knowledge like a battering ram. I was in my head—she was in her heart. She listened to me, and she almost never argued. Even so, it was no contest really. Her heart was being transformed by the love of God and the presence of his people in her life. I was increasingly isolated and angry. Eventually it was I who was battered down, not by arguments, but by faith and love—hers first, then others'.

We dated most of that year and the following summer. When Mimi graduated and moved away to go to college, I immediately felt her absence. At the time I believed what I missed was her daily presence in my life. I did, there is no doubt. But I later realized that in her, the presence of Christ was also reaching out and loving me. When she left to go to school, one of the main channels for love in my life evaporated. The pain was acute.

I experienced a lot of pain that year: isolation, anger, and depression—even self-hatred. But then something remarkable happened. Intoxicated (as usual) at a high school football game, I ran into a local businessman who volunteered with a parachurch ministry at my high school. I had known him for a few years. We had met at a youth group weekend retreat where I had gone to scope girls. During the retreat we got into the habit of staying up at night and talking "philosophy." He made an impression on me, not so much because he said anything revelatory but because he simply listened to my friends and me. Now he was standing in front of me and for some reason, that night, he asked if I would be interested in meeting with him and a few other guys to study the Bible. For some reason, that night, standing there drunk and high in front of him, I said okay.

I don't know who was more surprised, he or I. Even though I cursed myself the whole way there that following Sunday, I went. Even though I was the only guy who ever showed up, I kept going. The two of us met every Sunday afternoon for a couple of hours and studied the Bible and talked. He humored my "intellectual" protestations with a straight face and honest answers. Pretty soon he began picking me up on Sunday mornings to take me to church with him. We drove to an elementary school gymnasium where a new church plant was meeting for worship. A man with a sharp mind and a true teaching gift led the community, and as I sat and listened to him every week, my mind forming its arguments and objections, he somehow answered them before my own thoughts were fully formed or realized. I was quickly and truly welcomed and absorbed into a community of Jesus's people. When I say that I was saved, I mean it literally: God in Christ saved my life through a girl and a group of people I used to scream at and call "Jesus freaks."

The ground of my life had been broken.

Living an *Organic* Way of Life

Thus the first stage of my journey was drawing to a close as I graduated from high school. You often hear that said at high school graduations, but for me it was more than a saying. The first part of my story truly was over. My family, at least as I had known it, was functionally gone. I would have to learn a new way of being a son. My younger brother had to make a new way for himself in the midst of this fractured reality, but I never returned home. With twelve years of school behind me, I was ready to move on, strike out on my own. My days of self-destructive behavior were put to rest. More importantly, I was looking forward in a way that had never been available to me before. I was a new disciple of Jesus Christ, and that was changing everything for me. It was a new way of living my life. It was in this next stage that my sense of calling and ministry was given shape.

Following high school graduation I left Kansas City and moved forty miles west to Lawrence and the University of Kansas. Mimi had graduated the year before me and was attending Baylor University in Waco, Texas. Over the next three years we had a long-distance, on-and-off relationship. I spent the first two years of my life at KU living in a fraternity, where initially only one other guy besides me was committed to living and walking as a disciple of Jesus, but it didn't really affect me. Even though my freshmen pledge brothers seemed intent on going insane with the freedom college afforded them, I had already done all my self-destructing. I wasn't tempted in most of the ways people serious about faith are in those environments. Instead, the environment became a crucible where my faith was exercised, refined, and placed on display. I loved it. During my sophomore year in college two significant things happened, two transitions marking an important crossroads at the beginning of the journey that ultimately led to the church I now pastor, Jacob's Well.

The first was that I became involved in a student-led campus ministry called Icthus. The second involved a change of focus in my studies: I switched my major from the liberal arts school to the school of fine arts—from English and journalism to design and illustration.

Within a semester of being involved with Icthus, I was on the leadership team. Icthus was birthed in the 1970s during the Jesus movement. A Presbyterian church in Kansas City experienced explosive youth ministry growth, and when its students went away to college, this church had the foresight to develop a ministry to provide continuity, community, and support for these new disciples as well as opportunities to develop leaders. They also created an intern program that provided these students training, instruction in their faith, and opportunities to participate in ministry over the summer months. Fifteen years later it was still going strong on four different regional university campuses. At the time Icthus had no paid staff. That was the main part of its genius, I think. It depended on the instincts and willingness of its student participants to make things happen. There was very little program. We met weekly to worship, and someone spoke to us. The leadership team came out of the group itself, and current members nominated peers—women and men who seemed to demonstrate fruitfulness over time in the community.

In many ways the ministry was very *organic*. In saying that I mean that we weren't intentionally strategic about what we were trying to do. Rather our activities and life grew out of the people and the environment in which we found ourselves. It seemed to us that as people of God, maybe we should meet regularly for prayer. So four mornings a week people gathered in the campus chapel from 7:00 to 8:00 a.m. to pray. Jesus talked about the poor, so we tried to serve the poor by regularly working at the Salvation Army shelter. We also included in our community people in need from the city of Lawrence who found their way into our gatherings, even when it was clear they were neither students nor college age. Once a month we met in homes for "Friday Night Worship," a time of intense and focused singing and prayer. The leaders were expected to lead a Bible study weekly during the semester. Over time, more and more people began living together intentionally and sharing more and more. It was attractive. Hospitality was part of the culture. We weren't so much trying to *reach* people as much as people were being reached as the overflow of a community living its life together in an integrated and consistent manner. Most of us didn't know what we had until it was over. It was a life-defining experience. Better, it was a way-of-life–defining experience. And maybe not so amazingly, the ministry grew. But it was really the community that grew, and ministry was simply a by-product of that common life.

Becoming an art and design student was the other major shift in my life back then. The lessons I learned by accessing my imagination, my intuition, and my creative impulses never left me. I have increasingly come to rely on such faculties in my role at Jacob's Well. Working in a studio alongside fellow artists/designers in a collaborative manner to solve design problems that were beyond any individual's abilities modeled for me a way of approaching challenges that is less about the individual and more about the community and how each person has a voice and a part to play. Submitting myself to my peers and my professors by placing my artwork on a wall for critique gave me courage to hear and accept feedback that was tempting to perceive as rejection but was really about my growth and development as an artist and a human being. Finally, learning to live and work among an incredibly diverse and expressive group of people (in the way studio artists live and work), often different from me in every imaginable way, birthed in me a hunger for environments that can hold diversity in such a way that creation and life happen. I loved my education and experience in the school of design.

I didn't, however, become a vocational artist. To the befuddlement of my professors and peers, I went into vocational ministry. I figured that part of my life, while wonderful, was behind me. It might be expressed as a hobby, but nothing more.

Seeds had been sown.

Losing What I Didn't Know I Had

During the winter break of my senior year of college the on-again, off-again relationship that Mimi and I had underwent a significant transition: we married after she graduated from

Baylor. Throughout her time in college, Mimi had also been involved in student campus ministries and spent her summers doing missions work or working at a Christian summer camp. To that point we had been dating fairly consistently for five years and realized that we wanted to move into the life that was waiting for us after college through marriage. She graduated with a degree in elementary education, we were married, and she took a job teaching in Lawrence. Later that spring the next stage of life unfolded as I accepted a job as the first youth pastor of the very church where (just a few years earlier) I had been reluctantly driven to worship, connect, and learn. My life had dramatically changed in just four years' time. It was about to change again.

At first I loved the opportunity that working at this church created. I loved the staff, the people of the church, and an environment that was innovative and permission giving. The opportunity to learn and experiment was always present. During my first year on staff, the leadership of the church also made the requisite 1990s pilgrimage to Willow Creek, a very innovative community located outside Chicago, Illinois. Sometime in the year or two that followed that initial visit, our church's leadership made the challenging decision to become a seeker-targeted church in the language that Willow Creek coined. It was over this issue that I first witnessed a divisive church conflict.

Youth ministry, at the same time, was turning out to be something different from what I expected. Students who graduate from college and want to go into ministry have few options—the main one being youth ministry, the other, continuing education. That was a hard transition for me. In the early 1990s youth ministry was (and may still be to some extent) about creating and running programs that stimulate churched kids. That was a world I was neither comfortable in nor equipped to engage in. Nor was it the way I experienced ministry in college. Within a year I was feeling a rub that I couldn't quite put my finger on. I interpreted it as vocational disconnect. I was not cut out to be a youth guy. After two more years, I was struggling hard and couldn't seem to understand what was going on inside me and with my faith—after all, I loved the kids, my co-workers, the people of the church, and the opportunity to create and develop ministry in relative freedom. But I felt as though I was going through the motions. It seemed like I was constantly practicing for a game I never played.

Throughout that transition the leaders of the church listened and sought to coach me, refusing to see me as a person filling a job description that wasn't working. They saw *me* first and sought to shepherd me into a place of vocational integrity, and for that I am incredibly grateful. Mimi and I struggled and prayed and tried to figure out what we might do. We both loved ministry and felt called to a vocational expression of it. So how could we resolve this conflict? After a lot of counsel, conversation, and prayer, we did what most people confused about their faith and vocational identities do: we went to seminary.

After almost four years of youth ministry in a local church, I packed up my family (now including a one-year-old son) and drove to Colorado. I went west, like settlers before me, full of hopes and dreams. Going to seminary was something I had always hoped was in my future. When I became a youth pastor, for some reason I figured I would never really get there. Maybe it was because when I became a youth pastor I dove into that vocation with the conviction that I had fulfilled my calling and would labor there until some indeterminate time far in the future. Thus seminary education seemed like a casualty of that decision.

That first crisp September morning, when my new seminary professor began to teach a Gospels class (exploring the inter-testamental contextual landscape!) I almost couldn't believe it. It was exhilarating. More than the thin, cold mountain air exhilarated me. For the first time I was going to school because I had made the decision to do so. It almost felt selfish: surely God could not be so good as to allow me the experience of studying something I loved so much. What I had been doing informally for years I was now able to do in a formal and focused environment. It seemed unbelievable that I had the opportunity to submit myself to the teaching of extraordinary men and women given the task of plumbing the depths of one specific discipline for the benefit of the church. That was what I had come to seminary to do: to sit under the teaching and lives of brilliant men and women and go deep. I loved that. I wanted depth.

The largest living organism in the world is a grove of aspen trees in the Wasatch Mountains in Utah. Originally the trees of that range were seen individually, but it came to be understood that beneath the surface the interconnected root system made it a single organism. This biological phenomenon became a metaphor for what I was hoping would happen to me through the means of seminary training and subsequent learning. I came to seminary with a bunch of saplings that seemed disconnected: New Testament, Old Testament, counseling, philosophy of religion, leadership, preaching, to name a few. To get deep enough beneath the surface to see how all those disciplines were interconnected and reflective of a whole greater than the sum of its parts was important in helping me gain a more holistic picture of life, faith, and ministry. In such an approach to learning one might come away looking only marginally more mature on the surface but in reality having grown infinitely more complex and connected below the surface. What I understand of the Old Testament narrative influences how I counsel people, which influences how I lead, which alters my philosophy of religion, and so on.

But if my experience of life and ministry in the local church following the organic and communal reality of what I had experienced in college was ultimately frustrating and confusing, seminary was worse. The writer of Proverbs speaks truly when he writes, "Hope deferred makes the heart sick" (Prov. 13:12). I loved the learning I was being exposed to, especially the scriptural and historical studies. However as I worked my way through the master of divinity track, I had a sense of unease, a growing realization that something felt off-kilter in this environment too.

Part of that dynamic was the difficulty of navigating a master's degree while working two jobs and trying to be a passable husband and father. That struggle is not unique to seminary students, though—it is part of life, especially when a person is working to establish himself or herself in a vocation. Instead, my struggle increasingly was the character of the master of divinity program itself. It seemed as though the seminary was uncertain about what it was seeking to do with its students. In addition to the pressure to succeed academically, the school leveled a host of other requirements that became overwhelming: mandatory chapel attendance, mandatory marriage retreats, campus small groups, internships, mentoring programs, and on and on and on. The master of divinity program seemed like a pastiche of competing interests by groups vying to have their particular discipline or set of competencies represented. Unfortunately, no one seemed to be attending to the overall picture and what it was costing students to have so many demands placed upon them. The proverbial forest was lost for the trees, and these trees didn't seem nearly as interconnected as those of the Wasatch Range.

This was hard on my family and me. To the student trying to juggle so many requirements amid so much life—including the attempt to not go up to one's eyeballs in debt—it was detrimental. In its effort to do all that could possibly be done to educate and prepare students, the seminary program did not enrich us; it flattened our understandings and our lives. As we met to study, I remember hours of discussing this struggle with fellow students. At the time I was angry with the school, but I have since learned that seminaries face a number of tensions because of the unique space they occupy as both academic and ministry training institutions.[4]

So the first half of my growing unease stemmed from the nature of the educational program to which I was submitted. The second half of my struggle related to the world in which the seminary located itself. As I wended my way through four years of education, I realized with a growing and startling sense of clarity that the seminary was educating and training me for a world that no longer existed. Moreover, the posture of this particular brand of Christianity toward the surrounding culture was one of enormous suspicion and at times hostility. It seemed that part of this evolving designation involved a posture of entrenchment and argument toward culture. But I loved culture. I loved the freedom to engage with people for the purpose of friendship and dialogue, not simply evangelism.

I had gone to seminary hoping to gain greater clarity. In fact, it did just the opposite. I knew the world in which I was going to live and breathe and have my being as a pastor, and it was not the world the seminary was engaging. The longer my program went on, the more grueling it became.

Finding a New Path

One bright spot was a church plant I became a part of during seminary. It helped me begin to see a way forward.

A pastor named Ron Johnson started Pathways Church in Denver in the mid-90s. Ron's passion was to create a church for Generation X at the time people were just beginning to take such things seriously. Because of the ubiquity of Willow Creek community and its influence as *the* most innovative church related to reaching out and *doing* evangelism, Pathways, seeking to be relevant and make an impact among a specific group of people, was also a seeker-targeted church. I got involved on the ground floor of the church and labored alongside Ron, his wife, Kim, and others for two years leading worship, doing creative programming, and even being involved in a little bit of pastoring. It was through Pathways that I also attended a ministry conference where I heard the word *postmodern* for the first time. In this one event, all the frustration that had been roiling within me coalesced and found an outlet. For the first time I heard people describing out loud an expression of Christian faith in a language that was native to me, that named the tensions I was holding inside myself related to the church, our culture, and the gospel. This experience created a new lens on reality for me by which the frustration of my seminary experience came into sharp relief. I realized what wasn't happening in my seminary world relative to those issues.

It was also at this conference that I began to understand why, while totally respecting Willow Creek and its faithful response to God in South Barrington, Illinois, I was struggling internally with many of the presuppositions upon which the church growth movement and seeker-targeted approach to ministry was based and how it was then being replicated in different contexts as leaders attempted to reproduce the "Willow Creek model." I reflected back on my experience as the youth pastor of my home church and began to have insight into why I had grown increasingly uncomfortable in ministry there. One part of it was a vocational disconnect, to be sure. But it was also a philosophy and theology of ministry, culture, and even gospel that was ill-fitted to my experience of reality.

The conference was hosted at the Navigators' Glen Eyrie retreat center in Colorado Springs and put on by the Young Leaders Network, a subministry of the parachurch organization Leadership Network. It was there in 1996 that I first met people like Chris Seay, Doug Pagitt, Dieter Zander, and a whole host of others who were nascent leaders in the emerging church movement, though it was not referred to as that at the time. Over that week I heard the call to church plant. At the end of this gathering someone stood up and said something to this effect: "If you think God is calling you to plant a church that will seek to reach future generations, then stand up." I was on my feet before I knew what was happening. Truly, I believe my rational mind was bypassed by something deeper and more primal. The next thing I knew I was surrounded by six or seven people laying their hands on me and praying for what God might do. I was in.

That was more than just another seminal moment in the story of my journey. By the end of seminary, I was honestly ready to hang it up. I felt like the settlers who had gone west in hopes of finding fertile farmland and within a couple of generations were harvesting the dust bowl of Depression-era Kansas. I now look back at that time and think, to continue the growth metaphor, it was then that the seeds of grass had begun to break open and reach for purchase. It was a time of being watered and baked. It was a time of being hid beneath the surface of the ground where growth was happening, but not in any way visible to the human eye.

The growth had begun with my experience in the local church as a youth pastor. It continued during seminary, where I struggled through an expensive master of divinity program that in many ways seemed irrelevant to the call I felt on my life and brutal to my body and soul and on my family's finances. It concluded as I searched for words to describe why I could not simply co-opt Willow Creek's model of church and apply it in a church like Pathways one thousand miles to the west. At twenty-seven, I felt like a curmudgeon. At times I wondered if I was simply proud and unteachable. I truly didn't know. I knew I was tired of struggling. I was tired of complaining. I was tired of the *via negativa*, the negative way whereby you determine what something is, or what you believe about something, by what that something is *not*. I wanted to be *for* something, not just against something.

A *Kairos* Moment

As my seminary career was coming to its conclusion, I took more and more opportunities to go to the mountains to hike, think, and pray. I remember hiking in Golden Gate Canyon State Park and coming through a stand of trees and into a meadow surrounded by mountains. The vista before me brought into relief the chasm I felt inside. All the passion that had up until then been true of my life in God and animated my desire to serve him in ministry had finally run out—drained out of me by the very things I had hoped would help me faithfully take the next steps of obedience and faithfulness. I had finally begun to go through the motions.

I was done.

Standing there, I reached a crisis contemplating my future. I think every person has one or two of these moments of existential crisis sometime in their life. It is a time of crisis, to be sure. But it is also a time of possibility. Desperation makes new things possible; it is a pregnant time. The Bible sometimes uses the Greek word *kairos* to designate this time of possibility. It is different than *chronos*, that is, chronological time. It is the time of God's activity. It is comprised of a string of moments that possess extraordinary clarity—clarity frequently brought on by pain of one kind or another. Singularity. In these moments a person is absolutely present: to himself or herself, to God, and to the experience of reality that he or she is facing, and these moments can lead to some sort of discovery or declaration that has been previously hidden or unknown.

I think of Martin Luther, backed into every conceivable corner. Instead of retreating, he leans forward and says to the religious, civic, and militaristic powers of his day, "Here I stand. I can do no other." Crisis can crystallize what is at stake in such a way that tepid responses are not really options. At the same time, let's be honest. I was certainly under nowhere near the pressure that Luther was—not by a long shot. Nor do I consider myself in any way analogous to Luther except as a fellow pilgrim striving to be faithful to God as hundreds of thousands of Christians have been before me. But as I reflected wistfully back over the experience of the gospel and community that I had during college, of the environment and way of life that had produced such generous and compelling community in such a seemingly effortless way, in a fit of exasperation I actually cried out loud at God: *"I cannot believe that you intend the best years of my life as a disciple of Jesus Christ to be experienced between the ages of nineteen and twenty-one. I cannot accept that I have peaked in my experience of you and the church and that I am to spend the rest of my life going through the motions. I cannot accept this!"* It woke me up. It was my moment of clarity.

Looking back, I see that moment clearly—the realization that came out of my desperation and pain. It was the point of hope from which I was launched into the work that ultimately became the community I lead and live in now. I didn't—couldn't—know that at the time. What I knew was that I had hope. For the first time in a long while I had hope that was born in honesty. That hope was a thin carpet of green grass breaking the surface of the ground.

I began to see a world of possibility before me that I could live in and invite others to live in with me. I don't presume to know what the kingdom of God is, but it had that feel to me. Through my time at Glen Eyrie, I had an experience among other leaders that began to create a community of fellow sojourners, brothers and sisters committed to moving forward creatively and faithfully toward the birth of this new thing, whatever it might be. It was the makings of a new community of sorts, a new way to be vocationally connected. I also knew I had already experienced in college something of what the future might hold—a picture of sorts. It was certainly not a model—more like a deposit of what had been and might one day be again. Somewhere in that time I stumbled onto a passage in Isaiah that gave voice to all this.

> Forget the former things;
> do not dwell on the past.

See, I am doing a new thing!
Now it springs up; do you not perceive it?
I am making a way in the wilderness
and streams in the wasteland.
The wild animals honor me,
the jackals and the owls,
because I provide water in the wilderness
and streams in the wasteland,
to give drink to my people, my chosen,
the people I formed for myself
that they may proclaim my praise.

Isaiah 43:18–21

I knew I had been called to help develop a new church for a world that I was a part of and that was emerging within and around and before me. I knew this way was as much for my own benefit as it was for anyone else's. I knew (and prayed) the Spirit of God was out there ahead of me leading the way. I knew it was going to require more perception than comprehension to find this way, more intuition and creativity than skill and strategy (though they would be needed as well). I knew that wilderness was a more apt metaphor than the Promised Land, and while I didn't know how or even where this wilderness would ultimately be, if God was present in it, then that was enough of a promise for me.

Finally, I knew I had to learn. Seminary had opened the door of academics to me, but just barely. I needed theology. I needed history. I needed philosophy. I needed missiology. My education had just begun.

Back to a Beginning

As seminary wound down and the specter of my future drew closer, Mimi and I had some decisions to make. Initially we were hesitant about returning to Kansas City—you can't go home and all that. We thought we might remain in Denver and plant a church. There had also been some talk about moving to Seattle to join something already in progress. I had a college friend who had begun a Bible study in his home, and it had quickly grown beyond his ability to lead it and do all that was required of him in his job at Microsoft. Processing all this, Mimi and I both had a sense that we didn't want to generate something that was dependent on us. We knew as leaders we would be responsible, but being responsible is different than being the focal point that generates the work. We believed that wherever we were headed, God would be ahead of us, already working. Our simple task would be to discern where God was already at work and then join that work in the role that was given to us. Through that paradigm, it slowly became clear that Kansas City was the place to which we were being summoned. So in December 1997 we packed up our family (two kids now in tow) and belongings and returned back east down a long, flat stretch of I-70.

While the fertile plains of western Kansas were dormant, covered in snow, the surface of my soul stirred with the green of new life.

3

Making Sense of My Story

interpretation and experimentation

The best criticism of the bad has always been the practice of the better. If much of the old church has to die (and I think it will, even without our pushing), then maybe it is because we have neither criticized the bad nor practiced the better with any social vigor. We have daintily gone to church while living like the rest of the world. Now I find people who are living the mystery of the church, and from that place going to the world. The church has always been a movement much more than this institution or that, a continual torrent of the Spirit flowing through the grist mill of human structures and human history.[1]

> Richard Rohr, "Holy Fools: Ushers of the
> Next Generation of the Church," *Sojourners*

I was not sure where I was going, and I could not see what I would do when I got [there]. But you saw further and clearer than I, and you opened the seas before my ship, whose track led me across the waters to a place I had never dreamed of, and which you were even then preparing to be my rescue and my shelter and my home.[2]

> Thomas Merton, *The Seven Storey Mountain*

Vocation does not come from willfulness. It comes from listening. I must listen to my life and try to understand what it is truly about—quite apart from what I would like it to be about—or my life will never represent anything real in the world, no matter how earnest my intentions. That insight is hidden in the word vocation itself, which is rooted in the Latin for "voice." Vocation does not mean a goal that I pursue. It means a calling that I hear. Before I can tell my life what I want to do with it, I must listen to my life telling me who I am.[3]

Parker Palmer, *Let Your Life Speak*

Listening to My Life

Mimi and I had an ever-increasing sense that we inhabited a unique time with unique opportunities. Exactly *what* was unique about the time and the opportunities before us was unclear. That we seemed to be living through a time of significant cultural transition seemed obvious. But at that time we had very little language to describe what we were experiencing personally and culturally—mostly what we had was some kind of intuitive sense that we were shifting, internally and externally. As a result we struggled to express, even to ourselves, what it was we perceived and what we wanted to do in response to God and this context to which, with others, we sensed we were being called. In light of that uncertainty and the opportunity we sensed before us, the language of experimentation seemed the most appropriate way of understanding what we were about to do. And in order to experiment and move forward well, we needed to look backward into our story and do some *interpretation*.

Reflecting back on my time in college—the place where I had unwittingly experienced God, gospel, community, environment, ministry, and myself—I recognized that in that time I had experienced something true and good. I had participated in a way of life that was generative for myself, my community, and even the surrounding university campus. In this experiment, that college experience became a starting point. I wanted that same thing again. That was a big part of my motivation, and I want to be honest about it.

In the midst of this process, however, I was wary of forming an idol out of that experience and pursuing or worshiping it rather than God. It is so easy to do that. Rather than receiving the gift and moving on with our gaze fixed on God, we fix our eyes on the blessing and seek it instead. Wrongly aimed, we become increasingly dissatisfied when the thing we seek eludes us. Disillusionment and cynicism can quickly follow. As much as possible, I didn't want this previous experience, no matter how rich and good, to become an end in itself.

Faith as a Way of Life in Community

The first thing I began to discern during that critical time was that the life of faith I lived was just that: a life. There was no sense of separation or compartmentalization in anything I did. Faith was a way of life that centered on being a disciple of Jesus Christ, and that played out holistically in every arena of my life. Everything was included in my faith, and my faith included everything: art, school, fraternity life, ministry, living arrangements, friendships, church, community, recreation . . . it was all of a piece. Even more significant, I exercised my faith alongside other people. I was not in this by myself. Further, there was no separating the secular from the sacred, no subculture Christian ghetto. The university campus begged engagement. If our faith wasn't robust enough to engage the complexity of the environment we were in, we struggled until it was.

We lived out our faith within a specific context. Christian faith does not teach that the flesh became Word, that human beings struggle along until they transcend their creatureliness and are subsumed into some kind of divine union in an *a*cultural state of detachment. God revealed himself in a specific time, in a specific place, among a specific people. God did not create a divine subculture and then wait for humanity to wise up and join in. God joined a story. God got dirty. God entered. God engaged. And this is the calling of the church as well—to join in and participate in God's story at work in the world. In that sense to be incarnational is to live in the world the way God lived in the world. Somehow this was the spirit of our life on that campus. It was our story. But we did not do this as if we were trying to do something unique or strategic. It overflowed with a naturalness that is hard to explain.

Maybe part of this dynamic had to do with how the ministry itself was structured. As I mentioned before, the ministry I was a part of, Icthus, was a student-led ministry. There were no paid staff people. No fund-raising apparatus. No vision or mission or strategic plan. A group of students lived and played and served and learned and worked and worshiped together. We shared life and practiced hospitality without knowing we were doing it.

The genius of the structure was that there was very little structure. Structure is not a bad thing. Structures either support or inhibit life. The more the structure is in tune with the environment in which it exists, the greater its chance to stimulate rather than short-circuit life. The less the structure reflects the environment in which it exists, the more it struggles. Our structure was very loose. Our structure had very little distance between the top and the bottom. In a very real sense, it was flat. That does not mean it was without authority. There was a leadership structure that perpetuated itself from the inside out: student leaders recognized student leaders and invited them into a leadership *core*—a group of people who lived in all the same ways as their peers and sought to steward the life of the community in simple ways. There was generally no sense of *us* and *them*, either between the student leaders and the student participants or between the Icthus community and the broader life of the campus.

There was no real program to speak of: a Thursday night meeting was about the extent of it. But to equate that gathering with the overall life of the community it represented would be to miss the point of the whole thing. That gathering simply gave shape to the day-to-day, week-to-week, semester-to-semester community that existed in such an organic fashion. The community was an organism responding incarnationally, missionally, intuitively, and creatively to the environment in a holistic manner.

Implicit in all the characteristics I describe above is a fundamental understanding of our identity, first and foremost, in *group* terms. We were a part of something bigger than ourselves as individuals: we were a community. We were greater than the sum of our parts. We were a body of people seeking and following Jesus Christ, and our common way of life and friendships overflowed into our context. What is more, the flow of influence moved in both directions. We were not outside of the culture influencing it from a position of privilege. We were part of the culture. We were indigenous. We were engaged in life, a way of living held in common. We were a people among people.

Losing Community, Losing Faith

After my experience as a new disciple of Jesus Christ in college, suburban American Christian culture (or more accurately, subculture) at the end of the twentieth century was a tough place for me to land at twenty-two years of age. I had naively assumed that what had been so powerful, so life-giving, and so fruitful for so many others and myself would simply be continued in the next chapter of life. It wasn't. While many great people and opportunities greeted me, so did struggle and confusion.

At the time I did not possess the perspective relative to my maturity and experience to interpret what was going on and how that might affect me. As I observed people around me, however, I was able to see a number of friends with whom I had lived so intimately begin to lose their faith following college. That sounds dramatic, and I don't mean it in the way you might initially read it: I don't mean they lost the content of their belief system or became apostate doctrinally. I mean that upon leaving college and entering the world of twentieth-century suburban Christianity, they lost their way of life. They entered a way of life that was compartmentalized, disintegrated, individualistic, subcultured, ghettoized, programmed, and purpose-driven.

Christian faith, like almost anything else in American life, can easily become one more compartment like so many other compartments. In a culture consumed with separating the public from the private, faith can easily become privatized. Again I am not saying that this, in and of itself, is necessarily bad. I am simply pointing out that some kind of common, organic, and environmentally attuned way of life is nearly impossible when such a division is given primacy.

What had been for me a way of life became instead a job, a system of doctrine, a program to run. To be sure, that is not all it was, but even in the midst of some good stuff, I couldn't deny that I, too, was losing my faith. I saw it first in others, but I quickly came to realize that it was happening to me in all the same ways. Deep as I was in "ministry," it was hard to see at first.

I began to go through the motions. Occasionally I came to myself, got honest, and took a look around. But when I looked around, people either seemed uncritically satisfied or altogether out of the game. I tried to process what I was feeling, but as inchoate as most of these rumblings were, I was often met with confusion, dismissal, or misdiagnosis. The horizon of Christianity in America held little that awoke any sense of expectancy or hope for me. Everyone knew exactly what to expect: from God, from the Scriptures, from the church, from the world.

I know it sounds arrogant to pass judgment on so many different Christian communities and their expressions of faith.

I never intended to be arrogant or to pass judgment. I was desperate. I was constantly on the lookout for signs of life: in myself, in others, in communities. I just couldn't find any. And as I began to explore what it might mean to plant a church, I couldn't believe the number of already established churches that seemed to be simply running other churches' ministry programs, posting banners out front advertising prepackaged programs that seemed to me to be the adult version of the newest children's Sunday school curriculum.

Even church plants seemed trapped in this dynamic. I thought it was so ironic. In my mind, new church starts had the greatest relative freedom to engage and experiment in response to their environment. Instead they, too, had everything fundamentally locked down before they ever began. Just drop the franchise in whatever city you want to target and follow the directions.

The Sins of Reductionism

One of the marks of emerging churches is the rediscovery of the particular and local and of the resulting necessity of story for interpreting our location and identity, as I discussed in the first chapter. This (re)discovery in some ways is a corrective to the many different ways churches in the West, in the wake of modernity, became wedded to notions of knowledge and truth that removed the particular and the local in favor of what could be known universally, objectively, and with certainty. To say that knowledge and truth are *universal* is to say that if it is true in one place, then it is true in the same way in all places at all times for all people. Further, if it is universal, then it is universally accessible to all possible knowers regardless of their location and situation. To say that knowledge and truth are primarily accessed *objectively* is to say that there is some place available to human beings where we make judgments free from bias, and thus we believe these judgments correspond precisely to reality *as it is*. Finally, to hold a position that seeks some measure of certainty is to pursue knowledge and truth in an indubitable manner, that is, impossible to doubt and thus unquestionable.

Theologians John Franke and Stan Grenz describe this epistemological approach to knowledge, "foundationalism," with its limitations in their book *Beyond Foundationalism*.[4] In light of more in-depth, nuanced, and intelligent treatments of this material, I do not want to spend a lot of time trying to unpack epistemology in this book. But because these kinds of considerations influence how we engage and respond to reality so significantly, it is worth a few more comments for the purpose of clarity.

When truth and knowledge are seen primarily as those things that are universally available, objectively accessed, and held with certainty, it begins to create a corresponding culture of reductionism. Reductionism is a philosophical theory that the nature of complex things can always be reduced to simpler or more fundamental things. When we reduce something, we observe a complex reality and reduce it to simplified abstractions that are devoid of all contextual considerations. Reductionism is an attempt to get at first causes and basic foundations or essences, and it can be a very effective tool, to be sure. In fact, in the first chapter I confessed to using this tool to reduce the historical context and complexity of modernity for the purpose of telling a story that locates us somewhere other than the place described. But a tool used too frequently or too indiscriminately can end up mangling and misrepresenting more than it helps. I fear reductionism can be and has been just such a tool.

We live in a culture of reductionism. Or better, we are living in the aftermath of a culture of reductionism, and I believe this culture has a profound affect on churches. For example, we have reduced the complexity and diversity of the Scriptures to systematic theologies that insist on ideological conformity, even when such conformity flattens the diversity of the Scriptural witness. We have reduced our conception of gospel to four simple steps that short-circuit biblical narratives and notions of the kingdom of God on earth as it is in heaven in favor of a simplified means of entrance to heaven. Our preaching is often wed to our materialistic, consumerist cultural assumptions, and sermons are subsequently reduced to delivering messages that reinforce the worst of what American culture produces: self-centered end users who believe that God is a resource that helps an individual secure what amounts to an anemic and culturally bound understanding of the "abundant life" (see John 10:10).

Let me give one example that I believe is familiar to anyone at all involved in local church leadership and that captures the nature of my struggle following my college experience of faith. There is a great pressure on churches to be "successful." Of course, this notion of success is often derived through unquestioned and culturally defined lenses and metaphors. In such an environment we come to depend on markers that have been predetermined to have value that are easily observed and measured: size of community, size of building, staff, budget, number of programs, market share, etc. Because this system of metrics is largely about external markers, it results in a corresponding push to find ministries that are currently successful by those terms. Once these are located, they are often reduced to models that can be duplicated, following the logic that if it is true in one place, it must be true everywhere else, regardless of context.

Witness the increasing dependence of pastors and leaders upon pollsters and demographers to tell them what is happening in their own environments. Every few years a new book comes out in which such a pollster unearths some new, groundbreaking take on what is going on culturally and how the church must respond. The loss of connection between churches and neighborhoods creates a corresponding loss of localized imagination and creates an addictive-like dependence on acontextual experts who scan the physical and spiritual horizon for "success."

Witness the succession of churches that direct-mail slick brochures to churches around the country and world touting their ministry and the conferences (distribution arm of research and development) they host so you can come and learn how to become more effective relative, presumably, to the brochure images: huge crowds, stunning campuses, smiling people. Then witness a Christian marketing machine that rushes in to capitalize on this phenomenon and sell you the newest method for "winning" (if that isn't a culturally conditioned word, I am not sure one exists) the culture for Christ.

Finally, witness titillated, then exhausted and bored pastors and congregations fed up and frustrated by the next new thing but at the same time trained (often unknowingly but nevertheless masterfully) in the art of technique reproduction.

We have a mounting leadership crisis in the church. We are facing a crisis of imagination, an ill-fed spiritual attention span nourished by novelty. I believe this dynamic has debilitated local churches and is part of the diagnosis for what plagued me in the years following my college experience.

Am I being too harsh? Maybe I am. I honestly have a hard time telling most of the time. These dynamics that I have witnessed with increasing alarm over the last several years produce in me an almost irrational level of frustration and even despair at times. I am not trying to say that huge crowds, stunning campuses, and smiling people are bad, per se. In fact, in our community at Jacob's Well we have pretty big crowds and hopefully some smiling people. I am also not saying that all churches with big crowds, stunning campuses, and smiling people have achieved those things because they pursued them directly in an unreflective quest for success. This is not my point. My point is that this posture toward knowledge and truth, our environment, ourselves, metrics, culture, and even God is incredibly dangerous.

We are missing leaders like the patriarch Jacob, who are willing to wrestle with God as Jacob wrestled the angel on the bank of the river at Jabbok, refusing to release God until he blesses us—even if it means hobbling the rest of our days. We are missing prophetic leaders who are able to read the sign of the times, who listen carefully, thoughtfully, and theologically, who respond in faithful and creative ways based on an imagination baptized and engaged in a missional reading of Scripture, the environment, the people God has provided in their midst— not to mention the resources at hand that God has supplied. ("Therefore you do not lack any spiritual gift as you eagerly wait for our Lord Jesus Christ to be revealed," 1 Cor. 1:7.)

At its worst, this reduced picture of reality has drained the landscape of color and creativity under God, and imagination has been lost in favor of a very small and uniform version of life. Our churches are the religious equivalent of strip malls with the same ten massive retailers located in Anytown, USA. I am truly afraid that in our desire to attain success, defined as it has been and accessed through supposedly reproducible programs, models, and technique duplication, we have instead become technicians. We have given away the harder and truer path that would produce the more enduring fruit of character, discernment, and creative contextual responsiveness. Like Esau, we have traded our birthright for the proverbial bowl of stew.

Three Kinds of Experimentation

Is there an alternative? I believe there is, and I am beginning to hint at it with the concepts of story, community, and experimentation. When we think about creating an environment that might give rise to life in response to the Holy Spirit and the world we live in today, we must cherish and engage our context. *My* context is my life, the city I live in, and the church where I am working out, with others, what it means to be faithful to Jesus Christ—regardless of so-called measures of success. What are the particulars of your context? I believe this is the *stuff*, the raw material, out of which God creates, calls, and constitutes life for communities and the people who make them up. Tragically we often dismiss these things, relegating such precious resources to the slag heap in favor of that which has already been mass-produced somewhere else and then imported for easy consumption.

We must engage in interpretation and experimentation. Interpretation looks backward and analyzes what has happened in order to learn and know where we are *now* and in what direction we might head in the future. It asks, "What does that mean?" Experimentation asks a different question: "Where are we going, and how might we get there?" To experiment is to explore and to move within a location. Experimentation is historical in that it comes from someplace. Experimentation is teleological in that it is going someplace. And in the space between, experimentation is a dynamic engagement with where you are *right now*.

Experimentation, used in the way I am suggesting, implies an uncertainty regarding outcomes. Experimentation connotes looking into an environment or some kind of phenomena for possibility—for a sign of life, for something different than the status quo. Experimentation begins when a person's intuition or experience of reality does not match the explanation or current map of reality; an investigation of the discrepancies becomes necessary. The experimenter is responding to *something* in the environment. Whatever that something is, it gets under the skin and begins to irritate; it excites a reaction.

There are many different ways we experiment in our culture that provide metaphors for how we might approach this concept. There is the experimentation of big business: research and development tied together by big money, intellectual property, and science in ways never before seen. This kind of experimentation seeks to expose and isolate the method or particular pathway one must traverse to realize the goal of the experiment. What is really being investigated in this first metaphor of experimentation is the *means* by which a *predetermined outcome* is realized. It might be better described as research or experimentation for the purpose of development. For example, pharmaceutical companies identify outstanding, unresolved medical issues in populations and then do research and development to create drugs that treat these problems. Once the goal is realized, the drug is then mass-produced, hopefully to great advantage. The initial experiment becomes reproducible when the experimenters or, by that point, technicians, reproduce the same outcome by re-creating the environment that gave the desired results.

Experimentation can also imply playing with something for its own sake—such as the kind of experimentation that happens when jazz musicians gather to improvise or play variations on a theme. Sometimes it works, other times it doesn't. Jazz musicians work from musical motifs with loose structures and then experiment in a more intuitive fashion. When such a jam session happens, the result (a specific collection of sounds) dissipates as quickly as it emerges. It is never reproducible in the same way a scientific experiment is because all kinds of environmental variables are present in a jam session that can never be exactly re-created. It will never be replicated in the exact same way that a drug company can endlessly reproduce the same pharmaceutical product to meet demand.

And sometimes experimentation is nothing more than pure novelty. This third kind of experimentation is the kind that rises out of boredom or self-indulgence, an often uncritical and indulgent chasing of one's whims. Recreational drug use or sexual experimentation are examples of this type.

Have you experienced experimentation in local churches of the three types I have described above? In churches there are those of us who experiment with the intent of discovering, isolating, reproducing, marketing, and then distributing innovation—out of our context and into everyone else's. When this is our posture, we are like those experimenters who do research and development out of the amalgamation of big business, intellectual property, and science. We already know what we want; we simply want the best, cheapest, and most effective means to get us there. We have become technicians in search of profit. Others of us are bored and simply flit from one experiment to the next without reflection or intention, seeming to be more excited about the possibility of ministerial titillation than actually producing offspring. Finally, a few of us engage in a type of experimentation that is more intuitive and disciplined, that develops through the dynamic engagement of leaders who are like jazz musicians tuned in to themselves, a melody, their fellow musicians, and the environment where they are playing.

When Mimi and I left seminary I wanted (and still want) to pursue experimentation in this creatively engaged way as a faithful response to my story and my calling. I believe such a response is integral to my discipleship personally and communally.

Telling the First Part of Our Story

It is important to say that Jacob's Well Church didn't begin as a concept, theory, or model. I resist giving any concrete examples of what life at Jacob's Well is like or how we got started. In light of what I have said so far, perhaps you are beginning to understand why. I don't want to tell too much of the specifics of the story for fear that what is merely descriptive of what has happened in one place will become prescriptive for others who want to likewise engage in their place. We are not trained to engage. We are trained to duplicate. We are often not able to read stories and allow them to ignite our local imaginations. Instead we try to mine stories for timeless principles that can be readily applied.

In light of that I would rather set the stage, describe the environment, tell the story up to a certain point—and then no more. Jacob's Well was birthed out of the complex and interconnected stories of a specific group of people who over time began to let themselves follow God together without a predetermined grid for what that would look like or what the result would be. Experimentation.

Jacob's Well is the story of God hovering over the chaos of my life and calling forth life. It is the story of God hovering over a community of people in a place and calling forth life. It is a story of discovery, frustration, and hope birthing new life. It is a story, for better or worse, of engaged and intuitive experimentation. It is an ongoing attempt to have integrity and be faithful and responsive to reality as it is being engaged.

Some people do not think it is acceptable to begin a church as an experiment. I truly do not believe they could be more mistaken. Not only is it acceptable in my reckoning, it is vital that we do so. It is what churches have been doing for two millennia in the wake of the scandal of the incarnation of God in Jesus Christ.

I graduated from seminary in 1997, and Mimi and I quickly left Denver to begin an experiment in Kansas City, Missouri—the birthing of a new faith community. We had been in contact with the church where I had formerly been the youth pastor. They were interested in church planting. Initially, a return to Kansas City was not on my radar screen, but the more Mimi and I talked and prayed about it, the more it seemed to be where we sensed life. That was incredibly important to me. By then I had been involved with three church plants. I knew firsthand the hard work and demanding nature of beginning a faith community from scratch. In light of that it was equally important that we prayerfully discern where we were to begin this work. I believed God was already out in front of us somewhere at work.

The first step of faithfully responding to the call we felt was to discern where that work was happening and position ourselves to join in it. I had no interest in getting a group of people worked up around a vision that was largely dependent on my ability to rally them to something they otherwise would have no inclination to do. In a couple of the places I initially explored to plant a church, it quickly became clear that while I might be able to generate some momentum or gather some people around me, nothing was happening independent of my instigation.

When I began to talk to people in Kansas City, however, I had the opposite experience. There was a sense among a diverse group of people that they were interested in being a part of a faith community that would approach church in some ways that were different from what they had experienced up to that point. Further, we would be in an urban setting. That created even more resonance and excitement. As we talked with the leadership of my former church, they said they had initially thought of planting a church in either Columbia, Missouri, or Wichita, Kansas, both more than an hour's distance from Kansas City. Although I was interested in neither of these locations, they said they were still interested in helping us plant a church in the midtown community of Kansas City. In all those conversations we sensed what we had hoped to discover: the movement of the Holy Spirit out in front of us, preparing the way and birthing in others a similar dream for church and community, hazy and indistinct as it was at that time.

That is how we decided to go back home. But as the saying goes, you can never truly go back home. You change. Home changes. A new reality has to be forged. You can't just pick up after years away and seismic internal and external shifts.

Given the way I have told the story of my journey following college and beyond, you can probably see the difficulty that was looming before me. The partnership with the church where I had been the youth pastor ended up being quite painful. I think for a number of years following our community's launch, I was regarded in many ways as the black sheep—or goat. The difficulties we experienced can be traced to a number of sources and dynamics, but what it came down to in my reckoning was that the community I came out of as a youth pastor and the one I desired to develop lived in two different stories and metaphorical orientations to the environment.

My former church was a suburban megachurch functioning under Willow Creek's seeker-targeted church paradigm. I was a naive and idealistic twenty-seven-year-old wanting to call off all bets in order to creatively engage everything in the pursuit of God. When we discussed church planting, I think the Kansas City church imagined we would be some kind of satellite extension of their ministry—a franchise that would run the same program but at a remote site. I had no clue this was what they had in mind. They had been a church plant from a traditional denominational church and went in a totally different direction with the parent church's blessing. In the same way I imagined they were supporting me and thus the calling I was discerning and trying to pursue in community. The collision of these two very different orientations was painful for both.

I have learned subsequently that over the last decade this dynamic has played out in countless churches and ministries. One part of the equation is the relational element and the difficulty of navigating conflict and misunderstanding between sinful and broken human beings. The other part of the equation is the reality that the fault line between the former world and the emerging one often (but not always) runs directly between the Baby Boomer generation (the last generation to inhabit a version of American life and culture that is modern, isolated, monolithic, and largely Christian in worldview) and the Baby Buster generation or Gen X (the vanguard of a world that is increasingly postmodern, globalized, pluralistic, and post-Christian). Such sociological observations didn't make the relational process any easier, however. That drama played out in a number of different ways in the years that followed.

One of the gifts the Kansas City church provided for us in our transition back into life there was a platform from which to tell our story or, in terms that were more ubiquitous at that time, to cast our vision. As that happened, I struggled to articulate what it was this church plant would be about. It was not an easy thing to describe at that point. I remember saying the word *community* a lot. I also remember telling quite a few stories and talking about location. And slowly we began to attract a small group of people around us. But interestingly, not nearly as many from our former church came to join us as we had expected.

Generally, we began to develop a small community from three different places. There were those at the original church who heard our spiel and connected with us. There were those with whom I had been connected in college during our time together in the ministry of Icthus. We had already done this thing once together, and when I talked about what we might try to be about in this new work, they needed very little convincing. The final group of people who were initially drawn to what we were doing came from the part of town in which we wanted to live and work and worship: midtown. This midtown group of people was an interesting lot. They were mostly unchurched Christians. They were urbanites committed to the community and unwilling to drive to the suburbs to do church. At the same time few of them were able to find church communities in the city that were vital in a way that allowed them to fully engage. Many had been involved in urban churches that slowly died around them, one after another.

Over the six to eight months that followed my family's return to Kansas City, we slowly assimilated back into our city. We bought a house. We told our story. We gathered together this band of people. I wanted to be slow about starting to "do" things. I wanted to be patient, to explore, and to listen first. As a result we only did a very few things that accorded to some of my own critical values. We prayed. We ate meals together. We began to experiment with creative expressions of corporate worship. That was all.

Once a week, on Thursday mornings from 7:00 to 8:00 a.m., a small group of people gathered to pray. We opened the Scriptures, not for the purpose of Bible study, but rather in order to animate our life together before God in a way that had its imagination set in God and the church's story. We prayed for one another. We prayed for our neighborhoods and the broader community. We prayed for our church. We also gathered in those very early days to share a meal together. Sometimes we ate in each others' homes and sometimes we dined in local restaurants. We had fun and got to know one another. Food is a staple of what we do at Jacob's Well. It is easy to discuss hospitality and its importance in a postmodern world on a theoretical level, but if you never actually sit down and eat with each other you are not practicing hospitality. We began to practice sharing our table with one another. Finally, we began to meet very informally one Friday night a month to worship God together through music and interact creatively with the Scriptures. It was very intimate and participatory. When I shared something from the Bible, it was rarely much more than a simple meditation that would stimulate conversation and help us to connect with God and one another.

Most of 1998 was spent transitioning and doing those three things. There was not much to see, but by the end of that year a constellation of around fifty people had gathered around this dream of birthing a new community in midtown. We began in 1999 with the feeling that it was time to invite one another into a more intentional relational community. During January and February we hosted a series of six desserts where people were invited to people's homes in small groups to talk about where this developing work might go next. In those times together I asked people to reflect on the many ways we were experiencing shifts in our world, internal and external. But rather than seeing those things as indicative of a coming dark age, I interpreted and described our contemporary cultural context through the lens of the pluralistic and syncretistic world that churches thrived in during the first three centuries following the life, death, and resurrection of Jesus Christ. I talked about a world of emerging possibilities and hope and my desire to engage this world among a community of people who were more than a collection of individuals. I talked of and interpreted my own history with the church and my ongoing passion for her. I talked of my hunger and desire to be part of a people who would strive to live creatively, imaginatively, and faithfully in our time and place in the same spirit that God's people had always done (sometimes more, sometimes less) throughout time and space, demonstrated in our Scriptures and in our history.

I used words like *authenticity*, *depth*, *transcendence*, *inclusion*, and *impact* to paint a picture of our call. I also described the necessity of experiencing the reality of God's life and love in our own lives before seeking to try to give it away to others. Then I listened. Or better, we listened. We listened to one another talk about the hopes and dreams we had for this community that was being birthed in our midst. At the end of the night I explained to people that I believed none of these dreams would come to pass if we were not willing to join ourselves to one another in this experiment. I did an altar call of sorts. Over these six desserts I asked this ragtag band of roughly fifty people to covenant themselves to God, to one another, and to this dream. Out of that group thirty-five people did just that.

At the same time I began looking for a place to call home, so to speak. I started out with a part-time office at my former church, but more often I worked out of local coffee shops. In February I connected with a woman who was the pastor of a Presbyterian church struggling along in the heart of midtown. I went to her and her board of elders for some office space. They greeted me warmly and gave me a tour of the building. The tour culminated on the third floor of this seventy-year-old church. Most of the space had not seen active use for over a decade, but within a week the third floor of Roanoke Presbyterian Church became our home, for $100 a month. Shortly after that our community began to gather there on Sunday nights to worship, pray, eat, and learn. By the summer we began to think about opening our doors, as it were, for public worship. Once again we approached the leadership of Roanoke. We loved their beautiful sanctuary and wondered if we could worship there on Sunday nights? After some deliberation, they agreed and raised our rent to $250 a month. We had a beautiful relationship with the people of this community, and in many ways the hospitality and generosity they showered upon our little group blessed us and marked us in ways that I hope we are worthy of.

We held our first public worship gathering on September 12, 1999. A couple hundred people showed up: obligatory well-wishers, family members, curious onlookers, and people from our broader life invited into the intimacy of this new thing. And then a couple more weeks passed, and we settled back down into the life we had been slowly growing during the preceding eighteen months, a little bigger than when we had begun.

Dreaming Up a Name for Ourselves

In the months that led up to that public launch, we received a wonderful gift that we have continued to unwrap in the years that have followed our genesis. We received a name. I say we received it because that is in fact what happened. It occurred to some of us as this new church community was unfolding in the spring of 1999 that we ought to call ourselves something beyond "midtown church project." We actually had our first church conflict over the issue. But in the midst of the conversations and brainstorming sessions a young man in our community sat down next to me at a community dinner and told me that he had had a dream. He had dreamed of our church and somewhere in the midst of that dream he heard the name "The Well." He then drew my attention to the passage in John 4 in which Jesus encounters the Samaritan woman at Jacob's well in Sychar.

As we dove into the story that is recorded by John in his Gospel, I was overwhelmed by the interaction that takes place between Jesus and a woman living at the margins of her culture.

Reading it we began to discover that it had at its core many of the elements that caused our hearts to pulse with passion and hope as we considered our vocation as a community. This story became another way of understanding and describing our dream and our mission. In this story, Jesus encounters a woman with great hunger and great need. She is an outsider in every way that mattered in the first century. Her gender is wrong. Her nationality is wrong. And her morals are wrong. She is a Samaritan woman joined to a succession of men, the most recent not even her husband. In many ways she seems the perfect candidate for a lecture: relational, moral, theological. But the first thing Jesus does is ask *her* for something—a drink of water. There is vulnerability and mutuality right at the start of their relationship. They then begin a dialogue that is spirited, theological, and honest. They spar with one another. But even in the midst of this sparring, Jesus sees her heart, reaches out to her, and invites her into his life and kingdom. In so doing she becomes a part of a new community, a place where people worship not in this place or that place but in spirit and in truth because of the revelation of Jesus Christ, the Messiah. And at the conclusion of that encounter, the woman leaves, rejoins her former community, and then brings them back to Jesus.

In the same way, our new little church wanted to become a place—like the biblical Jacob's well—where outsiders could not only receive but also contribute, regardless of all externals that might seemingly disqualify them from participating in the life of the kingdom of God's Son. We wanted to be a place where people who were searching could join us, ask real and probing questions, and together with us seek God in spirit and truth. We wanted to create a space that would allow us to form a community that would be hospitable to the people in our lives whom we wanted to bring to the Messiah. And to do this we experimented our way into finding the kingdom that Jesus declared is in our midst.

4

A Cautionary Leadership Parable
recognizing an alternate temptation

The old story asserts that resistance to change is a fact of life. Bound by a world view that seeks stability and control, change is always undesirable. But the new story explains resistance not as a fact of life, but as evidence of an act against life. Life is in motion, constantly creating, exploring, discovering. Nothing alive, including us, resists these great creative motions. But all of life resists control. All of life reacts to any process that inhibits the freedom to create itself.[1]

Margaret Wheatley, *Finding Our Way*

Resisting Change, Relying on Tradition

If one possible response to a rapidly changing environment is to scan the horizon for signs of success that can be reduced, modeled, mastered, and then replicated in another context (as was discussed in the last chapter), another potential response is to do *nothing at all*, or rather to depend on those who came before and did the work that then allows a church to go through the motions. We might label this option the *anti*-experiment.

Because of its ubiquity, this potential but inadequate response bears examination and interpretation if we want to engage the leadership environment of our age.

Often traditional churches that come out of mainline denominations are tempted to respond in this way, but by no means do they have a corner on the market. Churches that continue to do what has always been done die a slow death caused by aging, atrophy, and irrelevance. That is ultimately what happened to Roanoke Presbyterian Church, the community that graciously hosted Jacob's Well and then passed to us the ministry baton. After an attempted leadership coup that cost the church its pastor, the already diminished community lost any remaining momentum and finally made the decision to put an end to their journey together as a church. The leadership crisis was the straw that broke the back of this community, but it was strained for a long time before. As Roanoke's context changed, the church struggled to know what to do in response. Eventually they chose to continue to do what they had always done.

In such a situation, instead of engaging in the world we are living in so that we might discover new possibilities, we rely on past history and former expressions of common life and engagements. This is often done in an attempt to avoid the confusion and difficulty of engagement, experimentation, and change.

People and communities often work hard to ignore evidence of change (usually experienced as a drop in either worship attendance or income or in the graying of a congregation), and when it somehow breaks through anyway, we sometimes redirect our attention to removing whatever harbinger of disruption came our way. But any system that ignores changing realities in order to minimize pain and confusion only forestalls or anesthetizes it temporarily. In fact, the irony is that forestalled or anesthetized pain eventually must be felt, and when it is, the problem is often worse in scope and degree than what it might have been had it been engaged sooner. Maybe it is not surprising to hear that we are not the first people of faith to experience upheaval and transition, and this way of reacting comes with a deep history and pedigree: the reaction that is *no* reaction is also part of our story.

Israel in Transition

The first book of Samuel in the Old Testament tells the story of a transitional time in Israel's national history. Leadership is a nonexistent commodity. Israel is a nation without a king. In fact, Israel has never had a king, and the fact that all the surrounding nations have kings irks the Israelites. That they demand one irks God, Israel's true King. Israel is long past the patriarchy, long past the leadership of Moses, Aaron, and Joshua. Coming to a close is the age of the judges—a time of chaos, relative blessing, and decisive judgment that corresponds to living in and out of sync with God's intentions. There is true horror to be found in the book of Judges as well. In dramatic fashion, the last verse of Judges declares, "In those days Israel had no king; everyone did as they saw fit" (Judg. 21:25).

The book of Ruth bridges these two stories—the chaotic world of the judges and that of the emerging monarchy—by telling the amazing story of a foreign woman who steps onto the stage of Israel's history at a crucial time of transition. The main character of this drama is Ruth, a Moabitess who joins herself in marriage to an Israelite family living exiled on foreign soil due to a famine in their homeland. Life in Bethlehem ("House of Bread") has grown barren and lifeless. Ruth engages in a radical and risky experiment when all the men in the family die and leave three childless widows. The outcome of Ruth's radical and risky experiment ultimately produces, several generations down the family tree, King David—a beautiful illustration of the fruit of experiment.

When we pick up the narrative of 1 Samuel, we still inhabit a world in chaos and transition, this time with a different, desperate woman in the opening scene. Hannah, childless and despairing in her barrenness, is praying at the temple for a son. Israel's leadership crisis is painfully obvious when we read that Eli, the high priest overseeing the spiritual life of God's people, mistakes Hannah's passion and desperation in prayer (in the temple!) for public drunkenness. Discovering the true origin and nature of her behavior, however, he blesses her, and she finally conceives and gives birth to a son, Samuel. Hannah pledges Samuel to God, and when he is weaned, she brings him back to Eli to serve in the temple as a priest.

Through Samuel's young eyes we see the extent of Israel's paucity of leadership. Eli the priest no longer hears the voice of God, and his two sons, Hophni and Phinehas, are described by the text as "scoundrels [who] had no regard for the LORD" (1 Sam. 2:12). They are known for their violence, for satisfying their gluttonous appetites by pillaging the people's sacrificed burnt offerings intended for God, and for sleeping with the women who serve at the entrance to the temple. Through the young man Samuel, God finally speaks and in speaking pronounces judgment on Eli and his household.

Of Arks and Totems

We will return to this, but for now I want to go further into the story, to the battle that is recorded in the next chapter between Israel and the enemies who surround them, the Philistines. The text tells us that Israel goes out to fight these Philistines. However, the battle goes against Israel, and they lose this engagement at the cost of four thousand soldiers. For the Israelites, this is more than the simple loss of a battle or a breakdown in strategy. Loss in battle provokes theological crisis: Yahweh has lost to the gods of their enemy. This reality provokes enormous confusion and an identity crisis, to be sure. What follows is instructive to us in our discussion of how to respond to transition and crisis when our maps of reality aren't working, as is surely the case for the Israelites in this instance. Two conversations ensue following the battle: that of Israel trying to figure out how to respond, and that of the Philistines reacting to the Israelites. Israel's reaction is recorded in 1 Samuel 4:3: "When the soldiers returned to camp, the elders of Israel asked, 'Why did the LORD bring defeat on us today before the Philistines? Let us bring the ark of the LORD's covenant from Shiloh, so that he may go with us and save us from the hand of our enemies.'"

Now remember, Israel is navigating a difficult stretch in their history with no leadership to speak of. They are in uncharted territory. They experience defeat at the hands of their enemies, and in their confusion they ask the question, "What happened?" This is where it gets interesting. Notice in the text what *doesn't* happen. Do you see it? *They never answer the question.* They ask the million-shekel question, but rather than staying in the confusion and pain of an outcome they never anticipated, they go straight to a solution. What is their solution? "Go and grab the ark of the Lord."

In other words, what Israel does in their moment of crisis is revert to their past. In the past the ark of the Lord's covenant represented the power of God and, furthermore, a time in Israel's history when a strong leader, Moses, guided them. Israel could have said, "This was the pattern of God's activity in the past. Based on that, how do we discern what to do *now*?" But in the confusion and pain of their environment, Israel looks to her glorious past. Implicit in this move is an assumption that because God operated in such a manner in the past, he will do so again.

Israel creates a totem. I am using this word anachronistically, but I think it is appropriate in this context. A totem is an object believed by a particular society to have spiritual significance and thus is adopted as an emblem. Israel, faced with confusion and pain, makes of the ark a totem to symbolize God's presence with them. But remember in the current set of circumstances

God's presence is not with them; God has not spoken, and when he finally does speak, he pronounces judgment on Eli and his household. We are told in verse 1 of chapter 4, "Samuel's word came to all Israel." Everyone knew Israel was off course, and yet they made a totem with the assumption that in employing it, they would regain control.

The reality is that God's activity in the past can become a stumbling block in the present. When we refuse to engage the environment as it is before us *now*, we become prone to sentimentality, going through the motions, employing totems, and spouting meaningless God talk—all in an attempt to avoid the pain of answering the fundamental question that Israel asks but never answers: "Why did the Lord bring defeat on us today before the Philistines?"

We see the same thing again in 2 Kings 18. Israel (and now Judah too) has once again been in a cycle of obedience and disobedience to God, led by a revolving door of kings. In 2 Kings we meet Hezekiah, a young man who seeks to use his authority to restore Israel to right relationship to God. In order to do that, some housecleaning is in order.

> In the third year of Hoshea son of Elah king of Israel, Hezekiah son of Ahaz king of Judah began to reign. He was twenty-five years old when he became king, and he reigned in Jerusalem twenty-nine years. His mother's name was Abijah daughter of Zechariah. He did what was right in the eyes of the Lord, just as his father David had done. He removed the high places, smashed the sacred stones and cut down the Asherah poles. He broke into pieces the bronze snake Moses had made, for up to that time the Israelites had been burning incense to it. (It was called Nehushtan).
>
> 2 Kings 18:1–4

Same story, different verse. In Israel's past God had instructed Moses to fashion a bronze serpent and attach it to the end of his staff (Numbers 21:4–9). This came in response to a plague

ENTERING STORY

of serpents that God sent as judgment on Israel's incorrigible complaining against God and Moses. When they finally repent in the face of this serpentine judgment, it is the bronze serpent raised up that becomes the means of salvation. However, by the time of Hezekiah this bronze serpent has become more than a totem; it has become an idol that is being worshiped. So Hezekiah has it destroyed. Can you imagine destroying this symbol of God's past salvation? Yet this was necessary to give Israel the possibility of reengaging with God in the present, according to Hezekiah. This is what leaders can provide for communities in transition and what doesn't happen in the story of 1 Samuel 4.

We are constantly faced with the temptation to take the blessing of God and make it the object of our pursuit. In the short term it is often easier to do this than to pursue the God who judges us. But God is into reality, which makes the next part of the passage, the Philistines' response to Israel's securing of the ark, so interesting.

The Philistine Way

How do the Philistines respond to what the Israelites do? We are told, as the story unfolds, that when the ark of the Lord's covenant comes into the camp, it creates bedlam:

> When the ark of the LORD's covenant came into the camp, all Israel raised such a great shout that the ground shook. Hearing the uproar, the Philistines asked, "What's all this shouting in the Hebrew camp?"
>
> When they learned that the ark of the LORD had come into the camp, the Philistines were afraid. "A god has come into the camp," they said. "We're in trouble! Nothing like this has happened before. Woe to us! Who will deliver us from the hand of these mighty gods? They are the gods who struck the Egyptians with all kinds of plagues in the wilderness. Be strong, Philistines!

Be men, or you will be subject to the Hebrews, as they have been to you. Be men, and fight!"

1 Samuel 4:5–9

The Philistines hear the uproar that the presence of the ark creates in the camp of Israel and they, too, ask a question: "What's all this shouting in the Hebrew camp?" But rather than going straight to a solution, they engage in reconnaissance and reflection that ultimately birth resolve. The Philistines take a different route than the one Israel takes in their confusion.

The Philistines are confused too, but they allow that confusion to take them deeper into their environment to understand what is really happening. They assess the environment realistically. First, there appears to be a god in the camp of our enemies. Second, this is unprecedented and we are in trouble. In fact, woe to us! Third, these first two observations force another more informed and reflective question: "Who will save us from the hand of these mighty gods? And by the way, these are the gods who struck down the Egyptians!" They answer in an amazing manner. Who will save us? We will! We are resolved to engage *this* reality, fully engaged, fully assessed, fully responsible—no totems.

Israel turns to a totem and the Philistines face reality. Israel engages a totem under the assumption that God is behind them. In a way they seek to use God without ever seeking God. The Philistines, on the other hand, engage reality with the assumption that they are in trouble, and in humility they tune into what is happening and do what needs to be done. Going through the motions versus radical environmental engagement. Can you guess the result? "So the Philistines fought, and the Israelites were defeated and every man fled to his tent. The slaughter was very great; Israel lost thirty thousand foot soldiers. The ark of God was captured, and Eli's two sons, Hophni and Phinehas, died" (1 Sam. 4:10–11).

Stunning, isn't it?

Success, Power, and Presumption

God's activity in the past can be a stumbling block in the present, especially when life is hard and confusing and filled with the pain of transition and loss. We get in trouble when we say, "This is what God did, and God will do it again," rather than, "This is the pattern of God's activity, and based on that, how do we discern God in the present?" When we settle for others' formulations based on how they engaged once upon a time, we become vulnerable to the same kind of destruction Israel experienced in this story. And this is what is happening right now, at least based on my experience and the countless conversations I have had with struggling Christians, struggling seekers, struggling pastors, struggling district superintendents, struggling bishops, struggling professors, struggling seminary presidents, and on and on.

We are all living in the pain and confusion of a liminal time in history, where the forces of change have been in motion and moving inexorably along, away from where we have been and toward what we don't know. None of us has the luxury of stopping the ride to get off and get it figured out. So we are trying to live in the pain and confusion and into the struggle, and the ironic thing is that in the attempt, some of us are discovering life, joy, adventure, and a whole host of things that one can never realize or anticipate except by embarking and engaging the environment, even if doing so is terrifying.

In order to do this, we have to be willing to relinquish something we have grown quite fond of, if not addicted to. Is it surprising to you that the thing is power? What is certainty if not a kind of power over that which we, in reality, cannot control? To move intentionally into pain, confusion, and transition is a relinquishing of power, of saying with the Philistines, "Woe to us." But what is the alternative?

I would like to return to the story of 1 Samuel, specifically the exchange that happens in the chapters leading up to the battle in 1 Samuel 4. It seems to me that the opening chapters of 1 Samuel are about hearing and who is able to hear God in the midst of transition. As the story opens we meet Eli, the powerful person at the top of a theocratic political food chain who, ironically, cannot hear God. Into that setting comes a marginal figure: a powerless woman bereft of the only currency available to her in that culture—bearing children. She prays to God, and God hears her and grants her request. When she gives birth she names her son Samuel, meaning "God hears," derivative of the Hebrew word for hearing, *shema*. It comes full circle when the young boy, now serving alongside the aged priest, is wakened in the middle of the night hearing the voice of God, once again speaking to Israel.

Does our power limit our ability to hear God? When God speaks, must he seek out people from the margins, and if so, does he do so out of preference or because people in the margins have less proverbial territory to defend? It is amazing to realize how often in Scripture God, at the advent of a new work, engages a woman and child in the inauguration of his disruptive work. Perhaps it is even more amazing, or maybe sobering, to realize that whenever God begins to move in this way through the powerless, the powerful (pharaoh in Egypt, Herod in Israel) seek to systematically slaughter the children to whom they are vulnerable (Moses, Jesus). Is this still happening today?

Often it is our power, our previous successes, and the very ways in which we have heard and observed God's activity in the past that become stumbling blocks for engaging God in the present. Not only do we see this in the Israelites, the ark, and the story of their battle with the Philistines, but even before that, in the story of the transition of anointing that occurs between Eli and Samuel. It is powerful that the brass serpent must be destroyed for the nation to become attentive again. And it is even more instructive that in the battle with the Philistines, God allows Israel to be defeated and the ark, the symbol of the presence of God, to be taken into captivity. Yahweh would rather allow his name and reputation to take a hit (for the obvious conclusion was that Dagon, the god of the Philistines, was mightier than Israel's God) than simply go through the motions himself. Reality, indeed.

Moving toward Engagement

In this and the previous chapters I have outlined a few ways we have tried and, I believe, failed to engage God, ourselves, and our world faithfully for the sake of the gospel. I discussed the necessity of story for locating ourselves in a specific time and place, over and against the pursuit of timeless truths and principles that get translated into acontextual methods and techniques designed to produce success. I have also told my story and how that dynamic played out to a certain point in my own context. That my own particular story includes a significant amount of pain and confusion hopefully illustrates what I discussed next: the necessity of being present to what is happening in our context, particularly and especially if that context involves pain or confusion. We see why this is critical as we acknowledge that we are so easily tempted to revert to what has worked before in an attempt to regain our power in the face of our powerlessness. It is an age-old story.

We sin when we try to co-opt God without seeking God. Whether we do that by mastery of the newest techniques or by resorting to previous configurations, ultimately the outcome is the same: God is silent. We go through our self-determined motions, even to the point of our own destruction.

What, then, does it look like to engage experimentally, and yet faithfully, the reality of the world we are living in today? I believe there are three critical overlapping spheres that must be fully lived into—three radical engagements that mark faithful, communal discipleship. The first engagement is contextual: Where do we live, and what is the nature of our cultural environment? The second engagement is theological: Who is God, and what is the gospel? The third and final engagement is structural: Who is the church, and what does it mean to be the people of God in the world paying particular attention to the metaphors, symbols, systems, and structures that give shape to our identity and our common life? The exploration of these three engagements will occupy the next section.

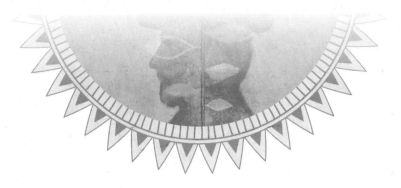

section 2
engaging context

5

Being There

grappling with the context of a "post" world

Environments are not passive wrappings, but are rather, active processes which are invisible. The ground rules, pervasive structure, and over-all patterns of environments elude easy perception.[1]

Marshall McLuhan, *The Medium Is the Massage*

Many people fervently hope that postmodernism—whatever they mean by it—will go away. And a lot of them are going to get their wish: Styles will change, of course. Some of the intellectual movements that have landed at the top of the academic pecking order will be deposed; this appears to be happening to deconstruction already. . . . Postmodernisms will come and go, but postmodernity—the postmodern condition—will still be here. It is a major transition in human history, a time of rebuilding all the foundations of civilization, and the world is going to be occupied with it for a long time to come. And, although it touches different people in vastly different ways, it is happening to us all. We are all emerging from out of the security of our tribes, traditions, religions and worldviews into a global civilization that is dazzlingly, overwhelmingly pluralistic.[2]

Walter Truett Anderson, *The Truth about the Truth*

Defining "Post"

In order to faithfully engage with God, the Scriptures, and the world in which we live, we must ask the following questions: Where *do* we live, what is the nature of our cultural environment, and what is the posture of a church engaged in and shaped by such a milieu? What is our context, and what significance, if any, can be attributed to our context? The first thing we must say in response to these questions is that we live in a "post" world. To be *post*-anything is not to be *anti*, however; to be *postmodern* is not to be against modernity but simply to exist in the time, age, or era that follows modernity. At the same time it is also true that when people self-identify as *postmoderns*, they are saying more than that they are simply past modernity. To claim postmodernity as a location means to exist in a cultural milieu that is in some kind of dialogue (explicit or implicit) with what has come before and is now moving beyond. There are many different "posts" in our transitional context with which we could interact, but I believe that conversations about the nature of our postmodern, post-Enlightenment, and post-Christendom world will be the most constructive in locating us in the world we are emerging from and into.

Postmodernity

When discussing the nature of a "post" world, postmodernity is the designation that has received the most attention by far. You are probably well aware of the cultural phenomenon of postmodernity if not its philosophical underpinnings. Trying to describe or approximate postmodernity as a philosophy or as a culture is no easy task: it calls to mind the parable of the blind men trying to describe the elephant, each universalizing to the whole what each individual's hands have revealed in one limited part. For some, the arrival of postmodernity is heralded with messianic anticipation while for others it is the portent of all that is evil and dangerous about our world. I would offer a more modest assessment: it is simply the context of the world in which we live, thus filled with possibilities and dangers like any other context.

Modernity's Narrative of Progress

Modernity was a time of grand narratives about the nature and destiny of humans freed from the constraints of ignorance and superstition. Under such themes, Western civilization sought to colonize both the natural and intellectual world, unifying it into classifiable systems by reducing material existence into distinct, separate, and easily identifiable categories. Knowledge was broken down into disciplines or fields of inquiry (botany, zoology, chemistry, physiology, biology, sociology, psychology, physics, etc.) that increasingly were bounded by unique language sets, practices, and guilds or academies distinct and separate from other fields of knowledge and their attendant subcultures. This approach subsequently gave rise to the cult of the "expert"—that singular person so focused in one field of knowledge that he or she proclaims the reality of how things are with a certainty and authority that thus dictates life for those who do not *know* in the same ways.

People and populations were likewise identified, reduced, and categorized, whether by race or class or some combination of both. The occupation and exploitation of foreign lands and native populations, called "colonialism," emerged in modernity as most European countries sought to expand boundaries and secure resources. Such privilege was an a priori assumption based on a combined sense of racial superiority, perceived theological mandate, and imperialized imagination. In the wake of the Protestant Reformation, religious authority and structures became tied to emerging nation-states. In several instances these state-sponsored churches were the forerunners of what we now know as denominations. Theologians systematized theology (Christology, pneumatology, soteriology, ecclesiology, eschatology, etc.) in much the same way scientists systematized the natural world (chemistry, geology, botany, zoology, etc.). Intelligence was given a measurable quotient. Merchants produced and distributed goods and resources mechanistically, that is, by assembly lines in factories and via progressively efficient, modern transportation systems. It goes without saying that those in control of the systems and structures that framed and supported modernity wielded enormous power.

Counting the Cost of Modernity

Modern travel, modern educational systems, modern manufacturing, modern medicine, and modern food production are just a few examples of the ways in which humanity's lot improved through the progress achieved during this era of history. However, as the twentieth century waned, a collective questioning of the assumptions of modernity emerged in many quarters. In particular, the very notion of progress itself was questioned. How is it defined and measured and by whom? What is the cost of progress? And how does power wielded in service to progress affect our ideas of what progress is and who benefits from it? While we unquestioningly "progressed" in some demonstrable and measurable ways, we have discovered that such progress often comes at the expense of something or somebody else: the environment, native peoples, time, families, neighborhoods, even our souls. In *The Challenge of Jesus*, N. T. Wright elaborates.

Modernity told an implicit narrative about the way the world was. It was essentially an eschatological story. World history had been steadily moving toward or at least eagerly awaiting the point where the industrial revolution and the philosophical Enlightenment would burst upon the world, bringing a new era

： . ： . ： . ： . ： . ： . ： . ： . engaging context of blessing for all. This huge overarching story—overarching stories are known in this world as meta-narratives—has now been conclusively shown to be an oppressive, imperialist and self-serving story; it has brought untold misery to millions in the industrialized West and to billions in the rest of the world, where cheap labor and raw materials have been ruthlessly exploited. It is a story that serves the interests of the Western world. Modernity stands condemned of building a new tower of Babel. Postmodernity has claimed, primarily with this great meta-narrative as the example, that *all* meta-narratives are suspect; they are all power games.[3]

Further, in the modern story, reality is that which is observable, measurable, and repeatable—the kinds of phenomena available, accessible, and verifiable to the five senses. Thus, reality comes to equal the scientific method. It should come as no surprise that in such a world the life of the spirit is ignored or marginalized (as well as a great many other nonmaterial things). This view of life subsequently birthed in human beings a ravenous materialism as matters of the soul were ignored or reinterpreted within this tightly controlled version of reality. When the life of the spirit is ignored, people will seek to feed the hunger of a neglected soul with the only nourishment available: in our context, the consumptive acquisition of material goods. If spirituality *is* engaged, it is often reduced and turned into one more commodity to be packaged, sold, and consumed like so many other aspects of modern life: in a radically individualistic way. As a result, to be human in the world of modernity means to understand oneself as a consumer who progresses by working to acquire the signs and symbols of a material world that are chosen on the basis of personal preference.

Churches existing within this framework for reality are often no different. "Church shopping" has become the *defining metaphor* for deciding which community of faith *satisfies one's needs*—it is the new mantra. Churches rarely possess a corporate understanding of themselves as a people but rather as one more collection of individuals choosing to be together based on similar preferences (music, preaching, programs, etc.). While leaders complain of the challenges inherent to such a paradigm, any honest assessment forces a humbling recognition that leaders are often shoppers too, though of a more professional sort. Seeking to advance a career, they move from one church to the next in an upward spiral that associates the numerical size of a church with success. In such a scenario, pastoral ministry is less a vocation than a profession. Because the rampant materialism of our consumer culture has so significantly shaped our self-understanding, the satisfaction of perceived needs based on desire and personal preference is now the determining factor for where a person or family worships and where pastors decide to serve.

In the latter part of the twentieth century, *church growth* and the megachurch phenomenon common to suburban America has functionally become the spiritual equivalent of a trip to the mall for large numbers of people. Churches have become one more modern institution gobbling up resources in order to increase in size and reach. For those churches not *fortune*-ate enough to exist in this way, their imaginations are nevertheless shaped by the paradigms inherent to such expressions and, as I have sought to demonstrate, are sold techniques by church-growth experts that will help such un-*fortune*-ate communities access the same kind of success.

Postmodern Realities

In the wake of modernity, the postmodern world responds in contradictory ways: fragmentation and polarization (of and between metanarratives, for example) on the one hand and syncretism (of different theologies, epistemologies, and ministry methodologies, for example) on the other. Such contradiction might seem schizophrenic, a condition whose obvious connotation is illness. While there is much that is not healthy about our postmodern context, there are profound creative and redemptive possibilities in these seemingly contradictory ideas, especially if we begin to embrace the dynamics of tension and paradox. While such words horrify moderns intent on banishing tension and paradox by dissecting the offending subjects in a misguided quest for resolution, postmoderns living in the aftermath of a world eviscerated by the need to control and dominate are often delighted by notions that defy such easy categorization.

A Fragmented World

Our postmodern world is a world of profound fragmentation. After modernity such fragmentation is certainly understandable. If power (in all of its different incarnations) is consolidated, held, and wielded by a select few within modernity, a corresponding splintering and fight for power following the demise of such hegemonic authority makes sense. Everything is up for grabs.

One word that can be used to describe this fragmentation is *balkanization*. This word is drawn from the former nation of Yugoslavia located on the Balkan Peninsula. When the Soviet Union dissolved, previously unified ethnic groups fought to stake out their territory. To *balkanize* now means to divide (by ever more precise means of differentiation) one place, one thing, one idea, or one group of people from each other for any number of reasons. The context of our world and our lives is a modern world that is breaking apart as modernity's hegemonic hold on us weakens. Life is being *balkanized*. It is fragmenting. The themes of progress and optimism that unified and undergirded the modern project have largely evaporated, and we have been left adrift in a disjointed world where meaning and value is constantly being contested by people staking out smaller and smaller patches of territory that they seem willing to defend unto death. Whether it is actual physical territory, the battle-torn terrain of the culture wars, or the polarized landscape of political rhetoric that is being defended, we have never been so aware of our differences. In the church our theological discourse and territorial disputes are often no different, nor any less bloody.

In a similar vein, other social commentators talk of the *atomization* of postmodern life and reality. They refer to the subatomic particles that are observed when matter is divided into its smallest parts. Much of the power that was consolidated, held, and wielded through enormous institutions and industries has been diffused in the postmodern shift as these former sources of authority are being put under the microscope, new pictures of reality are seen, and different stories are told. In one sense the world from which we have emerged was the world of the academy, and under the proverbial microscope, the academy has come under suspicion. From these academies, each filled with their different experts dedicated to singular disciplines, knowledge came down from on high. But that world of top-down knowledge diffusion (and power) is over. It is being *atomized*—broken down and diffused into smaller and smaller units of bottom-up, often independent yet networked grassroots organizations, communities, schools, families, and neighborhoods.

Medical care is another example of this postmodern fragmentation. Previously centralized and self-perpetuating, the medical industry has been atomized by an array of forces, including emerging alternative health practices, practitioners, knowledge, and information delivery systems that increasingly allow patients to take the custody and care of their bodies into their own hands and out of what often has been a Byzantine and dehumanizing maze of administrated health-care hell.

Educational systems governed by boards, bureaucracies, and unions at state and national levels have made way for homeschooling, charter schools, and new emerging paradigms for the holistic and lifelong pursuit of education.

News gathering and distribution, once held in the hands of a few print and broadcast media sources, now resides in myriad news outlets and in the hands of the people themselves through the emergence of new media such as blogs, news aggregates, and podcasts made possible by handheld devices like cell phones, PDAs, and video cameras that synchronize seamlessly to personal computers and the Internet. Intrinsic to all these shifts is the equalization of knowledge and the means to access it. As I type, I can hit one button on the keyboard of my laptop computer that directly links me to *Wikipedia*, an online encyclopedia created and maintained by a viral, atomized, global network of people who each contribute something to the conglomeration of knowledge formerly held in the hands of societies hidden behind names like *Britannica*. The entertainment industry struggles to keep pace with technology and how it is changing the ways in which people not only listen to music and view movies and television shows but also how they are being financed, created, and distributed. The list goes on and on.

Is it any surprise that new kinds of churches are emerging out of the husks of these former structures that are struggling to keep pace and adapt to this strange, new world? In a world of *balkanization* and *atomization* we are desperate for space to engage, create, and respond free from the power games that are being played in so many circles around us. In a shrinking, globalized world we are desperate to learn what it means to be in relationship to the *other*—the alien in our midst (or perhaps we are the alien in the midst)—for the purpose of dialogue and engagement. We desperately need to discover, recover, learn, and live out the ancient Christian practice of hospitality, which is the postmodern means of evangelism.

We do not need more Christian leaders building church empires at a time when our culture is dismantling other such structures around us. We must deconstruct ourselves in love. A postmodern context requires leaders who instead of seeking to dominate the environment are willing to become environmentalists—people who create spaces that allow God's people to have the possibility of an encounter with God and other people. Such an environment allows people to discover a future together under God instead of reducing them to mere pawns serving some larger agenda that comes from outside themselves.

A Remixed World

Another mark of postmodernity is an attendant move toward syncretism. The impulse to *blend* is a force that pulls together and merges disparate realities into a semiunified amalgam. This blending comes as a result of a world shrunken by globalization. The proximal realities of life in the twenty-first century put us into contact with people previously thought of as exotic. While religious, class, ethnic, and linguistic differences still define much of what it means to be a person in the world today, a cultural, racial, and ideological blending is happening in urban centers around the globe. Such blending is being made possible by new identity markers such as brand, lifestyle marketing, and technology, which are tied to transcendent values by an advertising industry that is evangelizing the world on the gospel of the American dream.

As communication technologies have shrunken our world further, we are beginning to have, by one degree or another, an emerging global youth culture in which previous boundaries are getting harder and harder to see. If modernity broke reality down into categorically differentiated and easily identified systems that quickly define what is what, who is who, and what belongs where, then postmodernity rejects such easy categories in the face of the complex and shrinking scope of our world. This is *pop postmodernity*, the version that is most easily recognizable to the casual observer and the place where most of society is intersecting. Postmodern culture is a culture with porous boundaries and loose definitions. Postmodernity is about the collapse of the rigidly defined categories of modernity and of the blending of previously untainted essences.

Postmodernity is a *sampled* culture. It is a culture of the *remix*, of borrowing ideas, images, and sounds from disparate sources and blending them in ways that are startling and at the same time stimulating. It is a culture that blends brand with art, product, and transcendence in a context of Web-based social networking that moves at the speed of sound (available for download). The rise of digital music downloaded electronically onto personal MP3 players and shared wirelessly across different types of networks is one obvious example of how this is playing out around us. The traditional music industry is struggling to keep up, and it is not a foregone conclusion that they will. Additionally, ours is a world in which news and entertainment are being merged into a new category of media labeled "infotainment." It is a world of designer and celebrity spirituality, the co-opting of religious impulses and traditions and then just as quickly the disposal of them in favor of the next new thing. Does the mixing of ideas, images, values, and words confuse you? Then there is a good chance you are not native to this world. But this is the world into which many in the emerging church are birthed and living. And while it has much to warrant concern, it is still a profoundly creative world.

Can the church engage in such radically creative ways, or are we destined to continue animating the imagination and practices of a response to a modern (or premodern/medieval) landscape? While there may be some people in today's world patient enough to wait and see how we will respond, many others have simply moved on. But perhaps such a move is too hasty. Postmodernity also affords us a way to look not just forward but backward as well—something modernity in its blind eagerness to move on combined with its arrogant confidence about the inevitability and goodness of progress refused to do. Consider more of my story.

I wrote that my story of faith emerges from many places and traditions, but most significantly it emerges out of the subculture of evangelicalism. In my early twenties I was weaned on the idea of the "quiet time"—private time set apart in devotion to God and marked by Bible reading, journaling, and intercessory prayer. As I matured in my faith, my ability to continue to faithfully observe this practice grew more difficult, and yet in my tradition, that quiet time experience seemed to be not only expected and normative behavior (and how one measured the quality of one's life in God) but really all that was available in terms of spiritual practice. Like many, I discovered Richard Foster and his book *Celebration of Discipline*,[4] and it had a profound impact on me. In the 1980s evangelical writing on spiritual practice was that book. Period. Fortunately he wrote more. From there, I moved to his *Devotional Classics*, a book sampling the writings of Christians throughout time and from different traditions. A whole world opened up before me and sent me on a quest and into a heritage that I did not know I possessed. I began to explore two thousand years of Christian writing available not only in books but also in and through traditions and communities alive and in greater proximity to me than I ever imagined. I discovered resources and guides to spiritual writing and practice beyond what fifty years of evangelical history and literature provided, beyond even what five hundred years of Protestant history and literature could provide.

In the second year after we planted Jacob's Well, I went on retreat to a Benedictine monastery, exhausted and nearly burnt out. There I met a monk who became for me a spiritual director and friend. Through him I was introduced to liturgical prayer and the daily office as well as to praying the Psalms, a practice our community regularly interacts with. In reading *The Rule of Benedict* I was confronted by the vow of stability. I am an entrepreneurial person. In the early days of this church, I had imagined that I might start this venture, get it going, hand it off, and then move on to something new. Benedict's words for monks, condemning them for moving from monastery to monastery, sounded prophetic and pertinent to my ears. The consumer mentality inculcated in me was being confronted by a monk who lived fifteen hundred years before me and a community embodying a way of life that had survived and thrived over that same period of time. Chastened, I made a public vow of stability to the community and now regularly challenge our people to resist the consumer impulse to change church communities based on whimsy and personal preference. While postmodern culture forces us to navigate the challenging waters of syncretism, it also offers access to a rich world of previously unknown possibilities, of *remixing* what has come before with what is now in a way that has the potential to bear life in significant, and even prophetic, ways.

A World of Suspicion, a World of Possibility

The posture of suspicion that postmoderns assume toward modernity illustrates how disempowered people have felt because of the real ways they have struggled to be acknowledged and heard as something other than a cog in the machinery over which they have no control. Sadly, this happens in church.

If people are questioning myths of progress, the ways in which the natural and intellectual world has been divided, the worlds of medicine, education, and news gathering (to name but a few examples of modern institutions under suspicion), if people are being *balkanized* and *atomized*, *remixed* and *sampled*, then we can be certain that religious faith, its categories and language sets, its practice, and the institutions that give shape to it are also being questioned and subjected to the same inspection and pressures. In fact most leaders of religious communities and institutions with which I interact are struggling as much as, if not more than, the average person both inside and outside such places. They often feel as trapped and disempowered as the most radical and articulate postmodern activist. Inasmuch as our context is postmodern, we must deal with the reality that many of the people around us (including ourselves) are suspicious of grand narratives that seek to define and commodify reality in service to some higher goal. In fact people tend to be suspicious of truth claims in general, and rightly so. Truth is not just an idea that can be *claimed*; for it to have any traction in the world today, it must ultimately be a relational reality that is embodied incarnationally in demonstrable ways over time.

As we assess where we are, we must begin to ask whether modern notions of *progress* have affected our understanding and subsequent articulation of the gospel. Through such a cultural rubric like modernity, what of the gospel was ignored, forgotten, or simply left out? What if the gospel was mangled by the media that carried the message? How has the gospel been domesticated in service to the goals and aims of modernity thinly veiled by the language of winning the world for Christ?

Listening, Embodiment, and Authenticity

In one way or another Christianity has often been party to the excesses and abuses of modernity, and so if people are not outright suspicious of our faith, they are often at least skeptical, if not cynical. The church of modernity often seems hardly distinguishable from other institutions within modernity that have enjoyed a long run of privilege and authority. We have too often assumed that since we have the "truth" there is no need to listen to those around us. *We* must be listened to. But in a postmodern world we must begin to listen—and not just in order to use listening as one more manipulative technique aimed at bringing another soul into our fold. To listen is to truly love another because it requires engagement and relationship as an act of hospitality. Wade Bradshaw of L'Abri Fellowship in England has written that in order to truly engage a postmodern world, we must listen to the voices of postmodern people around us. To listen to those voices is to hear pain, confusion, and longing. "As we listen . . . we will hear voices that are bored, cynical and profoundly unimpressed by a Gospel that all too often appears to them to be merely verbal or mental. These people assume the Gospel is simply another sales pitch with ulterior motives tucked away in the background. These presuppositions have huge ramifications for how our message will be heard by those we try to contact."[5]

Have you had these conversations? Often the suspicion we face can be hard to overcome in the short-term, and it is right that this should be so.

However, the move from modernity to postmodernity offers redemptive possibilities. The cultural context of postmodernity and its hermeneutic of suspicion offer us a reminder of the Christian virtue of humility, of listening, and of self-sacrificing love for one's neighbor that is free from the need to colonize or co-opt. To give the gift of oneself, of authenticity amid a world consumed by façade, is a necessity and a demonstration of the nature of the God revealed in Jesus Christ. If hypocrisy is the cardinal sin in a postmodern context, then authenticity is the cardinal virtue. Unfortunately Christians who have been consumed with the "truth" are at times less concerned with honesty and authenticity. While it seems that these ideas would exist seamlessly together, most of the time they do not. But where authenticity and honesty exist in people and communities, such postures go a long way in communicating to those around us a willingness to serve and not simply exploit for the realization of our own vision.

Such a humble posture also demonstrates the reality and nature of our trust and confidence in him in whom we place our faith. It seems that many people feel as if Jesus Christ cannot fend for himself on this contested field—that they must be his defender at all costs, shouting down every critic. What might it look like to trust God in this way? What might it look like to be the church in the wake of modernity's unfulfilled messianic claims, to be freed from the tyranny such assumptions place on our imaginations? What would it look like to actually love people separate from agendas and predetermined notions of progress, spiritual or otherwise? Bradshaw goes on to say that what is necessary in view of the cultural context of postmodernity is nothing less than a new kind of reformation: "The first Reformation was the rediscovery of the theology of Paul—of God's grace given freely to wholly undeserving sinners. A second, postmodern reformation will require the complementary rediscovery of the theology of James—that faith is always manifested. Postmoderns want to see the fruit of a message before they check into its doctrines. This is not a return to an anemic social gospel; this is a biblical response of gratitude to God manifested in concern for others."[6]

Our attitude and posture in the wake of modernity's siren call to control, power, and progress ought to be that of our Lord and Savior Jesus Christ. His self-emptying lifestyle and message witnessed prophetically to an alternate, hidden economy that has always animated and informed what is most beautiful, true, and thus *powerful* about the body of believers named Christ's bride, the church. In his letter to the church in Philippi, Paul quotes the lyrics to a song the early church regularly sang that poetically described for them their calling as the people of Jesus.

> Think of yourselves the way Christ Jesus thought of himself. He had equal status with God but didn't think so much of himself that he had to cling to the advantages of that status no matter what. Not at all. When the time came, he set aside the privileges of deity and took on the status of a slave, became *human*! Having become human, he stayed human. It was an incredibly humbling process. He didn't claim special privileges. Instead, he

lived a selfless, obedient life and then died a selfless, obedient
death—and the worst kind of death at that: a crucifixion.

Philippians 2:5–8, Message

Post-Enlightenment

To be post-Enlightenment means to begin to engage and
process ideas, social interactions, environments, reality even,
in ways different from those afforded us by modernity. As we
open ourselves to additional ways of knowing and engaging
beyond the accumulation of data surveyed objectively and sci-
entifically, we discover more *out there*—a larger sampling of
life, of reality, to be engaged. Engaged in this way, we have a
corresponding revelation *in here*, within ourselves. We begin to
discover that there is much we know that cannot be accessed
(or classified) if we are limited to modern, Enlightenment stan-
dards of knowledge.

In good modern fashion, epistemological discussions of how
we know are often largely philosophical in nature. But how
we know something involves much more than philosophical
considerations. How knowledge is accessed, held, and conveyed
is integral to what is actually known. Thus we must reckon
with the technology of communication, its rapid evolutionary
development, and how that technology impacts not just how
something is conveyed but also how it is shaped and changed by
the means of communication and then perceived or conceived
by those who finally receive it. Further, as human beings we are
not merely passive recipients for content, mere fleshy satellite
dishes receiving data packets out of the air to be reassembled
by our data processing systems. Human beings are complex
knowers with multiple intelligences beyond mere cognition.
How a person physiologically receives and processes information in relation to his or her environment rests on many
factors, and the exploration of how the technology of commu-

nication and the human brain interact is changing the way we understand and access reality—God, Scripture, theology, and church included.

The Technology of Modern Knowledge

In the first chapter I described modernity as that time in western European history following the Enlightenment when knowledge shifted in location from the local, particular, and contingent to the universal, objective, and indubitable. The Enlightenment gave us rationalism, the scientific method, and knowledge used in service (or submission) to some other aim. By observing and breaking down the world around us into smaller and smaller components, we were able to assert a certain kind of mastery over the environment in service to our worldview and goals. This kind of mastery over knowledge requires the ability to process information in a certain manner—enabled first by the technology of writing and later magnified by Johannes Gutenberg's fifteenth-century technological innovation, the printing press.

While it is natural enough to view the printing press as a technological innovation, it might strike many as odd to describe writing in the same way. Does it seem unusual to think of writing as technology? In his amazing book *The Hidden Power of Electronic Culture*, author and Mennonite pastor Shane Hipps describes how writing depends on the use of certain tools like pen and paper that give expression to a powerful symbol system "that can take years to learn how to decode (read) and encode (write)."[7] In the Eastern world ideographic writing (Chinese, e.g.) is based on over eighty thousand characters that "are pictorial in nature. A single symbol or character represents an entire world or concept and often bears a resemblance to the thing it describes." Contrast this with the phonetic alphabet of the West.

The phonetic alphabet, comprised of just over two-dozen characters (in the case of English), changed everything. Instead of inventing symbols that correspond with specific words or ideas, the people who formed phonetic alphabets made meaningless characters that correspond to meaningless "phonemes" or vocal sounds. For example, the symbol "t" corresponds to the meaningless sound "teh." These symbols are then assembled sequentially to re-create the sound of the spoken word. In other words, the phonetic alphabet is a symbol system that is totally abstracted from reality. Unlike Chinese, the English word *man* looks nothing like a man; it is just a collection of abstract, meaningless squiggly shapes used to create meaning.[8]

Created by the Greeks more than two millennia ago, the phonetic alphabet is structured in a sequential and linear manner that becomes nonsensical when the rules that govern it are ignored. Thus, the Western "phonetic alphabet is linear, sequential, and abstract" while Eastern, ideographic writing is "nonlinear, holistic, and intuitive." The impact of the technology of writing subsequently shapes not just the forms for knowledge acquisition and transmission but the very nature of how and what we know. "Ever since the Greeks perfected the phonetic alphabet, Western philosophy has been centered on linear, fragmented, and sequential forms of logic called syllogisms that perfectly mirror the form of our writing system. In contrast the nonlinear, holistic nature of Eastern philosophy can be summarized by a single symbol, the *yin-yang*, which mirrors ideographic writing."[9] Our very patterns and categories of thought are shaped and held by the nature of the medium that conveys the content. As our writing becomes linear, fragmented, and sequential, so does our way of engaging the world around us.

Yet even with the technology of Western, phonetic, alphabetic writing existing for thousands of years, it was accessible only to a relatively select and educated few. For the majority of its history, this technology existed alongside a dominant oral culture in the West. That all changed with the printing press. The printing press took language and encoded it onto the printed page and made it mass-producible.

> With this simple invention, Gutenberg unknowingly set off an explosion of such overwhelming power that we continue to feel its reverberations today. Printing made the alphabet perfectly uniform and infinitely repeatable. This mass production placed literacy in the hands of everyone, subsequently launching the Protestant Reformation. . . . By the 17th century, the medium had become the dominant means of communication. These conditions embedded the bias of the printed medium deeply into the Western worldview and gave rise to the modern mindset that represented a dramatic departure from medieval thought. This newly entrenched worldview was characterized by a strong emphasis on individualism, objectivity, abstraction, and reason, in contrast to the medieval worldview characterized by an emphasis on tribal, mystical, and sacramental experiences.[10]

Thus the introduction of the printing press had a number of effects on Western culture beyond the obvious ones: it introduced the notion of objectivity; it intensified linear, rational thinking, which in turn made us think more abstractly. We also became more individualistic. In such a context, that which is subjective, experiential, concrete, emotional, intuitive, and communal is marginalized.

Now many modern assumptions (individualism, objectivity, abstraction, and linear, rational thinking) are being profoundly questioned and renegotiated, if not held up for grabs altogether. The modern age of science and structures of control depended upon concepts that could be transmitted in an abstract, linear, and systematic manner. The technology of writing standardized, intensified, and unleashed by the printing press was suited perfectly to conveying such a conceptual paradigm of reality. In that environment the humanities were relegated to the margins. How does one reduce and then quantify beauty, love, transcendence, sublimity, intuition, awe, terror, or experience itself? In the postmodern milieu, the humanities are asserting themselves, not in terms defined by science and the limits imposed by the hegemonic and ubiquitous communication technologies of modernity, but in a new technological milieu that is expanding how we know while at the same time reaching back to a more primitive world.

Our post-Enlightenment culture is birthing a language all its own: creative, artistic, intuitive, organic, prophetic, and poetic. In the same way that our modern systems of education and higher learning are being atomized, so are our very ways of knowing. The ways in which we process information, make decisions, and interpret our environments are going through profound transitions.

But like much in postmodernity, it is not as if we are simply discovering something new; we are also in the process of recovering what has always been present in, around, and among us, yet marginalized, like so many other aspects of life in modernity. It is probably not surprising to learn that the context of the world in which we live today is a world that is increasingly and aggressively addressing and engaging intuitive, imaginative, and spiritual ways of being—and not just as a novelty. How human beings exist and engage with the visible and invisible world around them is a struggle that is unfolding all around us.

Marshall McLuhan, the Eastern Mind, and the End of Textual Hegemony

Communication theorist, English teacher, and media ecologist Marshall McLuhan has written extensively about the shift Western culture is going through relative to information and media technology and how such considerations shape how we think and engage the world around us. McLuhan coined the aphorism "The medium is the message" and another like it: "You become that which you behold." According to McLuhan "the message" isn't objective or timeless but rather malleable and profoundly affected by the vehicle that conveys it. With this framework it is not hard to see how within the conceptual frameworks of modernity, the Bible was transformed from a collection of diverse stories about Yahweh and his people through time to source material for systematic theologies based on linear, rational, abstract, and cognitive reasoning. Rather than concerning ourselves with living faithfully within these narratives, we became consumed with excavating "right" doctrine from text.

Further, we can see how the printed Bible, mass-produced and in the hands of every individual believer, enables and encourages a radically individualized expression of faith. That we developed in the West a gospel focused almost exclusively on the individual and the salvation of that person's individual soul by a cognitive assent to the right doctrinal configuration about salvation should not come as a surprise.

In his profoundly challenging book, *Unleashing the Scripture: Freeing the Bible from Captivity to America*, theologian Stanley Hauerwas addresses this state of affairs.

> Most North American Christians assume that they have a right, if not an obligation, to read the Bible. I challenge that assumption. No task is more important than for the Church to take the Bible out of the hands of individual Christians in North America. North American Christians are trained to believe that they are capable of reading the Bible without spiritual and moral transformation. They read the Bible not as Christians, not as a people set apart, but as democratic citizens who think their "common sense" is sufficient to "understanding" the Scripture. They feel no need to stand under a truthful community to be told how to read. Instead they assume that they have all the "religious experience" necessary to know what the Bible is about.[11]

The "common sense" Hauerwas references may be many things, but it is at least the common sense of the Enlightenment about what passes for knowledge arising out of that world. According to Hauerwas, such sensibilities have poisoned our reading of the Bible. Their impact on discipleship has been significant and long-lived. Read A. W. Tozer's description of the spiritual temperature of Western Christianity that is relevant today but dates to the 1948 publication of his spiritual classic, *The Pursuit of God*.

> There is today no lack of Bible teachers to set forth correctly the principles of the doctrines of Christ, but too many of these seem satisfied to teach the fundamentals of faith year after year, strangely unaware that there is in their ministry no manifest Presence, not anything unusual in their personal lives. . . . Thanks to our splendid Bible societies and to other effective agencies for the dissemination of the Word of God, there are today many millions of people who hold "right opinions," probably more than ever before in the history of the Church. Yet I wonder if there was ever a time when true spiritual worship was at lower ebb. To great sections of the Church the *art* of worship has been lost entirely, and in its place has come that strange and foreign thing called the "program." . . . The modern scientist has lost God amid the wonders of his world; we Christians are in real danger of losing God amid the wonders of His Word. We have almost forgotten that God is a person and, as such, can be cultivated as any person can.[12]

Certainly Tozer speaks prophetically to his time *and* ours, to societies gasping for oxygen amid the noxious fumes of reductionistic modern epistemologies. From a secular standpoint Neil Postman views McLuhan as a latter-day technological prophet. In his book *Amusing Ourselves to Death*, Postman states that McLuhan speaks "in the tradition of Orwell and Huxley—that is, as a prophesier, and I have remained steadfast to his teaching that the clearest way to see through a culture is to attend to its tools for conversation."[13] According to McLuhan, societies transition over time, and as we have seen, communication technology is a major contributor to such shifts. The shift that is made from alphabetic writing to the printing press, and later to electronic media, affects not only how humans think and perceive reality but also organize themselves socially. Postman elaborates:

> We know enough about language to understand that variations in the structures of languages will result in variations in what may be called "world view." How people think about time and space, and about things and processes, will be greatly influenced by the grammatical features of their language. We dare not suppose therefore that all human minds are unanimous in understanding how the world is put together. But how much more divergence there is in the world view among different cultures can be imagined when we consider the great number and variety of tools for conversation that go beyond speech. For although culture is a creation of speech, it is recreated anew by every medium of communication—from painting to hieroglyphs to the alphabet to television. Each medium, like language itself, makes possible a unique mode of discourse by providing a new orientation for thought, for expression, for sensibility.[14]

Echoing McLuhan, Postman later says that there have been three great crises in Western education. The first occurs in Greece during the fifth century BC when Athens transitioned from an oral culture to a written culture using the alphabet. The next crisis happens in sixteenth-century Europe with the invention of the printing press. We are in the midst of the third crisis, brought about by the electronic revolution beginning with technological innovations such as the telegraph and the telephone, continuing into broadcast technologies like radio and television, and finally fusing all of those innovations together with the advent of the Internet and increasing technological mobility that frees us from the constraints of geography (and places us into the world of the virtual). Such technologies rely on and enable myriad forms of communication and content, but none so significant as the reemergence of the image.

In the nineteenth century the West undergoes a "Graphic Revolution" that begins to move communication increasingly away from mere word conveyed through text into the world of image. Hipps elaborates:

> In many ways the Graphic Revolution returned us to the iconic world of the Middle Ages, only the images were recast at the speed of light and invaded our vision from every direction. Over time this iconic symbol system has been dissolving our dependence upon literacy. Corporate logos are the most obvious example of this phenomenon. There are hundreds of corporate icons that no longer require any phonetic descriptor for them to be recognizable. . . . The rise of image-based communication in our culture weakened our preference for abstract and linear thought patterns in favor of more concrete, holistic, and nonlinear approaches to the world.[15]

Such a move turns us to the East, whose ideographic, image-based language and subsequent patterns of thought and knowledge begin to renegotiate the ways in which we know and thus *what* we know and *how* we know it. As we are bombarded by rapidly successive, nonlinear images, the way we process what we are seeing and experiencing undergoes a transformation that can be understood in any number of different ways but perhaps most simply as a move from concept/conception to percept/perception. Text must be read linearly in order to understand and process the argument or information contained within the coded symbols of the alphabet. Streamed images work on a different level of consciousness, indeed in a different part of the brain. Is it any wonder, then, that into such contexts awareness and appreciation for mystery and transcendence is heightened? Further, we should not be surprised that experiential and holistic approaches to learning that make room for all five senses as well as the emotional and relational realities increase in importance as people look to engage more than their heads. Eastern religious experience is deeply rooted in these ways of knowing. And remember that Judaism is an Eastern religion, as are Greek and Eastern Orthodoxy. Each of these latter examples have experienced an increased interest in the wake of the emerging postmodern world.

As a young Christian, most of what I was taught as "evangelism" was merely apologetics—a particularly Western way of arguing people into submission by anticipating every possible argument they might come up with and having a rational argument prepared in response. Josh McDowell's book betrays his cultural context: *Evidence That Demands a Verdict*.[16] I have found that many Christians, consciously or not, try first to convert postmodern people into a modern, Enlightenment way of thinking before they can share the Good News of Jesus Christ with them. Why? Because we have encoded the gospel in the categories of modernity. You probably assume that I believe this is a bad thing. I don't. It is an incarnational and missiological necessity. But the missional context of our world has changed. Postmodern people reject these limited ways of knowing—they leave out too much life and reality. Meanwhile, many Christians sit wringing their hands and assume that the God of the cosmos revealed by Jesus Christ is confounded by a postmodern world.

The context of the Eastern world and our emerging culture is one that is not merely cognitive but profoundly somatic as well. Where is the actual human, physical body being addressed and engaged, not simply as a temporal prison for an immortal soul but as an integrated part of what it means to be human? Our domesticated faith has become functionally Deistic in nature, if not Gnostic. The reality described here has enormous implications for every aspect of our lives as people of Jesus Christ. What does all this have to do with life on the ground? Keep reading.

Recognizing that the Protestant Reformation was engendered and unleashed in many ways by the print revolution, we can trace the way in which the Word of God began to be understood as the mass-produced, printed Bible and how it grew in prominence. Subsequently, preaching of the Bible (a linear, abstract, and largely cognitive experience) increased in importance exponentially. If you remove authority for interpreting the revelation and will of God from a figure, like the pope, or a body, such as the College of the Cardinals, then authority must rest somewhere else—(human) nature abhors a vacuum. Modernity placed authority into hermeneutics, the science of interpretation. In such a world the pastor becomes the scientist mining and then appealing to the Bible for truth, the new authority. It is easy to see then how the Eucharist began to be pushed into the background within many Protestant traditions. In medieval, oral cultures, faith is practiced more sacramentally and thus mysteriously. Where the table or altar previously held the eminent place in worship in the premodern/medieval church, in the modern context of the Protestant Reformation we observe the elevation of the pulpit, often towering over the congregation and carved to look like a fortress. I have been to St. Peter's Church in Geneva, Switzerland, where John Calvin preached. The design and placement of the pulpit communicates volumes about what was significant in that context and where authority resided.

At Jacob's Well we have sought not to privilege either the ministry of the Word or the ministry of the table but rather to bring them back together, side by side, in our weekly worship gathering. If you want to engage postmodern people in a holistic way, what is better than the sacrament of communion? Communion, after all, is a first-century multimedia event: you taste it, smell it, touch it; you hear someone proclaim to you, "The body and blood of our Lord and Savior Jesus Christ." Additionally, at our church you have to physically get up and walk to the front of the sanctuary where you interact with another human being, likely making contact with him or her somewhere in the process. Communion in our context is the climax of worship and follows immediately after the preaching of the Word (thirty to forty minutes long). In such a liturgy, which part of the human person is not being engaged? We understand our worship gathering to be a corporate, public spiritual discipline. Because the congregation is made up of a diverse group of people with a variety of learning styles, personalities, and backgrounds, we know that if we want to be transformed to live, serve, and love in the way of Jesus, we must creatively and faithfully cultivate space (physical, emotional, intellectual, relational, artistic) where the whole person (body, soul, mind, spirit) can encounter God, others, and themselves in the context of creation. Because we understand that all areas of life are connected, we strive to be holistic.

The Revenge of the Right Brain

It turns out that linear, sequential, analytical ways of knowing are processed in one part of our brain, or more accurately, one hemisphere of our brain: the left hemisphere. Over the last several hundred years that make up modern history, the right brain was left to atrophy. In the emerging culture of the postmodern world we occupy, the use of the right hemisphere of the human brain is making a comeback.

One of the first places I began to learn about the right brain and its resurgence was, interestingly enough, in the technology and culture magazine *Wired*. I say it is interesting because *Wired* magazine claims Marshall McLuhan as its patron saint. I have subscribed to this magazine for several years and love the creative, diverse, and incisive picture it provides of the world of which I am a part. Flipping through its pages in the winter of 2004, I came upon an image that stunned me: an illustration of a human head viewed from above and slightly behind. The top of the head has been removed, and we immediately are confronted by the brain divided into two halves. The left half of the brain is a drab gray made up of mazelike cubicles filled with employees working with their heads down at desks. By comparison the right side of the brain is a verdant green where people work and live in a relaxed and creative environment of harmony. The image accompanied an article by Daniel Pink titled "Revenge of the Right Brain."

The world has changed. The future no longer belongs to people who can reason with computer-like logic, speed and precision. It belongs to a different kind of mind. . . . The left hemisphere of our brain handles sequence, literalness, and analysis. The right hemisphere, meanwhile, takes care of context, emotional expression, and synthesis. . . . Until recently, the abilities that led to success in school, work, and business [and I would add here church] were characteristic of the left hemisphere. They were the sorts of linear, logical, analytical talents measured by SATs and deployed by CPAs. Today, those capabilities are still necessary. But they're no longer sufficient. In a world upended by outsourcing, deluged with data, and choked with choices, the abilities that matter most are now closer in spirit to the specialties of the right hemisphere—artistry, empathy, seeing the big picture, and pursuing the transcendent.[17]

Most observations about the way the world is changing focus on externals. Pink argues that the most significant change is happening within human brains in the West. It is this change that is subsequently reshaping our world. Pink also wrote a book called *A Whole New Mind: Why Right-Brainers Will Rule the Future*. He sees us shifting out of the Information Age into the Conceptual Age. Sssshhhh. If you are quiet you can almost hear McLuhan giggling behind you. The revolution of knowledge that began with the Enlightenment and was enabled by the technologies of the textual world has reached its apogee in the "age of information." Now we are experiencing a new revolution with emerging ways of knowing and economies and structures of support that are birthing a new world. Pink continues:

Ours has been the age of the "knowledge worker," the well-educated manipulator of information and deployer of expertise. But that is changing. Thanks to an array of forces . . . we are entering a new age. It is an age animated by a different form of thinking and a new approach to life . . . "high concept" and "high touch." High concept involves the capacity to detect patterns and opportunities, to create artistic and emotional beauty, to craft a satisfying narrative, and to combine seemingly unrelated ideas into something new. High touch involves the ability to empathize with others, to understand the subtleties of human interaction, to find joy in one's self and elicit it in others, and to stretch beyond the quotidian in pursuit of purpose and meaning.[18]

For a person to be healthy and whole, both sides of the brain must be active and engaged. For a society to be likewise vibrant and a reflection of its people, how much more important is it for these two paradigms to engage one another. Unfortunately, this has not been the case, and we have suffered for it.

Using magnetic resonance imaging (MRI) we can see images of the brain that give us clues about how it works and what regions are active in response to different stimuli. Pink reports that for a long time the scientific establishment believed that the two lobes of the brain were separate and unequal. Scientists held the left hemisphere is what *makes us human*! The right brain, they thought, was the vestige of some earlier stage of development that humans had outgrown.

These discoveries become even more intriguing when you consider the impact of text on the brain. If you turn your head from the right to the left, the right brain controlled that motor function. If you turn your head from the left to the right, the left brain controlled that function. Now, move your head repetitively left to right. This is the physical activity we engage in when we read—a profoundly left-brained activity! "In Western languages, reading and writing involve turning from left to right, and therefore exercise the brain's left hemisphere. Written language, invented by the Greeks around 550 B.C.E., has helped reinforce left hemisphere dominance (at least in the West) and created what Harvard classicist Eric Havelock called the 'alphabetic mind.' So perhaps it's no surprise, then, that the left hemisphere has dominated the game. It's the only side that knows how to write the rules."[19] All our focus on abstract principles and doctrinal systems, all our linear, sequential arguments based on reason are tied intimately to our profound textuality and the lobe of the brain that can conceive, create, and dominate such a version of reality.

Now join me in recalling that over half of the original Bible is written, not left to right, but right to left! Ancient Semitic languages moved in the opposite direction across the page, thus engaging the part of the brain responsible for understanding context, metaphor, and synthesis.

> Certain languages depend heavily on context. Languages such as Arabic and Hebrew are often written only in consonants, which means the reader must figure out what the vowel is by the surrounding concepts and ideas. Unlike English, languages that require the reader to supply the vowels by discerning the context are usually written from right to left . . . which depends on the right hemisphere. . . . Context is also important in other dimensions of language. For example, many studies have shown that the right hemisphere is responsible for our ability to comprehend metaphors.[20]

Have you ever noticed how much most Protestant churches, particularly evangelical ones, love the apostle Paul and his abstract, theological letters? Given Pink's observations, is it any wonder that the Protestant Reformation, which in many ways was a rediscovery of the theology of Paul, occurred simultaneously with society's capacity to access ideas in an abstract and individualized way through the medium of print? And is it any surprise that we struggle mightily with Jesus and his confounding way of speaking (in Aramaic) in parables? We love the literal and avoid the metaphorical. That doesn't even begin to approach the ways in which the Old Testament confounds our categories. We do not have the brain for it!

I remember being told in a seminary homiletics class that I could preach the text of Genesis 14 (Abraham's rescue of Lot) in only one way because the text had a singular meaning. Such a position betrays captivity to a particular mindset. Regardless of the quality of my sermon at the time (which may well have needed some constraints), imagine what is lost when we domesticate the Hebrew narrative, imagination, and text to a set of predetermined meanings.

Several years ago I had the opportunity to hear author and former Catholic priest Brennan Manning speak. Manning recounted a story from his youth in Brooklyn, an amazingly creative community in which he grew up and was shaped. He told of one interaction with a longtime friend, the Jewish author, poet, and illustrator Shel Silverstein. In Manning's telling of the story, he remarked to Silverstein that he often noticed how differently the Jewish mind seemed to work—more creative in its perceptions and descriptions in the everyday nature of things, life, and stories. Manning wondered how Silverstein understood Jesus. Silverstein told Manning he would think about it and get back to him. When they came back together, Silverstein presented Manning with a children's book he wrote and illustrated as a response, a book that has become a classic for both children and adults, *The Giving Tree*.[21] The story describes the relationship between a young boy and a tree. The boy plays with the tree, but as he ages his needs change. Out of his love for the boy, the tree generously gives of itself in order to meet his needs: apples for money, branches for a house, trunk for a boat. Finally, it is only a stump. When the boy returns stooped and tired at the end of his life, the tree offers itself as a place to sit and rest, which makes the tree (stump) very happy. It is a poignant parable that communicates the power of self-sacrificing love. This ability to engage the imagination creatively and metaphorically is integral to the world we live in today.

None of this requires abandoning the left half of the brain (as if we could) in a slow descent into irrationality. In the twentieth century perhaps no one was more adept at creatively mingling these twin poles of reality into dynamic tension than C. S. Lewis. Lewis was not only a logician and apologist of the first order, he was also a poet and novelist steeped in myth. Louis Markos, an associate professor of English at Houston Baptist University, describes Lewis's unique contribution to Christianity in the twentieth century: "Had Lewis brought to Christian apologetics only his skills as a logician, his works would not have been as effective. The mature Lewis tempered his logic with a love of beauty, wonder, and magic. His conversion to Christ not only freed his mind from the bonds of a narrow stoicism; it freed his heart to embrace fully his earlier passion for mythology."[22]

Like so many others, I have lived my whole life in this tension between logic and magic. It took years for it to come to my attention, however. The awakening began when I enrolled as a student of art at the University of Kansas and came to a head halfway through my master of divinity program in seminary. The world of the arts/heart was being directly confronted and assaulted by the world of academics/head. Most of the time I simply felt conflicted and schizophrenic. I knew things that I couldn't "know" through the conceptual frameworks and language sets available to me within modernity's categories. Thus I struggled for more than a decade trying to discover abstract concepts and language to describe verbally and textually what I had known intuitively my whole life. Yet this emerging post-Enlightenment world—where new (and old) ways of knowing are coming into their own, empowered by new technologies that provide new space for the right hemisphere and what flows from it—cannot afford to jettison what has come before. We need to learn to live faithfully into the tension between the head and the heart, the left and the right hemispheres of the brain, the West and the East, the cognitive and the intuitive.

The Reemergence of Celtic Christianity

Throughout our culture are Irish festivals held in tandem with St. Patrick's Day. People listen to ancient-sounding Celtic music, and the stage production of Riverdance still sells out wherever it plays. Celtic whorls, crosses, knots, and so forth are everywhere. This ancient culture has experienced a resurgence within Christianity as well, and I believe it is the result of many of the hungers and dynamics described.

Celtic Christianity is a profoundly earthy faith, affirming the creation and our place as God's children in it. In her book *Every Earthly Blessing*, author and Benedictine oblate Esther de Waal describes her discovery of and journey into Celtic Christianity and its appeal to the world around her.

> Here was a Christianity that was not Mediterranean-based, but forged anew on the fringes of Europe by a people who knew nothing of Rome or urban civilization. It came out of a rural people, a hierarchical, tribal-based society in which personal relationships were of paramount importance—not only relationships between people, but relationships with the wild creatures and with material things, and not least, between this world and the next. . . . It was deeply influenced by the east, drawing much into its monasticism from the traditions of the Egyptian desert, and into its art from Coptic and Syrian sources. It comes out of the wholeness that the Church enjoyed before east and west were torn apart. . . . This Christianity was forged with a fire and a vigor that spoke as much to the heart as to the head . . . full of both tenderness and passion, with a dedication to beauty and yet a commitment to asceticism of the most extreme kind, a triumphant hymning of creation and yet an unswerving devotion to the cross. Here is a Christian understanding that is basic and universal, the primal vision which takes us into the heart of earliest Christendom, and which speaks to that primal vision within all of us. *It is something that many people today are looking for but tragically are finding that that search is carrying them outside the structures of the institutional Church.*[23]

In a Celtic expression of the Christian faith the imagination is stimulated and awakened to creation and our life in it. God creates and employs the raw materials of life and construes life from them. Thus we don't transcend those things in order to have a spiritual life; rather, in those things we discover the hand and presence of the Creator and awaken to the reality that everything is spiritual and has the potential to be sanctified in Christ. In such a conception of life, there is no room for a modern dualism between the secular and the sacred, the natural and the supernatural. The Celtic mind is like the Hebrew mind in this: everything is natural *and* supernatural.

According to de Waal, people long for creative and imaginative expressions of faith and are leaving churches in order to find them. But there are many who remain connected to churches with the conviction and hope that such expressions are possible. And it is not merely for selfish reasons that people are longing for these things. There is a desire to extend this kind of life outward into the lives of people around us who are likewise hungry and in need of spiritual nourishment.

Toward that end we discover that Celtic evangelism was unique in its efficacy. George Hunter's book, *The Celtic Way of Evangelism*, stokes the fires of our imagination.

> The Irish and other Celtic peoples were predominantly right-brained and, in reaching them, Christianity adapted remarkably from its earlier Roman reliance upon words, propositions, concepts, and theological abstractions. . . . Celtic Christianity was rooted more in the imagination than the intellect, and spoke in images more than in concepts. Celtic Christian leaders excelled at expressing their faith in symbols, metaphors and images, both visual and poetic. They had the ability to paint pictures in words, signs and music that acted as icons opening windows on heaven and pathways to eternity. . . . Celtic Christian communicators spoke from their imaginations to the imaginations of their hearers. They were less interested than the Church's Roman wing in "apologetics"; that is, rationally proving the validity of Christianity's truth claims; they seem to have believed that if you could make a Christian truth claim clear to the people's imaginations, the people and the Holy Spirit would take it from there.[24]

The irony of Hunter's and de Waal's descriptions is that the cultural shift I am seeking to describe is, in many ways, a return to this ancient world, regardless of the means by which we are getting there.

A Rekindled Imagination, a Community from the Margins

We must rekindle our imaginations, but we have grown bereft of material. Most of us don't know the lexicon of symbol, metaphor, image, analogy, or icon. We read the Scriptures from left to right in order to get them "right." We need to begin to engage the Scripture to fire our imaginations. I am not proposing that we ignore sound interpretation, but when the need to nail down the literal meaning and right interpretation is the primary or only lens through which we view Scripture, we are limited in what and how we see when we go to the Scriptures. Tragically, such reductive approaches will continue to marginalize the very people in our communities who can help us get out of this rut—those "barbarians" who know and intuitively understand these realities because they are native to them.

Many of us will never make the transition into a post-Enlightenment world. There is nothing wrong with that. However, we can allow others to begin to create environments, systems, and structures that will support such environments where this kind of life *might* emerge. We need every kind of intelligence fully engaged and playfully and creatively leveraged for the kingdom of God. We need women and men who have previously been on the margins to come forth and lead us. We need mystics. We need poets. We need prophets. We need apostles. We need artists. We need all these types of people to reclaim or discover faith in new ways.

We need a church from the margins, drawn from the places and filled with people and shaped by competencies formerly thought to be of little account. In fact perhaps it is from such marginal communities as these—the same way Ireland was marginal to the Roman world and yet was responsible for evangelizing Europe—that influence will begin to spread outward into communities and into new lands that have never been explored and also to those who have been domesticated in the modern world and thus rendered docile. We need a wild vine to be grafted into the branch. We need a church from the margins—a minority report that sees the unseen. We need alternate takes on reality and environments that nurture and release the imagination of God's people. No only so, this imagination must extend out into the creation of which we are a part for the love of God and the sake of the gospel of his Son Jesus Christ.

Post-Christendom

For the first three centuries following the life, death, and resurrection of Jesus Christ, that new community of people called the church existed in the margins of the societies where they found themselves living as disciples. To the Jewish faith from which they emerged, they were marginalized as heretics. To the Roman Empire intent on proclaiming Caesar as Lord, they were seditious. Early Christians were persecuted systematically and mercilessly. Yet the powerlessness and suffering that characterized the early church did not inhibit its life or growth. Rather, because they were shaped by the life, death, and teachings of Jesus Christ, legitimized by his bodily resurrection from the dead, these disciples of Jesus had imaginations that understood such suffering as normative to and demonstrative of the people of God throughout history. Chances are they never dreamed of a time when their religion would rule the day. And in an imperial context defined by power, a church from the margins was a profound countertestimony about what (and who) was powerful and life-giving.

Then everything changed.

In the fourth century the Roman Empire was divided; different claimants to the title "emperor" constantly waged battle against each other. One of the contenders was Constantine. In AD 312 Constantine crossed the Italian Alps to engage Maxientius. After securing northern Italy, he continued to Rome, where he once again met his rival in the Battle of the Milvian Bridge. Legend has it that Constantine had a vision: looking toward the sun, he saw the Greek letters chi and rho (the first two letters of the Greek name for Christ) and the phrase "*In hoc signo vinces*" ("In this sign, conquer"). Constantine had his army change their standard, painting on their shields the sign of the cross. Constantine was victorious in battle and ascended as sole emperor, Caesar Augustus, ruler of the Western Empire of Rome.

The veracity of this legend is a subject of debate, as is the sincerity of Constantine's ensuing conversion (he was not baptized until right before his death). Everyone agrees, however, that in 313 Constantine legitimized Christianity by legalizing it in the Roman Empire through the Edict of Milan. Christianity moved out of the margins of Roman society, where it had existed for three centuries as a persecuted minority, and into the mainstream of imperial life and power. Christians who had lived in the shadows with no power could now claim the emperor, the most powerful man in the Mediterranean, as one of their own.

In the centuries immediately following this transition, the church and the state became increasingly intertwined until they were one and the same. The Roman Empire, led by the emperor, became the Holy Roman Empire, led by the pope. This theocratic unity conferred on the man who sat in Peter's seat the power of the state, headship of the church, and command of the military. This religious/political/military reality defined the Western world for over a millennium.

Over the course of that time, the empire expanded and contracted. Often its reach exceeded its original Roman provenance, and at times the seat of power moved to places other than Rome. Gradually the Holy Roman Empire and the political landscape underneath it became known as "Christendom." Throughout all these transitions Christianity underwent a massive, even cataclysmic, conversion from the margins of society into the most exalted halls of power. Reconsider for a moment McLuhan's aphorisms, "The medium is the message," and, "We become what we behold." How does a Christian imagination steeped in power for over one thousand years imagine Scripture, church, culture, and the gospel?

In the sixteenth century much of this world began to unravel. Its dissolution had begun much earlier, but it was a Roman Catholic monk named Martin Luther who lit a fuse that blew this world apart. The Protestant Reformation ushered in a world remade, but it still saw itself within the rubric of Christendom. Though this new world saw its genesis as a divine necessity in response to political and theological corruption, it was also a world that would grow increasingly secularized, a world that would now begin to distinguish the head of the church from the head of state. Over time, the secular world and the sacred one grew more and more separate and distinct. This impulse toward secularization animated more and more of the common imagination, systems, and structures. In tandem with many other forces that shaped the world, humanity moved out of the Middle Ages and Renaissance and slowly but surely walked into the modern world. The world formerly known as "Christendom" gave birth to "Europe."

Enabled by fast sailing ships that shrunk the world and superior weapons technology that overwhelmed and dominated native peoples, the European imagination that reached into the new world was still enflamed by an imperial narrative of power and the posture of superiority and certainty that comes as a result of such power. Complicit in this was a church-sanctioned theology that intertwined and equated expanding national interests with spreading the gospel.

As these European nations sought to extend and maintain their sovereignty in the new worlds they discovered, within two centuries this way of engaging (called "colonialism") came into conflict in the new continent of North America (as well as Central and South America). European nations contended for supremacy in this world of abundant resources initially defended by "mere savages" and later by the colonists who lived there. The American Revolution was one reaction to the way European nations dealt with their colonies. The success of this revolution birthed a new political and theological reality that emerged out of this conflict and continued the process of transforming the political and sociological expression of the Christian faith. What had begun in the margins of Israel's first-century society and rose into power with Constantine in the context of the Roman Empire continued to evolve in the wake of the Protestant Reformation and its increasingly secularized European identity. American culture likewise continued the gradual process of this transformation. Former congressional chaplain Dr. Richard Halverson once said, "Christianity was birthed in Galilee as a relationship. It spread to Greece and became a philosophy. It spread to Rome and became an empire. It spread to Britain and became a culture. It spread to America and became an enterprise."

Christendom's Twilight and the American Experience

For the last century there has been a battle of Constantinian proportions being waged in America over national identity and how religious identity and conviction ought to be expressed in a whole host of ways. The question at the heart of this battle is whether America is a Christian nation, and if so, what kind and whose version. Interestingly, while most of these modern-day combatants disagree about what a society, Christian or otherwise, ought to look like and be based upon, they are virtually indistinguishable in their conviction that societal power, in the forms of cultural influence and structured political clout, must be won and used in the pursuit of their vision of society (and in the vanquishing of their enemies). In this, their captivity to the Constantinian heritage and worldview is obvious.

In their book *Resident Aliens*, Stanley Hauerwas and William Willimon describe the Constantinian worldview as the belief that "the church needs some sort of surrounding 'Christian' culture to prop it up."[25] However, the increasing secularization and radical individualism of American culture, combined with the relegation of faith to the realm of personal preference and private expression, have made the possibility of a cultural prop impossible to realize, to say nothing of the rightness or wrongness of striving for such a prop. Christendom, or a Christian culture, presupposes and requires a common language, beliefs, values, practices, and structures that support it and ultimately manifest it in a system of government and laws constructed to give shape to its identity. Such laws presuppose cultural buy-in and the attendant institutional and structural power to enforce such laws. Hauerwas and Willimon contend that the church has depended on, and thus has been corrupted and intoxicated by, Christendom and the power it takes to sustain it. To say we are now living in post-Christendom means that the church, for the first time since the fourth century, is moving back into the margins where it began.

I think this is an essential reality for followers of Jesus to embrace in the twenty-first century. We can no longer assume privilege, position, or control. We cannot assume a divine *imprimatur* because we have the power to back up our convictions. Post-Christendom tells us we no longer live in a society that by default shares the same language, beliefs, values, or structures that we believe ought to shape American identity. We are contending for a new story in a world that is balkanized and atomized and seeking to establish something new. In the absence of any agreed-upon cultural metanarrative (remember, we are a *de*-storied people), the default story seems to be the story of capitalism and conspicuous consumption. This is one of the challenges facing a society shaped under the metaphor of "melting pot." The culture wars we see being fought around us are about people and communities staking out territory in defense of worldviews perceived to be under fire.

God's people, when they are acting faithfully, place their trust in God, not in the structures of human power. The psalmist declares, "Some trust in chariots and some in horses, but we trust in the name of the LORD our God" (Ps. 20:7). The prophet Zechariah articulates the perspective of Yahweh: "'Not by might nor by power, but by my Spirit,' says the LORD Almighty" (Zech. 4:6). The "power" of God is a source of life and strength that comes from following Christ and speaking from and to the places Christ does, in the way Christ did. The world of Christendom has died, and its death has been a long time coming. Hauerwas and Willimon continue:

> In the twilight of that world, we have an opportunity to discover what has and always is the case—that the church, as those called out by God, embodies a social alternative that the world cannot on its own terms know. The demise of the Constantinian world view, the gradual decline of the notion that the church needs some sort of surrounding "Christian" culture to prop it up and mold its young, is not a death lament. It is an opportunity to celebrate. The decline of the old, Constantinian synthesis between the church and the world means that we American Christians are at last free to be faithful in a way that makes being a Christian today an exciting adventure.[26]

I look into the subculture of many versions of Christian faith that are operative in America today and see Christians wringing their hands in fear, hoping that Jesus will come back and get them out of this "mess." On the other hand, I look at the world around me and see a cultural context that is closer to the world of the early church than any other culture in the last two thousand years. The irony is that these same Christians are open about their desire for a return to a version of faith that was modeled by the early church and described in the pages of the New Testament book of Acts. In other words, we want the fruit of the early church but not the context of suffering and demand that produced such fruit. How American. How selfish. How consumptive. How anemic. Let us listen anew to the teachings of Jesus while we walk through the pages of Scripture to the cross. As we do, our personal and corporate imaginations will bring us into a new (and ancient) identity: sojourners and aliens testifying to an alternative life rooted in the revelation of God in Jesus Christ.

Twentieth-Century American Church History in the Context of Christendom

Describing the polarization that happens in modern expressions of the church in this context, Hauerwas and Willimon employ the categories of Mennonite theologian John Howard Yoder. If *liberal* describes the theology of the left half of this polarization, the way in which they engage culture is as an "activist church." An activist church is "more concerned with the building of a better society than with the reformation of the church."[27] The activist church's agenda is set by the agenda of the culture and as such runs the very real risk of being indistinguishable from any other social agency. The right half of this polarization, what I label as *fundamentalism*, is called by Yoder and described by Hauerwas and Willimon as the "conversionist church" for how it sees itself in and related to culture. "The [conversionist] church argues that no amount of tinkering with the structures of society will counter the effects of human sin. . . . The sphere of political action is shifted by the conversionist church from without to within, from society to the individual soul."[28]

The conversionist church often takes an adversarial/opposi-tional posture toward culture. Where the ability to distinguish the activist church from the surrounding culture is compli-cated by the virtual dissolution of any boundaries that would differentiate the church from the culture, the conversionist church erects fortresslike boundaries around itself and asks those who would participate in their community to convert out of the secular culture and into another—theirs. In both these contexts the implied context is Christendom. At stake is which version of the church is the faithful representative. Yoder argues that neither is. Instead he proposes a third option named the "confessing church," which Hauerwas and Willimon term a community of resident aliens, "a radical alternative . . . [that] reject[s] both the individualism of the conversionists and the secularism of the activists . . . the confessing church finds its main political task to lie, not in the personal transformation of individual hearts or the modification of society, but rather in the congregation's determination to worship Christ in all things."[29] Such an approach to the church is very helpful in interpreting the most recent history of the Christian subculture in America and how it has affected our imagination and given shape to many of the kinds of churches we live within today.

If the metaphor of *fortress* aptly describes such churches within this framework, then a dilemma arises: how will any-one *hear* if no one *goes*? It is hard to go anywhere if you are locked behind walls. During the 1940s and 1950s a new kind of ministry developed out of mostly fundamentalist/conversionist contexts: the parachurch ministry. A parachurch ministry oper-ates alongside a church and directly engages a specific culture usually outside the church. Its ministry is specialized to engage a specific subculture; it generally focuses on one unique vocation, goal, or strategy in a way that is often impossible (for a number of different reasons—financial, theological, philosophical, or otherwise) for any single local church to focus on. Thus over a span of almost two decades, ministries such as Young Life,

Campus Crusade for Christ, InterVarsity Christian Fellowship, the Navigators, Youth for Christ, and others emerged to reach high school and college-aged students in order to "win" them to Christ. Most of these parachurch ministries are evangelistic in their focus and seek to become bridges of relevance and translation to a surrounding subculture determined to be too hostile or difficult for churches to engage for one reason or another.

In some ways American nondenominational parachurch ministries mirror the many different orders, societies, and missions that emerged within the Roman Catholic Church in response to the Holy Spirit and the environment in which Catholics were disciples. Benedictines, Franciscans, Jesuits, and Carthusians are examples of orders that arose in different times and cultures to fulfill a specific purpose or exploit a unique opportunity the larger church was unable to see or meet. Two of the many differences between these two phenomena, however, are the length of the timeline out of which such orders emerge and the reality that in the Catholic Church an authority structure legitimized and regulated such expressions. Within the radically fragmented religious landscape of denominational and nondenominational churches and parachurch ministries in America, usually there is no authority outside that of the ministries themselves. It is through ministries like these, which emphasize biblical authority, faith fundamentals, personal salvation, and a concomitant engagement of culture, that a nascent evangelicalism is born.

The impact of parachurch ministries was explosive. Churches began to subcontract ministry to these specialists who could more effectively produce the kinds of outcomes, within a specific understanding of the gospel and salvation, that churches existing within the fundamentalist/conversionist paradigm had traditionally, though not exclusively, been inclined to value and pursue—inward change through forgiveness of the guilt of sin understood personally. Another by-product of the success of parachurch ministries on American religious imagination is that many churches began to imagine themselves within the same narrow framework of specialization. In fact, some parachurches actually began to look more like churches, and many more churches began to function out of a paradigm aligned closely to parachurch sensibilities. The seeker church movement is one example of this.

Church Growth, the Seeker-Targeted Church Movement, and Generational Ministry

In chapter 2 I briefly described my tenure as a youth pastor at a church. I shared that one of the first things I did as a member of this staff was travel to South Barrington, Illinois, for a Willow Creek Leadership Conference about building seeker-driven and seeker-targeted churches. I remember being overwhelmed by the massive campus, the people, the music and drama, and the founding pastor, Bill Hybels. He is an amazing pastor and leader, and I have great respect, admiration, and affection for him. Sitting in their massive worship space, I listened to Hybels tell the story of his conversion and how, in his excitement over his new faith, he brought a high school friend to church. Hybels described being horrified as he endured the worship service, now watching it through the eyes of his friend. It was hopelessly outdated, provincial, and inaccessible to an outsider. Hybels said this experience and others like it led him to try to discover a way to make the church and the gospel relevant to people such as his friend—people who were hungry for and open to Jesus but unable to reach him because of the seeming irrelevance of the church itself. Hybels then went on to describe, with passionate intensity, the need to make the church relevant by doing ministry with *excellence*, by using drama and music in creative ways, and by hosting all of this on a beautiful campus stripped of religious symbols and language inaccessible to the people of this world. Listening to this narrative while looking out giant windows at a beautiful lake, I was enraptured.

Hybels told us that Willow Creek had a specific "target" they were trying to reach with their ministry: a middle-class, thirty-eight-year-old male Baby Boomer, married with kids, who was beginning to experience a general dissatisfaction with life and was willing to seek out spiritual answers. Such a person was labeled a "seeker." According to Hybels's narrative, the seeker they were targeting grew up in a Christian home. Even if this home was only nominal in its Christianity, such a context provided the seeker with at least a basic understanding of the Christian faith, including its concepts and language. What the targeted person didn't have was any sense of its value or relevance to his life or the questions he was asking. Hybels said that if they could reach this specific target and make the gospel relevant to this person (through a number of means and strategies), they believed they could also reach a constellation of people around this person. Apparently they were right. I was one of several thousand people who had paid to attend that conference and who sat and took in this world that was being described and offered all around me. Its impact was instantly obvious: over fifteen thousand people in the greater Chicago area, most of whom had not been in church prior to Willow Creek, attended this church. Many people were skeptical, but most were mesmerized—and hooked.

Scenes like this continued to play out in the years that followed as more and more people made pilgrimages like my own to Willow Creek. This conference phenomenon has since expanded. Other churches that have experienced similar kinds of success in similar kinds of ways join themselves to the Willow Creek network that has sprung out of this paradigm for ministry. The impact of the seeker church emerging out of Willow Creek in the 1970s that later emerged into the popular consciousness of American Christianity as a movement in the late 1980s and early 1990s is hard to estimate, but I would venture to say that its impact on the church of twentieth-century America is unparalleled.

I have two observations to make about this. The first is that in its orientation, language, and sense of mission Willow Creek is much like the modern parachurch. In fact, I believe the Willow Creek/seeker church phenomenon is a direct by-product of the emergence of the American parachurch movement. Alongside a burgeoning evangelical movement, parachurch ministries birthed in the 1940s and 1950s came of age in the 1960s and 1970s. These ministries certainly were influential in the Jesus movement of the early 1970s, out of which Willow Creek itself came. As a youth pastor in a local church in Kansas City in the early 1990s, I was also concurrently on staff with Young Life—a parachurch ministry founded by Jim Rayburn in the 1940s to reach disinterested kids. The mantra of Young Life ministry is, "It's a sin to bore a kid with the gospel." All of the pastors of the church where I was on staff at one time either had been Young Life staff themselves or had served as volunteers in the 1970s and early 1980s. As we listened to the story of Willow Creek and heard language about programming and ministry designed to reach "seekers" with a gospel of relevance, it was as if we had stumbled into the adult version of Young Life. Willow Creek's vision and mission seemed to be to create a church that didn't feel like church. It seemed like Young Life's mantra had been co-opted into, "It is a sin to bore an adult with the gospel." For many in our leadership team, I think it felt like a homecoming of sorts. And it was—back home to a parachurch-oriented ministry aimed at *reaching seekers*. I am not saying Willow Creek was or is a parachurch ministry. I think Willow Creek's sensibilities were shaped under the influence of the parachurch first. It seems that only secondarily did Willow Creek come to understand what it means to be the church. This is not a value judgment; it is simply my interpretation of a context and a story that gave shape to a particular community that has made an enormous impact for the kingdom of God. Willow Creek is an amazing church incarnating and expressing the gospel in a faithful and multifaceted way in the context of their community. And besides, who am I to judge? I am grateful for them.

The reason I describe Willow Creek with this level of detail is because of their profound influence and because I think the landscape has radically changed around them. This is at the heart of the second observation I want to make about Willow Creek: Willow Creek represents the final creative response of the modern church in America grasping for identity, impact, and influence as Christendom gasps and breathes its last breath in the West. The language and assumptions of Christendom permeate the narrative, vision, and mission of Willow Creek. Remember, Christendom implies a shared vision of reality, common symbols and language sets, as well as a shared cultural landscape. Willow Creek's description of their target person is someone who has grown up in a Christian world and so possesses all of the background and language to engage what seeker churches offer. The challenge in that world is that this person must be convinced to engage. At the end of Christendom *the* issue is relevance. So the church seeks to show how it is relevant, mostly on terms dictated by the sensibilities of the seeker. The problem we now face is that Baby Boomers are the last generation to grow up and have their identity shaped under a modern, Christian view of reality.

In the 1990s generational ministry was all the rage. I attended seminars that promised to equip me with strategies to reach my generation. Living in Denver and going to seminary, I joined a Generation X church using a Willow Creek–based, seeker-targeted model to try to reach others in our generation with the gospel. We strove for excellence. We had creative programming (music and drama) that complemented the thrust of the sermon. The sermons were often aimed at felt-need issues relevant to seekers aged twenty- and thirtysomething. We regularly did surveys with sample groups from the church to try to gauge how effective we were and how we might add or subtract things (e.g., worship songs) in order to make these seekers more comfortable. We did direct mail. And we were successful. Yet something seemed off to me. The theory made sense—at least when I heard it at Willow Creek. Yet something was lost in translation, something that I knew intuitively but could not yet say aloud. It felt as though we were trying too hard. We had a lot of heart-to-heart, head-to-head discussions. For me the biggest part of it was that I began to miss God amid all of this effort and strategy.

It was in this context, in 1996, that I first connected to the community of people who later became Emergent. I have described in chapter 3 how I began to learn of postmodernity and all the cultural, theological, and structural issues around it. What we had previously understood as generational issues were really, in fact, worldview issues. If Baby Boomers were the last generation to grow up in a version of America that was modern and within a framework of Christendom, Generation X was the vanguard, the first generation of Americans to grow up in a world that is fully postmodern and post-Christendom in its sensibilities. Willow Creek's narrative and ministry model has become a square peg in a round hole. As we began to learn and discover the particularities of this world, our world, many things began to fall into place, including why we could no longer take a ministry model that was birthed in one (very different) context and translate and transplant it across geography, generations, and worldviews.

The Missional Context of a Post-Christendom World

I believe this same story could be told from the other side of the Christendom coin: the liberal/activist churches. Certainly theirs are different issues, and yet I know that mainline denominational churches were influenced by the seeker movement. However, such traditions have one big advantage over evangelicals: their theologians began describing the context of a post-Christendom world long before evangelical theologians did. One could posit any number of reasons for this, but one possible and perhaps plausible reason is that the evangelical movement in the 1980s was less likely to acknowledge any theory or theology that suggested their power and influence was waning. Moreover, as evangelicalism began to perceive its loss of influence, having only recently come into its possession, evangelicals were more likely to fight for it. Mainline, liberal denominational churches have less at stake. They have been in decline for some time and thus are more willing to examine the context of our culture in order to see it with fresh eyes and describe it in new ways. In both instances, most of the churches that exist today are churches whose entire mental framework was shaped within the narrative of Christendom, whether fundamentalist, conservative, evangelical, mainline, or liberal.

People native to the world of post-Christendom are struggling within these institutions, including leaders. Every week I receive numerous emails from pastors trying to faithfully serve God in institutions that cannot or will not engage the world in any meaningful way. For the most part, these are not angry, rebellious, or dissatisfied people. These are men and women desperate to be faithful and fighting to know how. Consider this email from a young pastor and seminary student:

I am a minister in a typical mainline Baptist congregation. I attend seminary in [Southern city in Southern state] at the [mainline denominational] Seminary. Our church looks nearly identical to the way it looked nearly 50 years ago. I am struggling to find a way to be connected to God communally since the congregation where I live out my calling is not communal but rather very modern. Simply put, we aren't relevant to me (25 years old) or to anyone my age. I am looking for a more excellent way. I have this calling and this heart for serving God through leadership in the church. Here is what I am looking for: a place to learn what you are doing. I recognize that church must be located with attention to local environment. However, the attitude with which your church carries out the beloved community in our world could help me understand the how behind the creation of community. At this point, seminary does not teach this. Neither does the church. So, I am asking for help. I want to do more than survive. I desire to be part of a community that is intimate and centered on Christ.

In this illustration, the young man uses the language of relevance—language I was quite explicit about deconstructing as it relates to the context of post-Christendom. However, it is such a common way to express oneself in a period of transition and dislocation that it is nearly impossible to avoid. How can he begin to discover how to respond in his context? All the systems and structures he inhabits are shaped in a world different from his own. However, the Christian theological discipline of missiology can begin to provide us resources to discern and respond to the context of post-Christendom, a world this twenty-five-year-old supplicant needs help navigating.

British missionary Lesslie Newbigin was one of the first missionaries or missiologists to describe the West as post-Christendom. His work has had an enormous impact on how many are now viewing culture and the context of the Western world. Newbigin and his wife were lifelong missionaries in India. After thirty-five years of ministry, Newbigin retired at the age of seventy-four and returned to England.

Missionaries must know how to read the context of a culture, discern its implicit and explicit narratives of reality, and listen and speak in the way language, concepts, symbols, and images function within a worldview. Because of this they are often not only missionaries but also theologians and sociologists of the first order. When Newbigin left India, he was a bishop and had led a fruitful life engaging the world where he had served and learned for those thirty-five years. It was with this experience and diverse set of skills that he returned to England and described the challenges and opportunities of a world similar to the one the young pastor describes above. Of course, when

Newbigin began writing these things, very few sensed a cultural transition. It took an outsider who was also an insider to be able to name the dislocation and transformation that was beginning to take place.

Newbigin declared the West was post-Christian/post-Christendom. Moreover, he said the West had domesticated the gospel within the categories of modernity and thus lost much of its power. When a community, church, or denomination lives within Christendom, *mission* is the activity or program it engages in when it goes to make disciples in a so-called foreign community, nation, culture, or civilization. In such an environment, *missions* is a subset of the life of the church. However, in a culture that has moved out of Christendom and into a marginal identity, the whole context of the life of the community becomes mission.

In post-Christendom, the church is that community of people who look to discover what God is actively doing in the world around them and then join themselves to that work. The church is that community of people gathered around Jesus Christ in order to participate in his life and incarnate it into the context where he has placed them. The invitation from God is for us to start *right here*, not just the exotic *out there*. Newbigin articulates the challenge facing churches that are trying to live missionally among people whose sensibilities were shaped within the narrow confines of modernity and the Enlightenment: "How can this strange story of God made man, of a crucified savior, of resurrection and new creation become credible for those whose entire mental training has conditioned them to believe that the real world is the world that can be satisfactorily explained and managed without the hypothesis of God? I know of only one clue to the answering of that question, only one real hermeneutic of the gospel: *congregations that believe it.*"[30]

Even though we are moving out of modernity, Newbigin's emphasis on the life of local church congregations as the primary means by which the gospel will be credible is truer than ever.

To be missiological in a post-Christendom world is not to be more committed to programs of mission but to hold resolutely to an ecclesiology that is incomprehensible apart from mission. Hauerwas elaborates: "The work of Jesus was not a new set of ideals or principles for reforming or even revolutionizing society, but the establishment of a new community, a people that embodied forgiveness, sharing and self-sacrificing love in its rituals and discipline. In that sense, the visible church . . . was not the bearer of Christ's message; it was itself to be the message."[31] In this context, we do not seek to "reach" a "target" group or demographic with a message. We live incarnationally in order to demonstrate the new reality that is being revealed in Jesus Christ and embodied by his people the church. A hunger for this kind of living is what I sense in the email from the young man quoted above. This longing is something for which the religious structures of his world, such as they are, have no imagination or framework. This is what I experienced firsthand in college that was transformational for so many.

The gospel is not a location to be defended. It is an alternate reality based on the person of Jesus Christ, who has called around himself a new community to live his life out in the world in hope, courage, and joy. We are called to live out our faith in the margins, witnessing to the gospel as communities of disciples following in the ways of our Master, Jesus Christ. The false dichotomies between evangelism and discipleship, between justification and sanctification break down, and we are joined holistically with God as we pursue Christ and his intentions for the world.

6

Being Here and There

discovering a wholly present, wholly other God

In the beginning was the Word, and the Word was with God, and the Word was God. He was with God in the beginning. Through him all things were made; without him nothing was made that has been made. . . . The Word became flesh and made his dwelling among us. We have seen his glory, the glory of the one and only Son, who came from the Father, full of grace and truth.

John 1:1–3, 14

If we submit everything to reason our religion will be left with nothing mysterious or supernatural. If we offend the principles of reason our religion will be absurd and ridiculous. . . . There are two equally dangerous extremes: to exclude reason, to admit nothing but reason.[1]

Blaise Pascal, *Pensées*

Representations of spirits and similar conceptions are rather one and all early modes of "rationalizing" a precedent experience, to which they are subsidiary. They are attempts in some way or other . . . to guess the riddle it propounds, and their effect is at the same time to weaken and deaden the experience itself.

They are the source from which springs, not religion, but the rationalization of religion, which often ends by constructing such a massive structure of theory and such a plausible fabric of interpretation, that the "mystery" is frankly excluded.[2]

Rudolf Otto, *The Idea of the Holy*

Functional Gnosticism

Modern Enlightenment notions about knowledge are often inherently dualistic (and Gnostic); they promote a separation between what is spiritual and what is physical. In such a dualistic conception of reality, we believe that what is spiritual/nonmaterial is good/holy, while what is physical/material is bad/evil. As a result, in order to access and know the spiritual, one must transcend the physical—whether it be the actual human body (as in classic Gnosticism) or actual cultures and communities of particularity that host physical human bodies. When a person has knowledge (gnosis) of the Divine, then what is merely material is left behind. Now I can't imagine that most people would avow such a position explicitly. Yet functionally, I believe this is often what happens. We imagine that our theological/conceptual systems are the means by which we know God *as God is*. I truly believe that such postures and perspectives put us in danger of conceptual idolatry, worshiping our ideas of and frameworks for God.

At one point I was considering ordination within a small, Reformed Presbyterian denomination. Preparing for my ordination exams I continued to read over the ordination vows to which I would have to submit myself. As I read and reflected over these vows, I kept stopping at this one: "Do you sincerely receive and adopt the Westminster Confession of Faith and the Catechisms of this Church, as containing *the system of doctrine* taught in the Holy Scripture?" (emphasis added). This stopped me short for a couple of reasons. First, I wasn't aware the main function of Scripture was to teach a system of doctrine. I figured if God had intended to give the church a system of doctrine, he would have given the church a system of doctrine, not the Bible I have studied, read, discussed, puzzled over, and preached for a period of nearly two decades. That a person or a community of people could faithfully systematize the Scriptures into a doctrinal framework I had (and have) no doubt. To be honest, that notion didn't really trouble me at all. But then I kept coming back to the use of the definite article just prior to the phrase "system of doctrine." If the vow had used an indefinite article like "a," instead of the definite "the," I might have been able to climb on board and say, "As a system of doctrine, it doesn't get much better than this." But to elevate such a culturally bound human artifact—no matter how good—to the functional level of Scripture seemed too much. It makes this system a form of gnosis that lifts us out of our boundedness rather than a sign of God's faithful engagement with a people in and out of particular context. Again, no one ever would say or believe such a thing explicitly, but functionally, it is what I perceived and experienced: we access the Scriptures through the Westminster Confession or any number of other confessions or systems arising out of and available to Protestant communities since the Reformation. Is it surprising to us that with such a perspective, imaginations stagnate?

The irony of such a posture is how significantly it betrays the Reformers and the spirit that animated them. At the heart of the Protestant Reformation are Latin phrases like *reformata semper reformanda est* and *Ecclesia semper reformanda est*. They can be translated, respectively, "reformed and always being re-formed," and similarly, "the church always *needs* to be re-formed." However, the spirit of these mottos has been lost within many Protestant communities and traditions, as the words of the Reformers have come to take precedence over the lives of the Reformers and how they engaged the Scriptures, themselves, and the world in light of their context. My friend and colleague Doug Pagitt has said, "We honor the Reformers not by saying what they said, but by doing what they did."

When we elevate our systems of doctrine to the level of "the" reality, to which they are merely and imperfectly bearing witness, we move into dangerous territory. We move into cultural captivity that domesticates the theological imagination, and when our imagination is bound in such a way, it ceases to be "salt and light."

Our ecclesiological structures always manifest our theological imaginations. If our theological imagination has stagnated, what does that say about our churches? I will go even further. I believe such a division between spirit and matter, between theology and context, betrays what separates Christianity from Gnosticism— the incarnation of God in the human form of the Messiah, Jesus Christ.

Conceptual Idolatry

The beauty and the mystery of the incarnation is not just that it reveals a God of humility and love but that it also reveals a God who dignifies his creatures *where they are* in creation. John tells us, "The Word became flesh and made his dwelling among us" (John 1:14). John does not say, "The flesh became Word, and when it had done so, it left behind its limitations and ascended, fully realized, into the presence of God."

Witness the ancient community of the Pharisees, whose imaginations were shaped by the exile of Israel to Babylon. They believed by strict adherence to the Torah, and the traditions they built up around it, they could keep Israel from ever coming under the same judgment again. By the first century AD, the Pharisees were a holiness and purity movement trying to usher in the messianic age through their observance of law and tradition. As they sought to leave creatureliness behind, they loaded "people down with heavy burdens they [could] hardly carry" while being unwilling to "lift one finger to help them" (Luke 11:46). This conceptual idolatry, however well intentioned, caused them to miss the reality and presence of the Messiah among them.

Because of the incarnation, people and churches must always contend with the limitations of our creatureliness. We always access and thus must subsequently express the life of God with and through the cultural tools at our disposal. This does not make all tools equal or valuable. The task requires discernment and wisdom. But because of the reality of our limitations, our language and communal faith expressions are always provisional and in need of reframing and re-forming around the continued revelation of God in Christ. Moreover, we must be in constant dialogue with those with whom we differ (in concept, culture, or class), whether they are contemporary or ancient, in order to access and submit ourselves to the full wisdom of the church animated by the Holy Spirit.

Modern, Enlightenment, Christendom-embedded portraits of God are faithful insofar as they acknowledge they are limited renderings of a reality that is only approximated by our language. We are accustomed to associating idolatry with the worship of an image, but I wonder if in the modern, Western world, birthed by the inky imagination of Johannes Gutenberg, we are more likely to commit the sin of idolatry by engraving an image of God in text? We have become adept in the world of the printing press at translating the words of the Scriptures into different languages. In such work, translators seek faithful equivalents to vocabulary, idioms, syntax, and genres of the original languages of Scripture. However, what we often fail to recognize is that such a move (the move from oral to written enabled first by the phonetic alphabet, then by the printing press) profoundly altered how people and communities accessed reality itself.

Knowledge (and its relational counterpart, wisdom) formerly resided in a living, localized community where learning and tradition were passed down orally from one generation to the next. The print revolution of modernity displaced knowledge from the community and into books that could store information and make it accessible to anyone possessing the technologies of literacy.

What if the world we are living in requires more than linguistic translation? What if we need people and communities to move beyond the inherited work of the modern, print revolution (exchanging one culture's word for another culture's word) and instead begin the equally vital work of conceptual translation. As I conjecture I confess that I am not even sure what I mean by this. However, I have an intuitive sense that this will become increasingly critical in the years before us—if not for our generation, then for two and three generations down the line. Will we be able to discover and faithfully create frameworks that ignite the imaginations of future generations—imaginations with which they can engage God, the Scriptures, and the world?

If the work of linguistic translation engages vocabulary, grammar, syntax, and idiom (to name a few considerations), then what are the corresponding categories for conceptual translation? In order to do conceptual translation, we must engage ideas, metaphors, frameworks, large-scale patterns, image, and symbols across multiple spectrums. Obviously this is not easy to do.

We cannot approach God *acontextually*. We always experience and know God provisionally within a context. We always use the resources, tools, and imaginative frameworks of our times to engage God and one another. We might wish we spoke only "with the tongues of angels," but Paul said that we also speak with the "tongues of men." Moreover, when we speak angelically, Paul demands translation back into the tongues of men that we might be edified and not confused (1 Cor. 14:1–25). We must be reminded that to such exalted, angelic creatures "the mystery that has been kept hidden for ages and generations" was kept back from these beings who "long to look into these things" (Col. 1:26; 1 Peter 1:12). Peter and Paul teach us that it was to finite, bounded, contextually specific people that God's revelation came and through whom the mystery was revealed, not to beings freed from such constraints.

We see these boundaries as limitations to be left behind, but this is one of the blessings we gain from the postmodern deconstruction of modernity: the recovery of the local, particular, and specific. These supposed limitations are in reality gifts that allow us to participate with God in his work in creation—a creation he loved and engaged within the cultural frameworks of first-century Israel. And God continues to meet his people in our own culture. We know this was not arbitrary because we are told by Paul in Galatians 4:4 that "when the set time had fully come, God sent his Son." How might we begin to perceive God at work in our time?

A Communal Imagination Shaped by Incarnational Theology

Communities engaging with the missional context of our age must be aware of the fact that they are *theology-generating* communities. I use the word *aware* because generating theology is not something we choose to do; it is something we do by default. Theology at the most basic level is nothing more than what we believe about God and ultimate things and, perhaps more importantly, how we live out of what we believe. C. S. Lewis writes in *Mere Christianity*, "Theology is practical: especially now. In the old days, when there was less education and discussion, perhaps it was possible to get on with a very few simple ideas about God. But it is not so now. Everyone reads, everyone hears things discussed. Consequently, if you do not listen to theology, that will not mean that you have no ideas about God. It will mean that you have a lot of wrong ones— bad, muddled, out-of-date ideas."[3]

Theology is always the by-product of an implicit or explicit dialogue that churches (personally and communally) are having with the tradition from which they arise and the living culture in which they reside. Thus the fundamental/conversionist and the liberal/activist categories proposed by Hauerwas and Willimon for how some communities of faith engage the culture are insufficient to generate an incarnation-honoring posture. One is too embedded, the other too distant. One seeks to be wholly immanent, the other wholly transcendent. But in Jesus Christ "all the fullness of the Deity lives in *bodily form*, and in Christ you have been brought to fullness" (Col. 2:9–10, emphasis added). Fully God, fully human. As a result, churches representing Christ must live in the incarnational tension of immanence and transcendence if they want to engage in a theologically and missionally faithful way. Though framed in the language of ethics, I believe what Hauerwas and Willimon describe in the following quote is broadly true of theology.

> Christian ethics [or in my argument, theology] arise, in great part, out of something Christians claim to have seen that the world has not seen, namely, the creation of a people, a family, a colony that is a living witness that Jesus Christ is Lord. Tradition, as we use the term here, is a complex, lively argument about what happened in Jesus that has been carried on, across generations, by a concrete body of people called the church. Fidelity to this tradition, this story, is the most invigorating challenge of the adventure begun in our baptism and is the toughest job of Christian ethics [theology].[4]

When we earnestly engage our context in a theological posture that takes seriously the incarnation, faithful engagement in the spirit of the gospel begins to be a real possibility, and life in the church becomes an adventure full of life. In Colossians, Paul tells a community of new, Gentile believers that the mystery of God, kept hidden for the ages, is now being revealed through the church. What is the nature of the mystery? Christ *in* them—the incarnation of the Holy Spirit of God in the new colony of Christ on earth, of which they are members. Have you ever noticed how much Paul entrusts to such seemingly ill-equipped followers at a time when the future of the church is no certain thing? Consider his words to the church in Philippi:

> I thank my God every time I remember you. In all my prayers for all of you, I always pray with joy because of your partner-ship in the gospel from the first day until now, being *confident* of this, that he who began a good work in you will carry it on to completion until the day of Christ Jesus.
>
> Philippians 1:3–6, emphasis added

Then later in the same letter:

> All of us, then, who are mature should take such a view of things. And if on some point you think differently, that too God will make clear to you. Only let us live up to what we have already attained.
>
> Philippians 3:15–16

Why is he able to say such things to such new believers, con-tending so strenuously for their faith in the face of opposition from Jews who think they are heretical and Romans who be-lieve they are seditious? Why? Because Christ is in them: the hope of glory. When the incarnation, the suffering, death, and resurrection of Christ constitute the shape and content of our communities, our theology follows suit.

A New Testament Church?

As soon as we arrive here, we immediately face a problem of translation. We are able to observe in the Scriptures how the Spirit leads new churches in ways that force them to engage in what I believe is a profoundly healthy and life-giving tension. On one hand they witness to an emerging theology that has at its heart the person of Jesus Christ and some basic convictions about what has happened around his presence in creation. On the other hand we see the church wrestling with the implications of his presence and what it means for how they live their lives *now* in light of what has come before. Circumcision or no circumcision? Meat sacrificed to idols or no meat sacrificed to idols? Sabbath observance or no Sabbath observance? Those in this newly formed community called the church constantly have to contend for the faith—and not just with their enemies, but within themselves and with each other as well. Yet as they contend, they do so in a locally responsive way that generates life and engagement with the issues of their time, culture, and geography.

The early church radically engaged their world as a community of sojourners located in a context under negotiation, a colony of heaven contending for their new faith and struggling mightily to understand the implications of the incarnation for life in the wake of Jesus Christ. Talk about having to reorient your theological imagination! We read the narratives of the early church found in the book of Acts, and we are captivated by what we see playing out before us. But rather than marveling at the ways in which the church responded to the leading of the Holy Spirit and learning what it means to be likewise discerning and responsive, we instead often want to duplicate these stories. We read Paul's instructions to the churches under his apostolic and pastoral direction and forget that the epistles were written in a context much different from our own. And as we displace the letters from the narrative that birthed them, we get lost to our own narratives and context and how God is working with us today in the same ways. Much in the same way that we try to duplicate the techniques of "successful" churches we see around us, we likewise seek to mimic the drama of the New Testament church. Unfortunately we often end up looking more like bad actors who cannot remember their lines.

Countless times I have heard leaders or congregants (or disillusioned ex-churchgoers) say, "If only we could once again be an Acts 2 church," or, "We need to be a New Testament church," or, "God wants churches to be Acts 2 communities." But if such declarations truly mirror God's intent for the church over time, God did a lousy job making it happen. As far as I can tell, the Acts 2 church lasted only about two or three chapters, and from there forward, we observe barely contained chaos as churches faithfully seek to keep pace with the life exploding under and around them.

Did God, in fact, do a lousy job, or are our expectations misplaced? You want a New Testament church? Try the letters written to the church at Corinth. There is a New Testament church. They are a mess. In fact, these messed-up New Testament communities that Paul and Peter and many others are fighting for and with (and sometimes against) look a lot like my church and probably yours as well. Often we are inhibited from dealing with the messy challenges and opportunities that are right in front of us in our churches—the raw materials of incarnation—because of our ideals, because of what we wish would be there versus what is there. Dietrich Bonhoeffer warns us of the danger of idealism in *Life Together*.

> Innumerable times a whole Christian community has broken down because it had sprung from a wish dream. The serious Christian, set down for the first time in Christian community, is likely to bring with him a very definite idea of what Christian life together should be and to try to realize it. But God's grace speedily shatters such dreams. . . . God will not permit us to live even for a brief period in a dream world. Only that fellowship which faces such disillusionment comes to an individual and to a community the better for both. . . . He who loves his dream of community more than the Christian community itself becomes a destroyer of the latter, even though his personal intentions may be ever so honest and earnest and sacrificial.[5]

In the New Testament I believe most of what we see is narrative describing the impact of the incarnation, death, and resurrection of Jesus Christ and how this story created local first-century communities called churches. As this story continued to unfold, these new churches were pulled out of their comfort zones and into the world around them in a radically engaged way. This kind of creative and redemptive engagement and struggle with what the Spirit was doing in and around them meant that their theology was likewise struggling to catch up.

Unfortunately, rather than living deeply within scriptural stories in a way that shapes our imagination, we use them in a way that kills it. We reduce these stories to prescriptions for how churches in all times ought to respond regardless of context. In my experience, leading in this manner does not take hard work and dependence on the Holy Spirit. Systems of control and structures of belief that do not reflect the witness of engagement and incarnation found in the Scriptures rarely do.

Quite a bit of the Scriptures is prescriptive—don't get me wrong. However, even the most conservative Bible interpreters recognize the necessity of placing such admonitions in context, that is, within a story.

There is a world out there that God loves and in which God is active. This world awaits engagement with the Spirit of Jesus Christ active and living in local communities demonstrating and proclaiming the emerging realities witnessed to by the incarnation, life, teachings, suffering, death, resurrection, and ascension of Jesus Christ. Again, Hauerwas and Willimon:

> The theology of translation assumes that there is some kernel of *real* Christianity, some abstract essence that can be preserved even while changing some of the old Near Eastern labels. Yet such a view distorts the nature of Christianity. In Jesus we meet not a presentation of basic ideas about God, world, and humanity, but an invitation to join up, to become part of the movement, a people. By the very act of our modern theological attempts at translation, we have unconsciously distorted the gospel and

transformed it into something it never claimed to be—ideas abstracted from Jesus, rather than *Jesus with his people*.[6]

N. T. Wright describes the story of God in time happening over five acts: creation, fall, Israel, Jesus, and the church. Each of these movements marks a part of the story that demonstrates God's faithful engagement in creation and redemption. In order to bring to fulfillment the creation project God initiates and ultimately fulfills in Christ, Jesus constitutes around himself a new people. The church is the human society that bears the image of Christ and participates alongside God in the redemption of all things. While each of the previous acts in this arc come to an end somewhere in our distant past, we still live in the age of the church. It is our vocation to continue what we see happening in the pages of the New Testament—the whole Bible actually—not exactly in the same way as those who have come before, but postured in similar ways in the power and under the inspiration of the same Spirit. To do so requires us to live deeply in the story of God, not in the collected facts about God.

In the book *Colossians Remixed*, authors Brian Walsh and Sylvia Keesmaat describe this story as an unfinished drama. They add a sixth act to Wright's five: the consummation of all things in God.

> We are now living in Act V and are on the stage as actors in this divine love story that seeks to restore the covenantal bond between the Creator and his beloved creation. Our task is to keep the drama alive and move it toward Act VI, recognizing that in this final Act God becomes the central actor again and finishes the play. But how do we move the drama forward? We turn to the Author and ask for more script. And the Author says, "Sorry, but that's all that's written—*you* have to finish Act V. But I have given you a very good Director who will comfort you and lead you." So here we are with an unfinished script, at least some indication of the final Act and a promise that we

have the Holy Spirit as our Director and we have to improvise. If we are to faithfully live out the biblical drama, then we will need to develop the imaginative skills necessary to improvise on this cosmic stage of creational redemption. Indeed it would be the height of infidelity and interpretive cowardice to simply repeat verbatim, over and over again, the earlier passages of the play.[7]

In the incarnation of Jesus Christ and in the witness of the imperfect and improvisational early church found in the pages of Scripture, we see a picture of what it looks like for a community of people constituted in his name to faithfully engage their environment for the sake of the gospel. When we begin to live out this fifth act of the story of what God has been doing, we will discover a robust theology that will allow us to faithfully engage in his name.

Language beyond Control

Just as it is difficult for us to come to grips with a theological framework for the church based in the incarnation, a transcendent understanding of God may be even more difficult. The Enlightenment project enlisted human powers of observation through sensory input, in tandem with reason, to know reality *as it is*. We see something, and as we try to strip away that which is conditional and subjective, we believe we arrive at what is ultimate and absolute.

Within such a paradigm, we look to our Scriptures and theology to deliver what may be known objectively and then held with certainty—particularly about God. Many systematized theologies approach the Bible from this perspective. The Bible becomes a natural resource to be strip-mined for precious and pure ores of theological truth. While we may enjoy possessing and looking at such shiny nuggets of theological wealth, when we go back to the Bible we discover that we have devastated the original resource, which once possessed a natural, magnificent, and even terrifying beauty.

Even as we admire these precious nuggets of "truth" (and perhaps our own reflections in their polished surfaces), we are nagged by the sneaking suspicion that we discarded other material, apparently less precious, in order to get to this "good stuff." Or perhaps these other kinds of resources, more alien and mysterious, embedded in the earth of the Scriptures were not accessible through the same methods of theological excavation. When our only tool is a jackhammer, we can discover only big, universal truths. Anything more nuanced, refined, or alien is beyond the blunt limitations of systemization and certitude.

I experienced this nagging sense throughout my seminary education and in the early years of my pastoral ministry. As I sought to engage the Scriptures with and before my community week in and week out, I struggled to live and lead in the world that described God and faith through these lenses. So much seemed to be left out in this approach: whole sections of Scriptures, emotions, a lot of my life and experience of reality. This was a prohibitively small world. Now it might be that the system of theology I was expected to affirm was internally consistent and sensible, and it might also be that the Bible employed in such a manner "worked" on some level, but I had to marginalize way too many things to make that system work.

I have written of this early struggle in an article for *Leadership Journal* called "Naked in the Pulpit."

At seminary, I learned about exegesis, and right after exegesis class, I went to homiletics class. For an entire semester, I was completely immersed in the biblical texts. One professor told our class that we should spend about 20 hours a week in preparation for any sermon. . . . Coming out of seminary, my head was full of information and I couldn't wait to dump it on people. Life and relationship with God became primarily about information transfer. I believed that if I were doing what I was supposed to be doing as a preacher, by the end of a sermon my listeners would know what I knew.[8]

Seeking to preach and lead in this way, I discovered that I was able to preach only certain kinds of things in very specific kinds of ways. But this posture and approach increasingly produced less and less life in me. And while people in the church were generous with me as I struggled within this discipline, my sense was that my sermons engaged their minds only, in very narrow ways.

That nagging sense launched me on a journey of seeking God beyond the categories and methods I had inherited and in which I had been trained. Several places along the journey were significant to my growth and discovery of what had formerly been hidden. The most significant, early on, was a trip I took to India, where I had to preach fourteen times in eleven days. Facing such a rigorous schedule, I knew I wasn't going to be able to prepare in the ways I normally did. Perhaps not surprisingly, I was angry. But in my anger, I sensed God inviting me to trust, to live in faith, and to believe that what was necessary for the context I was in would be provided by the Holy Spirit. I grudgingly acceded and dove in. It wasn't easy, and when I was done I was truly exhausted, but in the midst of that experience I had never felt more alive, nor had I ever sensed being used by God more profoundly.

Rather than trusting in my ability to mine the Scriptures in a quiet study for the right things to say about God, I looked into the eyes and lives of the people I was with—widows, students, children, the truly poor—and begged God for his words to fill my mouth. Maybe even more importantly, I looked deeply within myself and found God's Spirit staring back at me, awaiting my surrender that I might be empowered in his service.

It was a transforming experience. As I flew home, I was horrified and thrilled to sense the Spirit prompting me to continue to work out this way of listening, leading, and preaching in my home context. I could not argue. Going through the motions was no longer an option. But this was not going to come easily. I had to discover new ways of understanding what I was doing, and what faithfulness was in such a new way of engaging God, myself, the Scriptures, and the community and ministry entrusted to me.

As it unfolded, more than my preaching was transformed. I began to renegotiate all of the ways I sought to lead. I transitioned out of a mere dependence on the tools and frameworks of a theological education shaped in the mindset of the Enlightenment and into a more intuitive, creative, and mysterious engagement from a holistic place of total surrender.

In the *Leadership Journal* article I describe this transition as four movements that I underwent: the movement from *preparation to meditation*, from *composition to chaos*, from *answers to questions*, and finally from *comprehension to apprehension*. This is not the place to unpack what I have said in each of those movements, but I want to call attention to the movement from *comprehension to apprehension* because this categorical expansion began to open up the Scriptures and my lived experience in ways that had not been possible within the previous paradigm, ways that I was desperately hungry for.

Comprehension is understanding; apprehension is beholding. Cognitive people seek comprehension; contemplative people look to apprehend. In our preaching we often seek to understand God, to use language to describe who or what God is. That kind of description can be deceptive. It can be a form of control. Now, we know from the Scriptures that any god we can control is no real god but an idol. Our preaching must reckon with the reality that Yahweh is shrouded, mysterious and often inaccessible. How can we comprehend that though? Apprehension is simply stepping back and marveling at what it is you're beholding, even if you have no idea who it is or what is happening. . . . If the only kind of speech we have available to us is speech that deals with comprehension, then we will only talk about that which we understand. I believe that, as a communicator, I am invited to describe a reality that I am just beginning to get the hint of. That means being willing to not know, to stumble over language so I might tell a story. I'm not so interested in preaching in a way that people have more comprehension; I'm interested in describing things in a way that leaves some room for confusion.[9]

Perhaps you believe confusion is the enemy of the spiritual life, but when I read the Scriptures and submit myself to the accounts of men and women seeking to know and be faithful to Yahweh, I see stories filled with confused people in over their heads—people like myself and most of the members of my church. Confused but, even in confusion, seeking and capable of faithfulness.

The Wholly Other God

God is not contained by our words or by our concepts of him. Even in light of the incarnational revelation of Jesus Christ, Paul states, "For now we see only a reflection as in a mirror; then we see face to face. Now I know in part; then I shall know fully, even as I am fully known" (1 Cor. 13:12). God may know us fully, but we comprehend God only in part. Our Scriptures are filled with stories and statements that declare that God is complete and wholly "Other." Solomon prays at the dedication of the temple and rhetorically asks in recognition of the repre-sentational nature of what is happening, "But will God *really* dwell on earth? The heavens, even the highest heaven, cannot contain you. How much less this temple I have built!" (1 Kings 8:27, emphasis added). Even so, we read that God allowed his Spirit to abide and hover in the Holy of Holies. Why would we suppose that God would be able to dwell in the theologies that have been created by human minds if he wouldn't fully dwell in a sanctuary built by human hands?

In the modern world we don't build physical, architectural temples to host God; we construct elaborate theological systems to describe the God of the cosmos. But he is not contained by our descriptions. Just as God drew near to his people in the temple, I am sure that God draws near in such rational frameworks as well, but that is all—and that includes the framework I am offering. We must be careful to discern whether God's glory has departed from our temples, just as his Spirit departed the temple in Israel. The prophet Isaiah enters the terrifying presence of a holy God, who declares, "My thoughts are not your thoughts, neither are your ways my ways. . . . As the heavens are higher than the earth, so are my ways higher than your ways and my thoughts than your thoughts" (Isa. 55:8–9).

Even though we are told, "In Christ all the fullness of the Deity lives in bodily form" (Col. 2:9), we yet witness times when Jesus demonstrates the transcendent and shrouded nature of the God he incarnates. We discover, in Christ, God present and yet not fully accessible or subject to us, our senses and sensibilities, or our categories of how reality works. Witness the almost delirious response of Peter to the transfiguration of Jesus and his communion with Moses and Elijah on the mountain. Imagine the terror of the disciples out on the sea late at night as they discern a figure coming toward them on the water. What appears to them to be a ghost turns out in fact to be Christ. In a different seafaring episode, Christ is in the boat with them, but asleep, in the midst of terrible storm. When they awake him in fear, he chastises the raging elements and then the disciples as well. Their question, "Who is this that even wind and waves obey him?" alerts us to the fact that even though God approaches us in Christ in ways that are culturally embedded, Christ is not therefore bound or limited by these cultural reference points. He remains an ineffable Presence in their midst and ours.

Even that which is not terrifying but wonderful awakens us to the fact that all is not as we thought it was. After Jesus instructs some fishermen to recast their nets, they haul in such a load of fish that they can barely pull it onboard. Listen to Peter's stunned reaction, which mirrors Isaiah's response to discovering himself in the holy presence of God: "When Simon Peter saw this, he fell at Jesus' knees and said, 'Go away from me, Lord; I am a sinful man!'" (Luke 5:8).

The apostle Paul is no stranger to rational, logical thinking. Nevertheless he finds his senses and his rational mind overwhelmed at least twice in the manifest presence of the risen Christ recorded in the pages of Acts 9. On his way to Damascus, Paul comes into the presence of the resurrected Christ and is overmatched and rendered helpless. Paul has a suprarational experience of God in Christ. Almost sounding Gnostic, in 2 Corinthians Paul indirectly confesses of himself that he knows "a man in Christ who fourteen years ago was caught up to the third heaven. Whether it was in the body or out of the body I do not know—God knows. And I know that this man—whether in the body or apart from the body I do not know, but God knows—was caught up to paradise and heard inexpressible things, things that no one is permitted to tell" (2 Cor. 12:2–4). So even though in Christ we discover the fullness of God dwelling bodily, the Deity is not restrained by the limitations of this body but instead redefines what it means to be human in and through Christ. Different ways of knowing and responding come into play when we discover ourselves in this suprarational and transcendent world created by a holy Presence who refuses to be domesticated by the creatures he loves.

The reality is that while Christ is fully human and knowable as such, his godly nature is likewise uncompromised and subsequently *holy*, that is, Other, and thus accessed and engaged in different ways.

The Idea of the Holy

Just as the Scriptures themselves contain more than the doctrinal raw material for systematic theologies but testify to the mysterious Deity beyond the words themselves, so also are there traditions within Christian theology and practice that witness to knowledge that is more than mere comprehension. Traditional theology usually concerns itself with a certain approach to doctrine that focuses on the rational aspects of God. Alongside such traditional expressions of theology are mystical traditions that seek to apprehend and describe the nonrational, or perhaps suprarational, aspects of God.

In the early part of the twentieth century German theologian Rudolph Otto began to explore this nonrational approach to God and theology. At the start of his theological career in the 1890s, Otto taught systematic theology and gradually made his way up through the German university system. However, beginning in 1910 Otto made a journey that lasted over two years and carried him to North Africa, Egypt, Palestine, India, China, Japan, and finally the United States. As a result of his explorations Otto began to view his Christian tradition through a lens different from that of his own particular context (western European scientific materialism). Subsequently, Otto began to give careful consideration to a neglected aspect of theology of his native paradigm: those aspects of God that cannot be held within the theological frameworks of his scholastic tradition.

In 1917 Otto published *The Idea of the Holy*, which witnessed to the theological journey he had undergone. Massively influential in the West and never out of print since its original publication, this book explores the aspects of theology and faith that transcend or elude comprehension in the categories available through rationality. Otto likewise employs the word *holy* to represent what he seeks to describe but then quickly renegotiates the term. According to Otto, the word *holy* has devolved into a mere ethical category, a word describing a "perfectly moral will." Otto contends that this usage of the term is inaccurate and not original or constitutive "of the whole meaning of the word." Otto instead offers that *holy* suggests an "unnamed Something . . . so that [the reader] may himself *feel it*." He continues: "There is no religion in which it [the Holy or numinous] does not live as the real innermost core, and without it no religion would be worthy of the name. It is preeminently a living force in the Semitic religions, and of these again in none has it such vigour as in that of the Bible. Here, too, it has a name of its own, viz. the Hebrew *qadosh*, to which the Greek *hagios* and the Latin *sanctus*, and, more accurately still, *sacer*, are the corresponding terms."[10]

In calling attention to this reality testified to by several ancient words that convey the idea of holy (*qadosh*, *hagios*, and *sacer*), he posits an "'extra' in the meaning of 'holy' above and beyond the meaning of goodness"[11] and so coins the word *numinous* to describe the Reality beyond rationality. From the Latin *numen*, the numinous hints at that something outside oneself that transcends or eludes comprehension in rational terms but is nevertheless felt as an objective reality. Created beings in this Presence cry out, "Holy, holy, holy," and they are saying much more than, "Perfectly moral, perfectly moral, perfectly moral." This word suggests that which is holy, awesome, and distinctively and fully Other. To further describe this Reality, Otto uses the phrase *mysterium tremendum*.

Describing the category of *tremendum*, Otto identifies the modes by which the numinous is manifested, particularly as it excites a visceral response in the creatures who experience such. The *mysterium* is the Other whose presence induces stupor, a sense of "absolute amazement" and "blank wonder." "The creature, who trembles before it, utterly cowed and cast down, has always at the same time the impulse to turn to it, nay even to make it somehow his own. The 'mystery' is for him not merely something to be wondered at but something that entrances him; and beside that in it which bewilders and confounds, he feels a something that captivates and transports him with a strange ravishment, rising often enough to the pitch of dizzy intoxication."[12] Present throughout Otto's description of the numinous is the twin dynamic of experiencing both fascination and terror.

Otto used such adjectives as *awful, overpowering, majestic,* and *urgent* to describe the *mysterium tremendum*. All of these words function to describe and approximate a Reality beyond our normal ken, and yet such words are ultimately deceiving. For Otto, to submit the numinous to such categories was once again to bring it under the rationalizing tendency so prevalent in his, and our, world. Thus Otto draws our attention, again and again, to language that is metaphorical and symbolic to help us behold something we apprehend but never fully comprehend—or domesticate. These metaphors, symbols, and images seek to push us beyond the limitations of our rational minds and awaken in us affective response—the response of feeling and emotions that arises in recognition of that which exists beyond our rational categories: the Holy.

Hunger for Transcendence

Our culture and many in the church hunger to experience and know transcendence. Based on twenty years in ministry, I would guess that most Christians spend as much or more time watching television and movies as they do reading their Bibles. We expect movies to tell us stories. We expect no such awakening of our imaginations when we approach the Scriptures. Some conservative Christian analysts of popular culture decry movies that deal in the genre of horror, a genre laden with supernatural themes that are often demonic and on the surface appear to be anti-Christian. I believe such expressions of creativity do more than pander to base or macabre desires, however. Beyond the gore inherent to the genre, I believe these movies awaken the soul to realities that exist beyond the hyperrationalistic and material world and testify to the spiritual hunger inherent in people who intuitively sense there is more going on than meets the eye.

I wonder if people's rejection of Christ or the church is less about Christ and more about our precise formulations stripped of any awe-fulness, majesty, or urgency and the communities that are shaped by such hollowed-out (or should I say "hallowed-out") imaginations. Certainly a Celtic spirituality that hosts mystery speaks to this longing, as we have seen. I wonder if at least some part of the attraction of horror is that it acknowledges the hidden realities that exist beyond our neat pictures of life. Social critics witness these cultural dynamics at work and suppose a new dark age. Such unmediated spiritual hunger is understood to be a force that must be domesticated by a return to a right orientation toward doctrine. At its heart such an impulse presumes a lack of reason in the environment, but actually the opposite is true. There has been a surfeit of reason. In fact we are drowning in it.

We hunger for myth, the "true" stories that are not based in facts but nevertheless echo deeply in the eternal spaces of our creatureliness. C. S. Lewis and J. R. R. Tolkien knew this well, and while critics steeped in the sensibilities of modern criticism excoriated both men and their works, they nevertheless wrote in ways that evoked and sated the hunger for that which exists beyond the factual world—not in spite of their faith but because of it. This dynamic is at the heart of their enduring popularity. Their works testify to realities beyond the empirically verifiable that speak deeply to the inner sensibilities of creatures.

In the late 1990s the *X-Files* was a popular television series that followed two special agents, Fox Mulder and Dana Scully, as they sought to track down and investigate reports of paranormal and supernatural events. Mulder is a true believer looking for something miraculous, while his partner, Scully, is a skeptic determined to find a rational explanation behind every strange phenomenon. Chris Carter is the creator of the *X-Files* television series. Writing about the impetus that propelled him to create this show, Carter states, "I call myself a nonreligious person looking for a religious experience."[13] Could our totally rationalistic, domesticated version of Christianity be partly responsible for the fact that a creative person like Carter, unlike his predecessors Tolkien and Lewis, went outside the realm of faith in order to discover transcendence that was once the domain of the church?

Recently there has been a growing interest in kabbalah, that is, Jewish mysticism. This is one more example of the hunger that seeks life and reality beyond rationality. In *The Book of Lights*, Jewish novelist Chaim Potok tells the story of a young rabbinical student named Gershon Loran. Progressing through seminary studying Torah and Talmud, he is drawn into the world of kabbalah. At first he studies it academically. However, as he is drawn into this world he begins to have a growing sense of that which is accessible in only suprarational ways. His professor tells him that kabbalah is

> the heart of Judaism, the soul, the core. Talmud tells us how the Jew acts; Kabbalah tells us how Judaism feels, how it sees the world. We are Western secular beings today, embarrassed by Kabbalah, which is so irrational, illogical. . . . You do not care to know of the rabbis, the great ones who were filled with poetry and contradictions. There is deep, deep within us the irrational as well. It is our motor energy. You think we know the world only on the basis of what we observe or can deduce logically? The irrational completes us.[14]

Does the Christianity of the West have a heart or soul? Thanks to Descartes, we know we have a head. With its emphasis on solitude, contemplation, and prayer, the popular resurgence of and interest in all things monastic could be interpreted as one step toward a heart and soul. Nearly burned out from "doing" church, I stumbled into a Benedictine monastery where I found an oasis that helped me to discover and recover not only aspects of my humanity that had gone AWOL in service to ministry but also a broader Christian tradition and set of practices that helped me to attend to this heart and soul—the "irrational."

This discovery did not negate what I had formerly done. I continued to work, to do, and to engage in many of the same ways. But to that doing, to that arrhythmic pace and unbalanced orientation toward ministry and myself, I added the spiritual practice of pilgrimage—time and space in which to simply *be* and to engage God as being. And as I did this an interesting thing happened, a reversal of sorts: I found that increasingly when I went to the monastery, I was able to get a lot of things done. Conversely, my office became a sort of monastic cell where I could reflect and experience God in joy and peace.

Unfortunately our domesticated brand of Christianity in the West has little within it that speaks to such longings. Our problem has been that if we hear such soul longing at all, we speak to it either by filling it with material pursuits (thus numbing it), saying what we have already said with increased volume, or dismissing it as illegitimate altogether.

Fortunately, these limited responses are not the only ones available to us. In the twentieth century the rapid rise and expansion of charismatic and Pentecostal expressions of faith emphasizing a more *supernaturalized* and experiential expression of Christianity have been one way Christians have engaged the transcendent nature of God and fed both heart and soul in the process. The Orthodox faith that emerges out of the Eastern world is increasingly popular, I believe, for many of the same reasons. It recognizes the limitations of reason and even distrusts it, preferring to acknowledge the reality of mystery rather than seeking to expel it. Daniel B. Clendenin has written a book titled *Eastern Orthodox Christianity: A Western Perspective*. In it he discusses this tension between East and West.

> Following the legacy of the Enlightenment, the West has enthroned reason and logic as the final arbiters of all matters of truth, so much so that it is not uncommon for scholars to speak of the autocracy of reason in Western culture. In the West, all truth claims must pass the test of rational intelligibility that is administered at the bar of reason. . . . In contrast to its enthronement of logic, the rationalistic orientation has a positive distrust of, even a disdain for, concepts like myth and mystery. . . .

Eastern thinkers, by contrast, begin their thinking about God with a very different mind-set. . . . Orthodox theology is at its root apophatic. . . . This negative tradition of unknowing or of learned ignorance begins with the celebration, rather than the rationalistic extermination or explanation, of divine mystery. . . . When we begin to describe God affirmatively (he is omnipotent, loving, just, etc.), we must remember that human language is woefully inadequate to the task and that it always falls short of its object.[15]

In our former way of approaching theology we often see such hunger around us as demonstrations of a world gone apostate—particularly if we assume a cultural location within Christendom. But if we are able to live within a framework that holds in dynamic tension the immanence of God manifested in the incarnation and the church, as well as the transcendence of God that is always wholly Other, terrifying, and fascinating, we will begin to engage the Spirit of God at work in us and around us. Such cultural manifestations of hunger become bridges, not for mere engagement, but for discovery of that which has been previously inaccessible to our imaginations, limited as they have been.

What if we took on a theological posture beyond the one that attempts to tightly gift wrap (bind) God in a (pretty) box of our own conceptual and linguistic making to be gazed upon for our personal satisfaction? What if we engaged in the way that God engages? Such a posture would allow us to be missional in partnership with God. We too often approach theology as a final word about God. I don't believe what we get within such an approach is God, however. Do you? I want, and believe we can have, a robust theology of engagement that allows God's people the opportunity to join God in his life and work in creation, mysterious *and* revealed. In order to do this we will have to begin to do many things differently, including learning to reckon with emotions, feelings, and affective responses rather than treating them as secondary impulses to be sublimated beneath reason. As we do this we will begin to recognize such responses as different kinds of intelligences that, when valued and given voice, allow us to discover and respond to God in ways previously unknown or thought to be unspiritual.

Linguistic Opportunities and Necessities

In order to do this we will have to discover new ways of employing language. In creating and discussing theology we have come to rely on language that is primarily technical and descriptive. We will need to learn what it sounds like to engage theology imaginatively and poetically. We will have to give up the idea that poetic language is somehow less real than technical language. So much of our Scripture is poetic and not technical. We must develop new eyes with which to read and see, new ears with which to hear, and new tongues with which to speak. We will have to allow people with such perspectives a place at the table of our discussions. If such people were seen *at all*, they have likely been marginalized because the ways in which they perceive and approximate reality are not valued. Too much of our rich heritage is forfeited when the language of science becomes *the* language of theology. And too many people who could make critical contributions are left out because they speak in this alternative tongue.

We will also need to develop new forms of language that move us beyond the limitations of words so that we can engage the symbolic and visual world of images. This is what McLuhan describes as the anthropological move from the Western "literary man" to the Eastern, image-based "electronic man." In Colossians Paul writes, "The Son is the *image* of the invisible God" (Col. 1:15, emphasis added). In the original Greek text, the word translated "image" is *eikon*, from which we get the word *icon*. Jesus is the visual representation of the invisible God. Seeking to be known, God makes himself visible by incarnating himself in human flesh, not by sending a precise and technical treatise on the theology of incarnation accessed through words printed on paper.

In the preliterate world, churches made theology accessible and visible through creative expressions such as architecture, stained-glass windows that display the story of God, and in the East icons that become windows through which we peer in order to discern the eternal. For centuries the church was *the* patron of the arts. In commissioning artists to create beautiful and compelling artwork, glory was given to God, the ultimate Creator, and people were able to have a transcendent experience of faith that made visible and tangible that which often seemed inaccessible. In many ways the Reformation changed all this. Clendenin elaborates about this divide, again, between East and West.

> While the East was fixed on aesthetic images, the West had a preference for the written word. While the East wanted to see the Word in images, the West insisted on hearing it in the spoken word. . . . Whereas in the Catholic and Orthodox traditions the priestly functions were primarily sacerdotal in character, in the Reformation and subsequent Protestant tradition the pastor's use of the scholar's robe symbolized an extraordinary and inextricable link between ministry and scholarship. . . . The Reformation witnessed the general denigration of the image and the rise of text-oriented cultus.[16]

We have much to discover and recover. Rather than always approaching knowledge through the lens of correspondence (the referent described by words equals the object that is being referred), we must attend to the symbolic and metaphorical as we approach the Scriptures, as we engage God and develop theologies out of which we might live, and especially as we think and imagine what communities of faith shaped with a more expansive imagination might begin to look like. The Western theological posture I have been describing in this chapter has much to do with the ways churches have become dependent on technique execution rather than thoughtful engagement. We need to rediscover and reimagine ways of being God's people in the world, personally and collectively. This is a theological commitment, not merely a sociological one. And such a need brings us to our third critical engagement.

We have explored what it looks like to engage our context—a "post" world characterized by postmodernity, post-Enlightenment, and post-Christendom. In this chapter I have briefly sought to explore a theological posture that honors the reality of the incarnation while maintaining the Otherness of the God who draws near. With an imagination shaped in such a way, the church begins to have the ability to respond, not only to the environment around it, but also to the very longings present in itself, embedded as it is in its host culture. The final engagement explores the systems and structures that give shape to our theology and context. In what ways do we imagine and organize ourselves? How will we create systems and structures that honor the metaphorical, creative, mysterious, and imaginative realities we have been engaging?

Being Here, There, and Everywhere
waking up to the world of the twenty-first century

What matters is the internal poetry and consistency of the work, but it is also necessary that each work involve an outside reference typical and universal. The adjustment of all the requirements on an unconscious level is what takes time—on an unconscious level necessarily.

Claes Oldenburg

There is always an easy solution to every human problem—neat, plausible and wrong.[1]

 H. L. Mencken, "The Divine Afflatus," *New York Evening Mail*

If we are machines, we can only do as we are bidden to do by the mechanical laws of our mechanical nature. . . . But suppose we don't subscribe to this determinism. Suppose we don't believe that creatures are machines. . . . To confuse or conflate creatures with machines not only makes it impossible to see the differences between them; it also masks the conflict between creatures and machines that under industrialism has resulted so far in an almost continuous sequence of victories of machines over creatures. . . . It is easy for me to imagine that the next great division of the world will be between people who wish to live as creatures and people who wish to live as machines.[2]

Wendell Berry, *Life Is a Miracle*

Translating Theology into Structures

In the last two chapters I have sought to demonstrate how the context of our world, particularly in the West, is undergoing profound transformation. It is a "post" world, and such recognition causes us to reassess where we are and what we believe. While many of us feel the reverberations of such transformation shaking the foundations beneath our feet, we have a difficult time imagining what the implications might be for our churches, our ministries, and ourselves. How do these things affect how we live and respond?

It is not surprising that we have a difficult time taking these broad cultural and theological observations and grounding, or better, incarnating them into our own context. Why? Because we live embedded in structures. Our current structures largely reflect the world from which we are emerging. The story that developed from the landscape of modernity has given a tightly defined theological grid and corresponding systems within churches, denominations, and seminaries. These concrete frameworks reflect and facilitate our conceptual frameworks. Within such systems we have struggled to know how to respond to our emerging context. These structures are often closed, self-propagating, self-serving systems. When we sense disequilibrium between these systems and our larger environment, we have been conditioned to turn to experts *out there* who tell us what is happening and what to do with such observations. But such dependence has not yet given us what we had hoped it might.

Often such systems and structures are mediated through metaphors. And most of our metaphors are ill-prepared to deal with our emerging world and have few points of correspondence with the opportunities and challenges we discern before us. Even more disheartening is the reality that our systems, structures, and metaphors keep us from even *perceiving* these opportunities and challenges, much less responding to them.

The postmodern milieu in which we live is a world that seeks to bring the heart, soul, and body back into contact and balance with a dangerously enlarged and nearly detached head. In this environment a different imagination is emerging. As it does, it is creating a language set all its own: artistic, intuitive, prophetic, and poetic. This language and new kinds of competencies that are beginning to assert themselves in response to this environment are doing so not in terms defined by the categories and structures of the former world but in ways that are new—and in many cases, ancient.

But for us to respond to what is happening around us, we will also need to imagine structures and ways of understanding and organizing ourselves that go beyond these forms of control. This is why I contend, in chapter 4, that when the time comes for God to do something new within a culture that has grown stagnant or unresponsive to his movement, he often moves from the margins of a culture, symbolized in Scriptures by the woman and the child. Because systems and structures rarely like to surrender their power, the woman and the child are often vulnerable and endangered. Nevertheless, new wineskins make space for what is happening, as the old often burst, unable to contain what is fresh and new. Thus, new systems and structures must emerge to release the kind of imagination and creative thinking that I have been describing.

Systems Thinking

Everyone we know can be said to have an *outlook* on life. An outlook is a way of interpreting what is happening in the world around a person. There are myriad variations of outlooks: optimistic, pessimistic, solipsistic, altruistic, and on and on. But what about when a group of people have a shared outlook? When such tacit knowledge is held collectively within a culture, it is called either a *worldview* or a *plausibility structure*. The recognition that we inhabit and live out of such structures is what *systems thinking* addresses.

One of the things that can be frustrating for people who read a book like this one is that it awakens them to feelings or descriptions of life and faith that reach down deeply into their identity. We read or hear about a postmodern, posteverything faith and find our hearts strangely warmed within us. Yet when we return to our version of reality, whatever that may be, the experience is often brutal and immediate as we recognize the inability of our structures to respond to what we have come to know. Often, we feel schizophrenic. The systems and structures we live in inhibit the very life we hunger for and seek to create.

Social and Economic Structures through Time

We live within complex social and economic systems that exert profound influence over how we live and even what we perceive the very nature of life to be. These systems exist on many levels simultaneously and create the plausibility structures that give shape to our lives. No one illustration can be given as an example of such a complex system because their embeddedness and reach is such that we believe our experience of reality is reality *as it is*. Everything in our lives supports these tacit convictions, social agreements, and animating metaphors.

Ours is a capitalistic society that has developed a metaphor for what it means to be human based on production and consumption. Within such a framework people have come to believe that they are first and foremost individuals who consume. Churches have responded by creating structures that accommodate and reinforce such a self-understanding. Employing marketing strategies to increase their bottom line, churches merely adapt the metric system for measuring success that exists in business. Just as businesses use numbers to define success, so do churches.

As metaphors go, the business metaphor has its costs and benefits. All metaphors do. But we run into trouble when we fail to remember that this business orientation is *only* a metaphor and not the thing itself. Too often we come to believe that our experience of reality is not mediated by such metaphors. Church becomes business. We begin to believe such metaphors are the only metaphors available to us. And if it is true for us, it must be true for everyone else as well. Such a view seems hardly worth questioning—that is, until we experience upheaval.

In the United States, the events of the morning of September 11, 2001, were just such an experience of upheaval. All of a sudden the world around us looked quite different than it had two hours previously, as we discovered there were large segments of the world that were hostile to such a materialistic view of what it means to be human. When terrorists attacked the World Trade Center, they attacked the very heart of our capitalistic culture. And President Bush reinforced this view when he announced that despite such an attack "on our way of life," America was still "open for business."

In his book *The Rise of the Creative Class*, author Richard Florida employs systems thinking to analyze our culture. He describes the current social and economic transformation as a creative revolution. Like Daniel Pink's *A Whole New Mind*, Florida's book addresses the different ways people, businesses, and cities are beginning to adapt their systems and structures to identify, release, and maximize human creativity. After the introduction to this basic concept, Florida describes the previous economic and social structures and transitions that humans have animated and gone through since prehistoric times. According to Florida, human civilization has moved through four economic and social iterations and is now coming into a fifth economic age, the age of creativity. The previous four systems of social and economic organization have been the ages of agriculture, trade and specialization, industrial capitalism, and the organization.

It should be noted that these ages are not distinct and neatly grouped but broad and overlapping. In fact, one of the major challenges of globalization is that it shrinks the world so significantly that people and cultures at different stages of social and economic development exist simultaneously alongside each other. With instantaneous communications and ease of travel, there is little to buffer the inevitable confusion and confrontation that happens when people and cultures living in different plausibility structures come into contact with one another. To set the stage for how we can begin to conceive of new systems and structures, I will briefly draw on Florida's descriptions of the previous shifts that have moved civilization through these stages. Florida ties each of these major economic and social shifts to the harnessing of human creativity that explodes previous categories and creates new ones. Let's go back in time to get a better understanding of where we have come from and how our current environment emerges out of these previous contexts.

The Age of Agriculture

Securing a stable food source is a basic human need. We must eat to survive. As ancient human beings began to discover and create ways to do this beyond basic hunting and gathering (inherently unstable and unpredictable), a new social order that was inherently more stable began to be created. This ensuing economic stability (in the form of a consistent and accessible food source) is at the heart of the rise of agriculture and is the first significant shift in human culture. When people start to plant and harvest crops and domesticate animals as a source of food, life begins to operate in more stable and predictable rhythms. As agricultural society spreads, people begin to settle in more densely populated communities and villages that enable more and more people to participate in this agrarian economy.

Out of these growing communities and villages evolve more complex city-states that are urbanized and have administrative centers at their heart. Such administrative centers regulate commerce and the economics of agrarian society. These emerging urban communities, surrounded by farmland, live in sync with nature, and life revolves around the seasons of planting, growing, and harvesting. Much of the Bible can be seen to exist within an agricultural social and economic system. Most of the festivals of the Old Testament, for example, correspond to the agricultural calendar. With this new economic ordering of life, new social systems develop, including class structures, power relations, and occupations. As these new systems and structures emerge, more creativity is released, which enables the next stage of economic and social transition.

The Age of Trade and Specialization

As cultures begin to develop around urban administrative centers in emerging city-states, people begin to have needs for basic goods and services, particularly those people who occupy the wealthy upper and ruling classes. Into such a context skilled craftsmen begin to create specialized goods that merchants then trade. Guilds develop that reflect the diversification of products now available, and people are known by their specialized trade and product that they contribute. Baker, Smith, and Cooper are a few examples of last names that chart the correspondence between who someone is and what they do. The economics of this society follow a very simple formula: producers make specialized products, consumers consume them, and merchants live off the profits made by connecting those who produce with those who consume. Thus skilled craftsmen and merchants concentrate in towns and cities to serve wealthy rulers and subsequently begin to serve each other as well. Real economies begin to emerge in this age. Florida states that in such an environment, "cities became centers of specialization and diverse interaction—hubs of creativity."[3]

The Age of Industrial Capitalism

Perhaps you are able to see thus far how creativity and economic innovation drive cultures to develop and evolve new social structures that give frameworks for these new common expressions of life. Whereas the age of trade and specialization focused on the production of goods at the hands of a skilled class of craftsmen and then distributed them by means of merchants, the emergence of industrial capitalism creates a system that makes mass production and distribution a possibility. This level of production is achieved through the factory system, and later the railroad, among other means of transportation, enables mass distribution.

"The basic idea of the factory," Florida writes, "is to bring large numbers of workers together with all their various tools and materials in one place, with a high degree of division of labor, to produce goods efficiently."[4] In such a factory system, the structures and rhythms of society and life are once again profoundly altered. Large numbers of people work in locations different from where they live, and fewer and fewer people live on farms or in houses that connect to shops where they work.

Through the influence of inventions like the electric light-bulb, the division of the day into highly organized periods of time called "working hours," and the standardization of time in order to coordinate transportation between cities via the railroad, more natural patterns of everyday life are disrupted. The experience of time changes from something that is natural and local to something that is standardized and must not be wasted. People are increasingly separated from land. Mechanistic metaphors begin to dominate vocabulary (for example, food

: . : . : . : . : . : . : . : . ENGAGING CONTEXT is described as "fuel"), and people see themselves in many ways as machines—cogs in the mechanisms of production. As cities expand under such economic development, once again new classes and power structures emerge, and industrialized nations transform not just themselves but also the world. Developed industrial nations increase the distance between themselves and the "developing" world.

The Organizational Age

As we get to the age of the organization, we come into the stage in human history to which many of the people reading this book are native. Florida characterizes the organizational age in the following ways:

> The next great transition (late 1800s and 1900s) marked the rise of the large-scale organization. Its defining element is the shift to a modern, highly organized economy and society whose fundamental features are large-scale institutions, functional specialization and bureaucracy. This transition was premised on two basic principles: the breaking down of tasks into their most elemental components and the transformation of human productive activity into stable and predictable routines. Still more significantly, the organizational model came to prevail in places other than factories and its spread had powerful social effects. The notions of a finely honed division of tasks, of hierarchy and of bureaucratic rules came to define work virtually everywhere. Whether people made things or pushed paper, they filled prescribed slots: "Work, don't think." Even if you had a high-order thinking job, you were paid to think only about certain things in certain ways. The giant office towers with massive administrative, managerial, executive and clerical staffs were the vertical equivalent of the factory. . . . [However] the organizational system, as a means of harnessing human creativity, had proven to be inexorably self-limiting. The dominant form of organization was now the integrated, hierarchical, command-

and-control behemoth—not a good form for eliciting creativity from vast ranks of pigeonholed employees.[5]

So the organizational age is characterized by a highly organized economy and society in which large-scale bureaucratic institutions work to transform human activity into productive and predictable routines of functional specialization. What a stunning statement Florida makes—*that corporate office towers are the vertical equivalents of factories*! I think it is also remarkable to note his assertion that this organizational age model began to prevail in places other than factories (such as churches) and profoundly alter our experience of life. While the economic and social structures of this age change, people still view themselves through largely mechanized metaphors—this time through the ubiquitous corporate uber-machine, the computer.

As we move away from our agricultural, trade/merchant, and industrial past, we come closer to the systems, structures, and metaphors that are shaping our own imagination. Thus we can see this organizational dynamic at play in many places in the church. This reality is at the heart of the struggle I see most church leaders having as they try to respond intuitively and creatively in the midst of their context. The simple reality is that they cannot. They live in and out of structures and systems of control that are shaped with metaphors of the industrial and organizational ages—whether they be in denominations, seminaries, and churches, whether they are of the micro or mega variety. Structures that frame the church within an organizational paradigm often continue to push the metaphor into the business realm. Pastors default and become the functional equivalent of the CEO, elder boards become a board of directors, and congregations become consumers.

It is worth requoting Florida here: "The dominant form of organization was now the integrated, hierarchical, command-and-control behemoth—not a good form for eliciting creativity from vast ranks of pigeonholed employees."[6] These are struc-

ENGAGING CONTEXT

tures of command and control where only a certain kind of thought or product has value. Where can creativity happen in any of these places? I can't help but see a connection between this idea of pigeonholed employees and the contemporary understanding of spiritual gifts in many churches. In such a paradigm, we are "wired" by God with a certain set of gifts designed to help us find our place within a church as it seeks to fulfill its mission. Talk about functional specialization! In the secular version of the age of the organization, creativity arises mostly out of Bohemian enclaves and segregated artistic communities. In the sacred version of the age of the organization, creativity doesn't arise. Period. There are *no* sacred equivalents to "Bohemian enclaves."

Contemporary religious systems and structures are located within metaphors and imaginations shaped within and by the industrial and organizational ages. This reality draws our attention to a dangerous and ironic dynamic that religious organizations face. Organizations, as they mature, often lose sight of the original spirit that animated them. As they do, such organizations become self-propagating closed systems. When this dynamic comes into play, creativity and innovation become a threat as organizations seek to maintain the status quo. The ironic aspect of this situation is that without such an infusion of creativity and innovation, organizations will become irrelevant, serving only aging constituencies interested in preserving something historic rather than engaging the present. As a result many religious institutions and organizations are hemorrhaging their future in the form of creative young men and women who can no longer live within the systems and structures of a world that they themselves have never known or been a part of.

In his book *The Sky Is Falling!?! Leaders Lost in Transition*, Alan Roxburgh calls attention to the fact that most of the systems and structures of our organizations were birthed in a time of great stability. Consider that prior to the transitions described by the prefix *post-*, the world of the West was one that had been living within the multicentury narratives of modernity, the Enlightenment, and Christendom. Further, our economic and social milieu has been stable for at least two centuries. Roxburgh's point is that during times of stability, organizations have the luxury of specialization (pigeonholing). As it relates to religious systems, denominations, seminaries, and churches have become adept at producing one type of leader in a role that is functionally specialized to uphold the status quo: the pastor whose primary role is to teach.

Emerging Organizational Realities of the Fifth Age

Whether or not we are ready, and whether or not we like it, we live in an age of upheaval *and* creative potential, hence the title of Florida's book, *The Rise of the Creative Class*. For churches and other religious structures seeking to engage creatively and faithfully in this context, those that have pastors as the only expression of leadership are going to struggle. Domesticated in the narratives, theologies, and structures of the last two to four centuries, churches, denominations, and seminaries must begin to find how to engage in ways beyond what has come before, and in order to do this they are going to need different kinds of leadership.

Pastors in local churches and administrators and bureaucrats within denominations and seminaries are not going to be able to engage this future on their own within the systems and structures they have inherited. I am not saying there is no need for pastors or administrators any longer. That would be ridiculous. I am a pastor. I know firsthand the value of administrators and the chaos that is created within organizations when they are administrated poorly or not at all. These offices of the church are indispensable. However, we are missing some important offices and roles.

We need more and different kinds of people and roles in the mix. We need prophets, poets, apostles, mystics, artists, liturgists, and who knows what else. More than that, we need to allow the boundaries of our communities to become porous so that all kinds of different people see themselves as players in the life of the gospel beyond the traditional roles of leadership, both inside and outside the walls of our formal structures. But you know what? I am not saying anything new here. This is all in the Bible. For people who seem so terrifically devoted to a text we claim as authoritative, we seem to be missing several key leadership voices and postures toward culture that have been present in the history of Yahweh's people. Does this strike you as odd? One size does not fit all.

Take Ezra for example. Ezra is written during a time when God's people have been in exile in Babylon. Now the time of judgment is over and God's people are about to return to Jerusalem to take up residence again and rebuild their city. As the story unfolds we find an amazing cast of characters charged with the task of this rebuilding. But interestingly, there are more than builders engaged in this work. There is Ezra, the teacher of the Law; Nehemiah, the administrator; Zerubbabel, the builder; and Zechariah, the prophet, to name a few. The book of Ezra lists all the different people who returned to Jerusalem, some by family and others by vocation. Thus we find that for God's people to be reconstituted in the land, they needed priests, musicians, gatekeepers, and temple servants. I think this story provides a helpful paradigm for a church living within a context of upheaval and journey.

Tension, Paradox, and Chaos

The missional context of our culture is one that increasingly demands creativity, both because this is the currency of our culture and because in order to respond to an environment that is new to us, we must be creative. We cannot keep going through the same motions. Of course this does not mean that organization goes out the window. Rather, it requires a different kind of organization that empowers and unleashes creativity. Florida speaks directly to this dynamic when he writes, "Perhaps the biggest issue at stake in this emerging age is the ongoing tension between creativity and organization. The creative process is social, not just individual, and thus forms of organization are necessary. But elements of organization can and frequently do stifle creativity."[7] This is likely not news to you. Most of us inhabit social systems in which all the questions of organization were answered long before we arrived on the scene. This is why many within the emerging church movement have begun communities from scratch. Creative types are often unwilling to navigate labyrinthine administrative structures in order to get permission to do something they could more easily do on their own. It has worked this way throughout church history. In an environment in which most of the questions have been long answered and leadership is largely about execution, the main task of the leader is to give life to the organization. Ezekiel asks the question that exists in many people's minds: Can these dry bones live?

Creative people and communities often want to do more than simply reanimate that which has come before. Often there exists an impulse to create anew. In such a context creatives look for signs of life and then begin to participate in and with it. But most of our institutions go the other way. Rather than discovering life and building organic structures to give shape to this life, we have our structures and go looking for life. This is a Herculean task. Such organizational realities and dynamics expose and confront what we value. Our organizations have tended to value control, stability, and the ability to quickly resolve tension with a solution. However, one of the dominant currencies of creativity is tension—the ability to hold seemingly opposing forces in dynamic relationship without privileging one at the expense of the other or too quickly resolving it. New life is messy and doesn't always fit neatly into preexisting categories.

We can see this dynamic of tension that bears life in many places, including the scriptural narratives. We are told that Jesus comes from the Father full of grace *and* truth. We often know how to be graceful or truthful, but often giving grace can come at the expense of telling the truth, or vice versa. Authentic spirituality and life in God comes by grace through faith (Paul) and yet validates itself by what it does—works (James). In the Scriptures we discover a Deity who is simultaneously immanent (close) and transcendent (distant). We discover the Spirit of God hovering over primordial chaos in the opening chapter of Genesis and from chaos calling forth life. All of these tensions are life-bearing and creative paradoxes that are incarnational mysteries. They must be born out in life.

We are often concerned with orthodoxy (right thinking) or orthopraxy (right doing), but pastor and writer Dwight Friesen has suggested a third category, *orthoparadoxy*, that is, living rightly in the tension and mystery of the mysterious and revealed God of the Scriptures. Doing so requires and invites a radical dependence on the Spirit of God living in and working through his people in creation. Creativity values tension because it creates *possibility*, the chance that something might happen should the environment exist in a way that allows for life to emerge organically from it.

Roxburgh differentiates top-down, command-and-control structures from the kinds of leadership needed in emerging and missional churches. Twenty-first-century missional churches have skill sets that tend to be adaptive. The culture of such communities, formal or informal, tends to be community based within a networked and decentralized vision of a collective identity. In such environments, dialogue is more highly valued than input from experts; input flows from the bottom up rather than just from the top down. Knowledge of what is happening in the immediate context of an organization is critical. Feedback from a variety of sources is sought not for novelty's sake but as an expression of the reality that to apprehend the nature of the environment we are a part of, we must hear from many voices.

As a result, the linear dynamics of an organization oriented around a *plan* are not as important as creating an environment in which values shape a creative identity and expression comes as a result of adaptive engagement within a specific context. In this framework, leaders become, in fact, *environmentalists*, to use a different metaphor than the business one. Such environmentalists help to create and shape cultures of trust that respond and adapt creatively to their location and what God is doing there. But that doesn't mean that all of the organizational needs are lost in favor of a purely organic expression. Leaders who understand themselves as environmentalists must maintain a healthy regard for the operational aspects that give expression to the corporate identity and common expressions of life that flow from this identity.

Swarm Logic

We have seen how it is often our tendency in the midst of confusion to look for answers from the outside by appealing to experts. James Surowiecki deconstructs this practice in his book *The Wisdom of Crowds*. He states, "Most of us . . . believe that wisdom is concentrated in a very few hands (or, rather, in a very few heads). We assume that the key to solving problems or making good decisions is finding that one right person who will have the answer. . . . As sociologists Jack B. Soll and Richard Larrick put it, we feel the need to 'chase the expert.' The argument of *The Wisdom of Crowds* is that chasing the expert is a mistake, and a costly one at that. We should stop hunting and ask the crowd instead. Chances are, it knows."[8] Such a view is part of the new science of *emergence*.

Emergence is a developing branch of science that recognizes that in general the whole is smarter than the sum of the individual parts. Emergence theory says that coherent patterns exist and arise from interactions among simple objects when there is a commingling of bottom-up and top-down processes. In simple terms, this theory states that life emerges in unique ways when an environment is created that allows for bottom-up and top-down interactions; out of these interactions simple order arises without any kind of master plan. These *coherent patterns* are signs of life that can be recognized in a dynamic process that allows for all the players in a system to be engaged in creative processes.

Emergent Village, the organization, is a postmodern network of people, churches, and organizations seeking to respond creatively in an emerging context with little organization or master plan. People have a hard time understanding and believing this because when viewing groups of people who are semi-intentional about something, our collective mind/imagination defaults to structures of the industrial and organizational age that are top-down and aligned around a linear plan. Emergent Village takes its name from this emerging branch of science in recognition of the nature of this dynamic. It is structured accordingly.

In his fascinating book *Emergence*, author Steven Johnson shows how ant colonies, European cities in the twelfth century, and the human brain evolve structures that emerge without any overarching control center, whether it be a leader or a master plan. Johnson describes the dynamic of emergent behavior as it relates to the aforementioned ant colonies.

> While there's no single key to the success of the social insects, the collective intelligence of the colony system certainly plays an essential role. Call it swarm logic: ten thousand ants—each limited to a meager vocabulary of pheromones and minimal cognitive skills—collectively engage in nuanced and improvisational problem-solving. . . . *Local* turns out to be the key term

in understanding the power of swarm logic. We see emergent behavior in systems like ant colonies when the individual agents in the system pay attention to their immediate neighbors rather than wait for orders from above. They think *and* act locally, but their collective action produces global behavior.[9]

Drawing on this science of emergence, Roxburgh applies the dynamics of adaptive emergent structures to religious communities. Rather than operating with a predetermined direction set from the top down, emergent structures develop as the result of collective behaviors and interactions among many diverse players. This kind of adaptive engagement is integral in the discontinuous and unpredictable culture of change we occupy. These interactive and iterative processes can help to cultivate cultures that allow for experimentation and engagement. Leaders who create responsive and adaptive environments can help communities to discover where life is happening in, among, and around them. As they make such discoveries communally, they have the possibility to then adapt and respond creatively to these opportunities in not just their narratives and theologies but also their systems and structures. And such discoveries come as the fruit of the creative work of the whole group, not just a select few.

Practical Creativity

It is too soon to define all the characteristics of the age of creativity that is emerging before us. Florida's book charts this emerging world within the world of business, and in that context he makes some broad observations about the nature of creativity that nevertheless have implications not just for businesses but for religious organizations as well. He says that often creativity is viewed as a mystical enterprise that most people and organizations write off as impractical. However, across multiple disciplines we are seeing that many different kinds of organizations are seeking to learn how to be creative. Florida states that "researchers have observed and analyzed creativity in subjects ranging from eminent scientists and artists to preschoolers and chimpanzees. Occasionally but notably, they have studied its workings across entire human societies. They have pored over biographies, notebooks, and letters of great creators of the past; modeled the creative process by computer; and tried to get computers to *be* creative. From the existing body of literature . . . several main themes . . . surface repeatedly."[10] Florida then considers the following themes, and while not all are immediately applicable, several are nonetheless interesting.

Florida states that creativity is not the same as intelligence but requires an ability to synthesize from diverse and divergent sources of "data, perception, and materials to come up with combinations that are *new and useful.*" Another way of saying this is that while intelligence seeks mastery over a body of knowledge, creativity seeks to recognize patterns arising from the environment. Creativity requires the ability to take risks, and because it is often subversive to "existing patterns of thought and life," self-assurance is also necessary. Even so, creativity is not the province of "a select few geniuses with superhuman talent." There is actually a common pattern to creativity that often emerges out of a four-stage process of "preparation, incubation, illumination, and verification or revision." Creativity is a process that is "multidimensional and experiential." Quoting psychologist Dean Keith Simonton, Florida adds that

"creativity is favored by an intellect that has been enriched with diverse experiences and perspectives." It is "associated with a mind that exhibits a variety of interests and knowledge." Thus, the varied forms of creativity that we typically see as different from one another—technological creativity (or invention), economic creativity (entrepreneurship) and artistic and cultural creativity, among others—are in fact deeply interrelated. Not only do they share a common thought process, they reinforce each other through cross-fertilization and mutual stimulation.[11]

Here one can see another reason why leaders must be environmentalists. Good environmentalists create settings of trust that allow diverse people with varied experiences to come together in order to engage each other in nonterritorial ways that allow a community to apprehend all of the different potentialities that emerge in such an environment of engagement.

Lest we think such creativity emerges whimsically, Florida argues, and my experience bears out, that creativity is hard work: "90 percent perspiration and 10 percent inspiration." Many people (including leaders in the church) characterize artists/creatives as loosey-goosey, hippy-dippy, come-what-may, let's-all-dance-in-flowers silliness. If you have ever spent any time around artists, you know how far from reality such a portrait is. The simple economics of what it takes to make a living from creativity quickly defeats such stereotypes. Creatives are generally very disciplined people who balance a host of competing demands in much the same way small business entrepreneurs wear many different hats as they try to make their dream a reality.

Such commitment to creativity reveals that these processes often take a very long time to bring to fruition and demand complete commitment. In fact, creative work is often all-encompassing. Creatives tend to be driven intrinsically, that is they "are driven primarily by internal motivations." External motivations have very little to add to the force that drives creatives—passion. Even so, creativity is a social process. And this is where the rubber hits the road for our organizations. Florida states, "Creativity flourishes best in a unique kind of social environment: one that is stable enough to allow continuity of effort, yet diverse and broad-minded enough to nourish creativity in all its subversive forms."[12] This kind of creative engagement is more than a technique for growing our churches and organizations. It is embodiment of a theology of church that recognizes the profound value of the entire body of believers and structures common life accordingly. Such an ecclesiology demonstrates the reality that each person is a gift that brings to the whole unique perspectives and contributions that help the church to discern and be faithful to God's work in their midst.

Metaphors for Creativity

Have you noticed that the way we watch movies has changed in the last several years? Often people would rather watch a movie from their home than go out to a theater. Obviously there are several reasons why this might be the case, including better technology available for home viewing. But I think another reason DVDs have become so popular is that when the movie ends, you can go to the menu and choose from any number of different options that allow you to go behind the scenes and watch how the creative process unfolded and developed into what you just watched on the screen.

My favorite is found on the *Lord of the Rings* movie trilogy DVDs. Watching hours of these behind-the-scenes documentaries, it is fascinating to see how director Peter Jackson created such a dynamic and creative community of people with diverse skills, personalities, and motivations while at the same time obviously being in charge. It is clear from watching and listening to these creative people describe their individual parts in the whole process that they were given enormous latitude to imagine and create their piece of the whole. Peter Jackson surrounded himself with an amazing community of people and fostered environments and processes that allowed, even forced, creativity to develop and grow. It goes without saying that he allowed himself to be profoundly influenced by their input. At the same time it is likewise clear that Peter Jackson was listening to something within himself and sought congruency between the external input of this community and the muse that he followed with his head and heart. It is also clear that this creative community was being shaped by a text—in this case, Tolkien's fantasy masterpiece, to which they were seeking to be faithful, though not slavishly so. They were an interpretive community. Watching the process that allowed these movies to be created exposes any myths we have about the impractical nature of creativity. The simple logistics of mounting such an undertaking are staggering, and the fact that these movies were released to both critical acclaim and box office success demonstrates what is possible when a creative community engages in dynamic and integral ways.

The ways in which movies are made offer us a limited metaphor that nevertheless can help us begin to imagine ways that communities around us are responding to the dynamics of creativity and emergent systems described in this chapter. While not all movies are made in the same way Jackson's trilogy of movies was, his example helps us to see some structural possibilities. His movie production company is really a complex economic and social system living in a specific environment in relation to an animating text (a book translated into a screenplay). This system develops creative processes to engage this community in both top-down (studio heads, writers, director, producers) and bottom-up (actors, costume designers, special effects artists, caterers, makeup artists, location scouts) ways in order to release personal and communal imagination. Even so, it is worth noting that this system, creative and emergent as it is, still operates within organized structures with economic realities in play.

The burgeoning science of complexity and emergence cannot offer us new models for how communities ought to be structured in a liminal environment. Rather the ideas represented by the study of emergent systems suggest different postures for us to assume so we can discover the life that is developing organically in and around ourselves and our communities. These humble and open postures challenge the many ways leaders and institutions have conceived of themselves, and yet they provide us the possibility of seeing life emerge in unexpected ways. Leadership in this paradigm is about cultivation. Roxburgh states that within a transitional environment "the role of leaders is to *cultivate environments that release the missional imagination of the people of God*. Leadership as cultivation is about creating environments within which God's people shape their own missional life. This accounting of leadership takes seriously the biblical understanding of the people of God as the place where God's Spirit is most specifically at work. It is in and through God's people that God's future emerges."[13]

How well do our organizations create spaces that allow for diverse people with varied experiences and multiple intelligences to gather in order to discern signs of life intrinsic and extrinsic to our communities? How willing are we to do the hard and long-term work of creativity and contextual engagement? Will we create systems and structures that allow for new imaginations to emerge? Moreover, will we step aside and allow those people who are already engaged in this kind of work an opportunity to lead us and develop new frameworks that help us to identify and release our communities to be responsive to God's creative activity around us? How highly do we value control, and what is the cost we are willing to pay to continue to hold it in our hands alone?

The reality is that creatives walk into our communities, systems, and structures all the time, and when they do, they intuit the environment we have created and know immediately whether there is a space for them. Most often, they discover there is not. If we are going to have systems and structures that allow our communities to respond to the context of our world and what God is doing in such contexts, we must be allowed to create systems and structures that are organic to this emerging world. In order to do this we must be creative! We must allow our imaginations to be funded in new ways from new sources across multiple disciplines, ideas, and metaphors. We must allow emergence to happen in our midst by fostering the environments that will allow us to hear God through engaging each other.

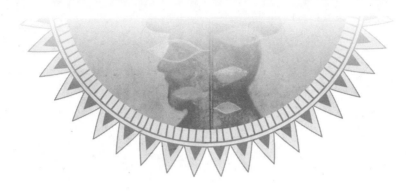

section 3

embracing
POSSIBILITY

A Modest Proposal

what we need is sometimes not what we want

At the heart of every good theology lies not simply a plausible intellectual vision but more importantly a compelling account of a way of life, and that theology is therefore best done from within the pursuit of this way of life.[1]

Miroslav Volf, *Practicing Theology*

Practicing a discipline is different from emulating a "model." All too often, new management innovations are described in terms of "best practices" of so-called leading firms. While interesting, I believe that such descriptions can often do more harm than good, leading to piecemeal copying and playing catch-up. I do not believe great organizations have ever been built by trying to emulate another, any more than individual greatness is achieved by trying to copy another "great person."[2]

Peter Senge, *The Fifth Discipline*

Moving Beyond Caricatures

Many people have been critical of the emerging church for bitterness, anger, arrogance, and its reactionary postures. While these charges are often aimed at proverbial straw men (and women), many of these accusations have some merit. I know this because I have been all of these things at one time or another myself. It is not something I am proud of. It has been part of my maturation process—my sanctification, if you will. I confess it. But there is something else going on beneath these visceral expressions.

In the last fifteen years I have heard a lot of stories about people's struggles to express their faith in ways that don't marginalize the truth of who they are as human beings made in the image of God. I have heard stories about people's struggles to find God in their church and the responses that label them as selfish for that hunger. I have heard of people exploring theological issues, inspired by their love of God, and being labeled dangerous. I have also met creative people who are tired of being excluded or, if not excluded, viewed and used only as a resource to be leveraged in pursuit of a leader's or church's vision. And I have heard stories about people's willingness to take great risks to find and embody something different in order that they might be part of the solution and not simply one more finger pointing at the problem. When they are subsequently labeled as "divisive" for going beyond traditional organizations and structures, most of these people are past the point of caring. In such stories I have heard a lot of pain. I have heard a lot of shame. I have also heard faith, hope, and love. Moreover, I have seen extraordinary perseverance.

Why do I say all that? Because when people characterize the phenomenon of the emerging church as bitter, angry, arrogant, or reactionary, I know what is underneath all of those things. I know that when people get just a taste of life, it is intoxicating. Intoxicated people do foolish things. But even that characterization misrepresents more than it illuminates because for every bitter, angry, arrogant, and reactionary emerging person or community out there, I know ten hopeful, passionate, humble, and creative counterparts that are actively engaging God, themselves, their communities, and the larger context of the world in which they live. I also know that they are bearing fruit in these contexts. And that too draws attention.

It is also worth observing that many of the people who initially get excited about the conversation that is taking place around postmodernity do so because they perceive postmoderns as their next target to be *reached*. But for most of us in the conversation, that is not the goal. We aren't trying to reach anyone, at least not in the way that phrase and the energy behind it has been understood. Yet people are being reached. It is happening accidentally or, better, as a by-product of something else. My experience tells me that when you try to *reach* someone or some group or some thing, you end up chasing not just a nonexistent caricature but the wrong thing altogether.

Exegeting the Experiences of Observers

Because we have a Sunday night worship gathering, we experience a steady flow of leaders and groups who come to observe what is happening in our church. When I see such people and groups arrive at our church, I always have mixed feelings. I hope these people arrive motivated by a hunger to meet God and participate in our life; more often they show up impressed by an outward manifestation of that life, whether it be the size, the number of young people, the worship liturgy, or the creativity. They then seek to discover what is unique in our environment that they can then export to their churches in order to *reproduce* whatever particular manifestation of life they see in our community and long for in theirs. Such efforts are doomed to failure.

But when people *do* come and worship with us, whatever their motivation, often something significant happens that most people aren't expecting. They have an encounter with God *among* us. That is not to say that every person who comes into our space and community has some kind of transcendent encounter and experiences something significant. Often people come and very quickly discover that there is nothing attractive to them about our church. But sometimes in the course of our time together some people there to *observe* stop watching as experts or leaders or spies or outsiders or tourists and actually begin participating as humans beings made to know God and people made in his image in the context of our community. When they snap out of it, they are usually confused. That is when I begin to hear stories. I have sat at countless meetings with people in Kansas City and all over the country and world and listened to people ask about or discuss their experience among us. As they do we begin to deconstruct their expectations and what they were coming for and then ultimately what happened and what the significance of that was—and what it means for them *in their context*.

People come to us and see the fruit, and they want to know *how*. I have spent a lot of this book describing the ways leaders have been trained to go questing for a silver bullet—a magical model or technique that, when placed in the barrel of their ministry gun and fired, will allow them to hit their target (some group of people their community is short on that they want to *reach*). In this scenario, emerging churches are the next stop on the "cutting-edge ministry tour" that began in the 1980s with the contemporary worship movement, went on to the small group movement, continued into the 1990s with the seeker-targeted church movement, and later evolved into packaged ministry expressions such as the Alpha evangelism ministry and Purpose-Driven Life curriculums like *40 Days of Purpose*. Let me give you an explicit example of this.

In the fall of 2006 our community was profiled in a large Christian magazine, *The Christian Century*, as an example of an emergent church. In the issue that preceded the one that carried the Jacob's Well story, the last page of the magazine told readers that an upcoming issue would profile an emerging church. This teaser prompted one reader to email Jason Byassee, the editor responsible for the article. He writes:

> I was just reading the latest edition of *The Christian Century* and noticed at the bottom that you have an article on the "emergent church" coming soon. I really look forward to that. Last week I attended a conference on worship our denomination put on. We heard the word "emergent" countless times, but after several hours of workshops and plenary discussions a classmate leaned over to me and said, "I still don't know what emergent worship is, but now I am convinced that neither do these presenters." It's true. I have heard these supposed experts and still have the looming question, "What in God's name is emerging worship?" My hunch is that it's not in God's name so much as it is in the name of meeting people's perceived needs, fueling our addiction to visual technologies and our ADHD culture, and mixing in a few ancient practices (a little incense burning here, a little chanting there) to make it seem edgy and new because the old edgy and new has ceased to be edgy and new these days. It was a total waste. Part of me wants to be wrong about emergent worship. Here's hoping that you can convince me I am wrong.[3]

Do you hear what is going on here? I edited out the silly experiential exercise that was given as an example of interactive preaching from the email because it was one more example of what is going on in the name of being relevant but in reality is too goofy and painful for me even to type. Emergent/emerging worship is being branded as the next new cutting-edge thing. Someone somewhere has extracted some principle of worship from some place and turned it into a technique that is being packaged now as "emergent." And here's the thing: it doesn't surprise me. It saddens me, mostly because I know the impetus and heart behind such attempts. I know the frustration and desperation many pastors feel leading their churches. Leaders want to connect and be relevant and make an impact. I get that. But when it is pursued in this way, it just ends up being plain silly, and worse, ineffective and misrepresentative.

I believe the main reason we are so desperate and thus vulnerable to such silliness or other more serious expressions like candles and incense is because we are ultimately chasing the wrong thing. We try to *reach*. We try to *do* ministry. We seek to *make* something happen. We want to be *relevant*. This is no new temptation. I think people of faith have struggled with this challenging dynamic for a long time. Chapter 4 gave an example from the Old Testament of Israel turning God's activity in the past into a totem for the present. Such totems don't have to come out of the past alone. They can also emerge from contemporary ministries down the street that we look to instead of God himself.

Learning from the Cistercians

Thomas Merton, a Trappist monk from the monastery at Gethsemani in Kentucky, calls attention to this dynamic in his day. To read Thomas Merton is to observe a man with a sharp and hungry mind searching everywhere for God. I love reading his journals because they allow me a window into this amazing man's life. Observe the following passage from his journal, *The Sign of Jonas*, as an example of what I am seeking to describe. In this entry he discusses architecture and how monastic communities can produce beautiful buildings. Even though he is writing about architecture, the underlying message is appropriate for our discussion. And as you read this, keep in mind the email to *The Christian Century* above. Merton writes,

> The perfection of the twelfth-century Cistercian architecture is not to be explained by saying that the Cistercians were looking for a new technique. I am not sure that they were looking for a new technique at all. They built good churches because they

were looking for God. And they were looking for God in a way that was pure and integral enough to make everything they did and everything they touched give glory to God.

We cannot reproduce what they did because we approach the problem in a way that makes it impossible for us to find a solution. We ask ourselves a question that they never considered. How shall we build a beautiful monastery according to the style of some past age and according to the rules of a dead tradition? Thus we make the problem not only infinitely complicated but we make it, in fact, unsolvable. Because a dead style is a dead style. And the reason why it is dead is that the motives that once gave it life have ceased to exist. They have given place to a situation that demands another style. If we were intent upon loving God rather than upon getting a Gothic church out of a small budget we would soon put up something that would give glory to God and would be very simple and would also be in the tradition of our fathers.[4]

Merton is talking about a community of monks in the twelfth century who were seeking God. And from this primary pursuit they produced, as a by-product of their holy longing, an architectural style that was beautiful and had integrity because it developed organically from their context. As a result the architecture was still speaking to people eight centuries later when Merton was writing. Against this backdrop, Merton laments the fact that in his day architecture is not allowed to develop in the same way it did in the Cistercian context. His peers, rather than seeking God, sought instead to *reproduce* a style, something mimicking the *rules* that arose from a different community's life. But reproduction is not possible because "a dead style is a dead style," as the context that birthed it is no longer available.

Ministry as Idolatry

I believe the most acceptable and common form of idolatry in churches today is *ministry*. I believe many leaders and many churches worship ministry—that is, what we are trying to *do* for God. Unlike the twelfth-century Cistercians, we often do not pursue God but instead pursue the fruitfulness that we are told accompanies God's presence in a person or community's life. Let me rephrase that statement: we rarely pursue God directly but instead pursue external expressions called "ministry" as a sign of God. But when we make ministry our pursuit, we make it impossible to realize the very thing we seek. Ministry is always the by-product of something else. What? The pursuit of God.

Jesus says as much in John 15:4–5: "Remain in me, as I also remain in you. No branch can bear fruit by itself; it must remain in the vine. Neither can you bear fruit unless you remain in me. I am the vine; you are the branches. If you remain in me and I in you, you will bear much fruit; apart from me you can do nothing." Do we take this seriously? I think rather than figuring out what it looks like for our communities to learn what it means to abide in Christ, we spend most of our energy looking for signs of life, manifestations of another community's lifestyle of abiding in Jesus. It reminds me of the old Alcoholics Anonymous adage: "You know why the grass is always greener on the other side of the fence? Because that guy stays home and works on his yard!" The healthy yard gets and stays that way because the person tending the lawn is not running around looking at everyone else's grass. According to Jesus, fruitfulness comes when the vine is intimately connected to the branch. Fruit is the natural outgrowth of a healthy tree. Trees don't try to produce fruit. They don't seize up and grunt real hard in an attempt to squeeze something out. Nor do they pick up fruit from other trees and tape it to their branches. Trees that are healthy simply produce fruit. They don't try to make it happen, and they can't stop it when it does. Fruit comes when everything else in the environment functions as it should.

In the same way I believe ministry, including the ability to *reach* people, is a natural by-product and sign of a healthy church ecosystem functioning as it should. You might have heard the word *organic* used often in the context of emerging churches. It means that we allow life to grow naturally out of the environment in which it exists. Unfortunately, many of us do not operate with this perspective. Rather than listening to God and discerning God's presence among us, rather than listening to our people and discerning God's provision through our people, we look beyond our communities and try to make something happen based on what has worked for other people. Tragically our people, whom we know and who support us as leaders, are often taken for granted as we go questing in an attempt to reach some unnamed, unknown person who will validate our relevance. But a converse leadership situation is often at work as well. Often leaders come into communities wanting to shepherd and disciple a group of people who would rather run programs and attract people. Such pastors are often chewed up and spit out for not producing the external signs of life our broader culture tends to value, particularly when shaped through metaphors of the organizational age.

My Expert Answer: "I Don't Know"

When I was speaking on this topic at an event for evangelical denominational leaders, one pastor raised his hand to ask me a question. He said he was a pastor of a seventy-five-year-old church in the Pacific Northwest. As he introduced himself and described his community's context, I knew what his question was going to be before he asked it. He listened to me describe the context of a "post" world, the necessity of engaging incarnationally in contexts of specificity, and how we work within systems and structures that either inhibit or empower such engagements. He wanted to know how what I was saying applied to him in his context, an aging denominational church, as compared to Jacob's Well, a first-generation, independent Christian community. It is a great question, and it is one I hear all the time.

The first answer I always give is simple: I don't know how to answer that question, at least not in the way it is often asked. The expectation is often that I can reduce these complex realities down to simple, acontextual answers that will apply in another pastor's context the way it has in my own. But I cannot deliver a step-by-step implementation manual because a manual assumes the transferability of a model. I have been trying to deconstruct this approach throughout the entire book. If I had a model, then it would be a model that is radically localized—in fact, so localized that the only way to come up with an implementation manual would be to write one for each community and to write it after the fact and with an open ending that allows for the possibility of additional chapters. Thus my answer, if it is to have any integrity with the rest of what I have written so far, must be, "I don't know."

The second part of my answer is not any idea or application but the community itself. *This* community, Jacob's Well, is how we have responded to the "post" world. And this book is in many ways my attempt to articulate and describe the context and the community that has developed over the last several years in this place as *our* faithful attempt to answer the question, "How are we to be the people of God here and now?"

We must seek to get away from looking for others to tell us what everything means and what the implications are. Instead we must learn what it means to engage. We must begin to intuit what is going on and learn to respond in ways that have integrity to who we are, where we are, and who we have been.

Is that all? Am I saying that you are on your own, and good luck?

No. There are ways I believe we should respond. But they will be challenging to us because we have been so masterfully discipled in technique reproduction. For most of us, the ways I believe we will need to respond will be counterintuitive. Nevertheless, I believe there are ways the evangelical pastor in Oregon can take what I have said here and go engage in his own context—but not because he has a new set of answers. He will be able to engage because he has a new set of postures that open him and his community up for new possibilities. I believe that in our world how we posture ourselves and our churches is a critical issue. I believe we have been postured in a way that has kept us from being able to be responsive: to God, ourselves, each other, the Scriptures, and our neighborhoods. The last thing we need is answers, because when we have answers, we assume the posture of an expert, and experts are a big part of the problem. We need to discover some basic postures of engagement that allow us to see and respond to the possibilities that are available because of God's activity out in front of us.

In closing, let me make a modest proposal:

> God is alive and at work in you, your community, and your context. Our world is filled with possibility because of who God is and what he is doing in creation. God longs for our participation with him, and at the same time God is on the move. Jesus said, "Follow me" and he meant it. He is going somewhere, and if we are to keep pace, we must follow. That means we must move. I can't give you any answers. All I can do is propose some postures—ways of positioning ourselves that allow us a greater chance of catching God at work among us.

It is to these postures that we now turn. As we do so, let us hope that, as the Cistercians did, we too can look for God in a way that is "pure and integral enough to make everything we do and everything we touch give glory to God."[5]

9

Opening Up and Leaning Forward
postures of engagement and possibility

The [prophetic] narrative creates the sense of new realities that can be trusted and relied upon just when the old realities had left us hopeless. . . . It is the [prophetic] task . . . to bring to expression the new realities against the more visible ones of the old order. Energizing is closely linked to hope. We are energized not by that which we already possess but by that which is promised and about to be given.[1]

Walter Brueggemann, *Prophetic Imagination*

The Language of Postures

When we use the word *posture* it often refers to the way a person physically holds himself or herself. But *posture* has another meaning. It refers to a person's bearing or attitude. People can be said to have a defensive posture, and such a claim means more than that they have positioned themselves to repel an attack, though that might be the case. It means they carry themselves in a way that interprets the world around them as hostile. As a result, such a posture toward life bleeds out into everything they do. They might be suspicious, passive/aggressive. They might misinterpret simple gestures as hostile, and thus they are easily offended or wounded.

We all have ways that we posture ourselves in life based on how we interpret our environment. It doesn't end with people. Institutions and organizations likewise adopt postures toward the environment around them based on what they have experienced in the past and now believe in and about the present. And these postures we assume are not supplementary to something else. They are a way through which we engage the world—both what we perceive as well as what the world perceives of us. They impact our lives, personally and corporately, in profound ways. These postures reveal something of who we are at the core of our identities and influence what we communicate, verbally and nonverbally, and conversely what we are able to hear.

We don't regularly inspect our own postures. We don't know what it is like for others to be in relationship with us. The closest we get to seeing ourselves and developing better self-understanding often comes from a haphazard or accidental interaction. Maybe someone makes an offhand comment or observation about us that gives us a clue about how our basic postures affect others around us. We are surprised to learn that the way we see ourselves and the way we are experienced by others are not the same thing.

Our postures reveal what we believe about God, the Bible, the world, and ourselves—things we are not usually very willing to engage about. It feels too vulnerable and important. Our posture hardens and we become stiff. Thus, there is often a disconnect between what we say with our words and what our postures reveal. We may say that God loves people, but do our postures demonstrate this in tangible ways? Many people around us sniff out inconsistency between what we claim with our words on one hand and what our postures reveal on the other. As we look around and notice that our postures have indeed had an impact, we discover that it has been one that we may have scarcely known or been able to recognize. In fact, many of us in leadership are just starting to recognize that we cannot continue to go on postured in the same way we have been.

While it may seem to many that embracing change is dangerous, it is no less so to stay where we are. Inaction makes us just as vulnerable as moving into unchartered territory. To continue in the same posture(s) and expect a different outcome calls to mind Albert Einstein's famous definition: "Insanity: doing the same thing over and over again and expecting different results."

In order to do the kind of creative engagement I have been talking about, we must explore new postures beyond those born of a previous age. Perhaps my approach in this chapter of trying to identify and suggest *postures* that allow us to engage in new ways versus our earlier posture of seeking out "answers from experts" that we then apply is an example of a different way of posturing ourselves. We have posture problems. Or a better way of saying it is that if we can faithfully reposture ourselves in keeping with God's life in and around us, the resulting opportunities may surprise us.

But this is no implementation manual, as I have said. Rather it is an invitation to cultivate new ways of being. It is an invitation to start or continue on a process of transition, to cultivate the imagination and allow a common life to flow from it in new and particular ways. As you read through these brief offerings, try not to think *application* but rather *implication*. As you read, ask how you can listen so closely to the voices of your story and your community that you are compelled by these voices and stories to particular, and even peculiar, postures and actions in your context.

I am going to suggest a series of nine postures that I hope will help you to engage God and your community creatively. You will see that many of these postures overlap and inform one another. In that sense they are less nine distinct postures than they are one posture that manifests and expresses itself fluidly in different ways. In order to help you engage these ideas more substantively, in some of the descriptions I will give a few examples of ways these postures are incarnated in the Jacob's Well community. In each proposed posture I suggest some questions for you to consider as you think about the implications for leadership and your community. As you prepare to read on, consider your posture. Is it one of openness and receptivity? Or is it one of defense and critique? Your posture will affect what you discover in the following pages, but more importantly, in yourself.

A Posture of Learning: From Answers to Questions

Leaders trade in answers. At least that is the common perception. Thus, the person in the community who is best able to answer questions is, by default, the leader. Pastors go away to seminaries and receive training in order to supply certain kinds of knowledge to a community. There are many good and important things that we come to know in this way. But when this is the dominant way a leader learns, he or she assumes the mantle of expert. That mantle places distance between a leader and his or her community.

I wanted to be that person. It feels good to have everyone look at you expectantly. But I am not so sure I want to be that person anymore. It's not that I have grown past the satisfaction of having my ego massaged. Nor am I in danger of being in short supply of answers. I am a recovering pontificator and can still distribute answers with the best of them. It's just that I am no longer sure that an answer is always what is called for. To be sure, sometimes it is. But if you look at Jesus and the way he engaged those around him, he often (if not nearly always) responded to a question with a question, not an answer. It seems he wanted to expose something more important than what the question itself presented—perhaps something more important hidden *behind* or *beneath* the question.

There is also the dynamic that if you accept the question on the terms it is asked, then only certain kinds of answers are available. But what if you don't agree with the premise of the question? I spend a lot of time renegotiating questions. Why? You can often learn more from a well-formed question than from a glibly offered answer. I am also finding that when people, myself included, ask a question, they are often asking more than the question reveals at face value. You have to excavate to get at what is really going on. As a result, I am coming to believe that questions require more work, more attentiveness to what is happening in the environment. It takes a lot more *depth*, *presence*, and *creativity* on the part of the leader to ask a well-informed, sensitive, and sincere question that engages the person on the other end of the relationship.

We have to ask in order to learn. I also think we have to ask in order to engage. If leaders are always in the position of answering questions, how can they ever learn anything in the environment where they are called to serve? If the only place a leader can learn is by reading alone in a study, then we become disconnected in a way that causes trouble. Our churches are filled with people with amazing resources to offer leaders, one another, and the world around them. In fact, that is what most of them do all week—share out of their area of knowledge and sphere of influence what they know with people around them. Are we accessing this resource?

One of the many ways this posture of learning plays itself out in my leadership is in my sermons. I have come to view my sermons more interactively. They are no longer mere monologues. It is no longer about the transfer of information. It is about engaging God through his Word in community. As a result, I solicit feedback from the congregation. When we open up the Scriptures and read them out loud in unison we also reflect out loud together about what we discover there. I ask questions. And

I am often amazed and challenged by what different members of our church see and hear in the Scriptures. When we come together communally in submission to God and his Word and engage with each other, something dynamic occurs.

Why is it we are willing to ask experts (whether they be commentators or consultants) but not our people about the important issues we are struggling with? When people become passive receivers of information versus active participants in the discovery of new realities, they disengage and go through the motions. What if instead people saw themselves as critical participants in the discovery of a local expression of life? What if leaders refused the posture of expert and took on the posture of humble and engaged learner? What if leaders learned the *art* of the question?

A Posture of Vulnerability: From the Head to the Heart

The ways in which we have framed our faith and theology have placed a premium on cognitive skill sets. These cognitive abilities are incredibly important skills to have. But they are no longer enough. There is a lot of material currently being written on the importance of the heart and the need to engage and live life with a heart that is fully alive. In order to secure right thinking, leaders in the church have often ignored matters of the heart and the competencies that flow out of emotional awareness and intelligence. The emotional aspects of faith in many quarters have either been totally marginalized or expressed in an unqualified and unrestrained way as a reaction to such marginalization. We cannot afford to do this any longer. Can you sense this? It is not *healthy*.

We need to discover ways to engage both the head *and* the heart, and our leadership must recognize the need people have to be engaged in more than cognitive ways. Not only do we need to learn to lead in ways that captivate the human heart,

embracing POSSIBILITY

but we also need to discover ways of leading that allow our own hearts to be engaged *as leaders*. Passion flows from a heart fully engaged. Does our leadership evince any signs of passion? What about brokenness and authenticity? If not, perhaps this is a clue that we are not fully engaged and leading from our hearts.

Ignoring the heart for very long is always dangerous because we are emotional and relational people. The heart always finds a way to get what it needs: legitimately or illegitimately. Does our faith engage our hearts, or do we have to go somewhere else to express what is inside us? Does our faith engage our people's hearts, or do they have to go somewhere else to engage what is inside of them? When our leadership does not allow heart expression, then the leader and the community lose out in important and dangerous ways.

The heart is not engaged or satisfied in the same ways the mind is. It cannot be domesticated, or at least if it can, it is only at great cost and is often the result of violence. To engage the heart, your own and others', you must be present, and that can be incredibly hard for many of us because it means engaging pain. When we give ourselves permission to engage our hearts (usually with the help of another), what we find there is often scary to us. But far scarier is what happens when we don't engage the heart: we pay a price personally and our churches miss out on an integral part of what it means to be a disciple of Jesus Christ. Worship is not *merely* singing songs to God for the sake of singing. The reality is that music engages the heart and the mind simultaneously in a way that I believe is intended to allow us penetrating access to God and ourselves. Musical worship allows us to begin the process of engaging God *in* worship because worship is the progressive surrender of everything I know of myself to everything I know of God— and that includes my heart.

The Bible speaks constantly and consistently about the human heart. We see examples of passionate God followers like King

David, Jeremiah, Peter, Mary, and Paul (just to name a few) throughout the collected stories of God's people. The dramatic last week of Christ's life on earth is called the *passion*. If you read the list of the heroes of the faith found in Hebrews 11, you can be sure what propelled these people to sacrifice was not merely their cognitive doctrinal affirmations (though doctrine can be amazingly inspiring) but rather the burning love of a living God that was stoked continually in the furnace of their hearts. What if leaders assumed a posture of vulnerability that allowed them to access their hearts and make them available to God and their people? What if leaders did the hard work of engaging hearts, theirs and others'? What if leaders became conversant in the language of the heart?

A Posture of Availability: From Spoken Words to Living Words

Have you ever noticed how much God required of his prophets in the Old Testament narratives? We often envision prophets as men who showed up, did a bit of yelling, and then vanished, like contemporary street preachers who bark at disinterested people as they pass by and then pack up and go home when their speaking gig ends. A lot more was going on in the ancient context.

The words a prophet spoke were more than mere words. When God calls a leader into his service, God is interested in shaping and molding him or her from the inside out. Old Testament prophets did not merely speak God's words; they embodied them with their actions. Although it is hard to imagine in our context, they were often forced by God to live lives that proclaimed God's message beyond mere words. Their words were the final expression of a process that began with God working internally. In fact, it seems like the work God did first *within* the prophet was what allowed the prophet to speak as he or she did. The prophets of the Old Testament manifested the words of God with their lives as a human embodiment of the divine message. Jeremiah was chained up and placed in a pit, just as Israel herself would be, captive in Babylon. Hosea was married to a prostitute named Gomer, a demonstration of Yahweh's persevering tenderness for his wayward bride Israel. Ezekiel lived in exile and struggled to find life amid the desperation of Israel's dry-boned existence, remembering and proclaiming the promise of their future restoration by God.

In each of these examples the content of the message is integrally linked with the person communicating it. The person of God hosts the word of God and there is a cost to be paid, even as John discovers that ingesting the living Word tastes both sweet and bitter (Rev. 10:9–11). This posture brings us into a spiritual domain where humility accompanied by fear and trembling is the order of the day. In this domain we tremble in awe as we discover the lengths to which God will go to engage *his* people. When we become leaders who serve *this* God, we discover that such things might be asked of us as well.

When God works within a servant who is wholly available an integrity emerges that cannot be manufactured. This life integration is vital for those who would host and draw out the words of God for and from a community of Christ's people. I hope that we who lead churches will become more concerned with embodying God's words than speaking them. Don't misunderstand me. It is not that we do not speak. Rather, we speak when God has done the work of shaping us internally first. To be available to God and the people we serve in our present age means accepting the invitation to suffer. If God engages us in a way that shapes our whole lives, we will have an authority that is real and weighty and devoid of pretension. It makes of us humble servants. To move beyond spoken words to living words, leaders must make themselves available to God in a way that makes our whole lives vulnerable to the message. When leaders are available in this way and allow God to speak prophetically through their lives, the congregation itself has the possibility of hosting and embodying God's Word collectively—the power of the gospel at work.

While God might work in and shape a person in many different ways, the most consistent way I have engaged God has come through suffering and pain. When I have chosen to embrace rather than evade or anesthetize pain, I die in order that I might live. Often we use our position as leaders to elevate ourselves out of discomfort and pain. When we do, we often cause those around us to face pain that we ourselves are unwilling to experience. We miss a critical opportunity to be molded in the image and likeness of Jesus Christ. Jesus, as the prophets before him, leaned into the pain of serving God. Why? Because as the writer of Hebrews says, "He saw the *joy* set before him" (Heb. 12:2, emphasis added). When we embrace pain in the service of God as the prophets did, we are shaped in the way of the cross and are postured in a way that opens us up to hear God's words, regardless of the cost to ourselves and our churches. Because we ourselves suffer first, we lead our people on a path that we have trod and know. We have compassion and can comfort. Moreover, we can challenge and provoke our people to persevere when they grow faint, knowing that God's love confronts and strengthens us to go places we could not otherwise find if left to our own devices.

Can we be so available to God that we allow ourselves to struggle in order to be instructed and corrected? Can we demonstrate to our people what it looks like to hear God's voice out of the whirlwind? Can we learn to help one another embrace our limitations and circumstances that we might be instructed through them rather than always seeking to circumvent or transcend them? What if leaders assumed a posture of availability that pursued God regardless of the cost to our comfort zones? What if suffering became a trusted teacher rather than a hated foe? What if leaders learned to live the Word rather than merely reading or speaking it?

A Posture of Stillness: From Preparation to Meditation

I invite you to consider making a move from seeking not just to *comprehend* God but to *apprehend* God as well—to behold the mysterious reality of God in a way that does not seek to place limitations on his nature that he doesn't place on himself. Remember that when we use words (even the ones I am using now) to describe God, they approximate at best. At worst, they distort.

When I went to seminary, I was taught to prepare. To prepare in this setting meant to do research—usually around a text—and then find materials to support and illustrate my research, particularly in relation to preaching. That was a good discipline for me to submit myself to for an extended season. As an art major in college I had very little background in traditional studies. After I had finished my initial liberal arts degree requirements, I spent most of the next two years in studio classes where preparation meant something much different. I never stopped working hard at my studies, but the kind of work I did didn't resemble what most college students conceive as class work or studying. Thus when I went to seminary I needed to develop and hone those particular skills—of study and research. And that is what I did. I learned the skills of preparation, whether it was for a sermon I was going to preach or later as the pastor of a church preparing for a meeting I had to lead. I buried myself in materials and tried to find a cogent line through the data so I could bring people to the same place I was and believed we were called to go.

However, as I sought to have integrity as a leader in the context of my community, I began to discover that spending most of my time preparing left me ill-suited for the kind of engagement I believe God wanted me to be present for. To be present to my people and the Scriptures, I first had to learn what it meant to be present to God. For me that was, and is, no easy task. Such engagement invites me to change my posture from one of activity to one that could be better characterized by stillness, a more meditative engagement. I think for many of us such an approach to God can be scary. Why? I believe it is scary, not because we are intimidated by the presence of God (or his apparent absence at times), but because in such a posture we slow down enough to reckon with the reality that we are not in control. And the predetermined outcomes we have pursued are often more about us than they are about God's activity.

If preparation means doing research and finding material that supports and illustrates your research, meditation is a deep and intimate conversation with God on God's terms—simply allowing oneself to be present in stillness before the God we serve. To be present to God in this way allows our souls to be shaped beyond the ways we often try to conscript God for some end that we are pursuing, even those we pursue in his name. Why is this so hard? Part of the reason is that when we discover ourselves in the role of leader, we believe that means we ought to be busy doing something. We definitely have to do things a great deal of the time, and it is right that we should. But when are we ever postured in stillness? When do we ever wait in silence? And how and when do our churches participate with us in this critical posture of humility?

Elijah, serving God at a time of enormous confusion in the identity of Israel, opposes Ahab and Jezebel and their altar to Baal. At first it seems that his labors have paid off: the offering of Yahweh is consumed by fire while Baal's priests work themselves into a frenzy that ultimately goes nowhere. But when his work does not result in the end that he had anticipated and Jezebel issues an edict to kill the prophet, he flees for his life. When he finally collapses, he finds himself on a sheer cliff burrowed in a small mountain cave. All of his preparation and work have amounted to very little, and in his despair he hides himself away. You know the story. You have probably lived it. It is in this very *hollow* of desperation that the *hallowed* voice of God comes to Elijah. It is in this place that Elijah learns that he had not nearly comprehended the scope of God's power or intent. It is to a servant of Yahweh emptied of his own agenda and strength that revelation comes.

Do we still ourselves only when we have come to the end of our resources, or do we create time and space to be present in a way that allows us to be exposed—to God, to others, and to ourselves? Can we stop ourselves from constantly preparing to do *something* so that we might have the possibility of engaging *Someone*? What if leaders began to posture themselves in stillness rather than constant activity? What if leaders began to invite their people with them into these kinds of spaces in order to engage with God on agenda-free grounds and discern the still, small voice? What if we slowly nurtured a desire to release the control and security that comes from preparing in order to have the possibility and ability to actually meditate and meet God in a space of deliberate hospitality? What if leaders learned to be still and know God?

A Posture of Surrender: From Control to Chaos

Most people react negatively to the word *chaos*. The idea of chaos strikes fear in the heart because when we experience it, it means we have lost control over our environment, and when that happens, something bad usually follows. Chaos theory posits that while we look at chaos and see only unpredictability, randomness, and erratic noise, actually patterns and a sort of order exist that, while not obvious, are nevertheless present. Within the seemingly random behavior of complex systems such as economic markets, crowds, expanding and contracting populations, order and patterns and life are pulsing, no matter how obscure, inaccessible, or arcane they may be to our senses and perceptions. Thus, in order to perceive this life and order, we must begin to look at different things with different eyes from a different perspective on a different scale.

Why is this befuddling concept of chaos exciting and helpful to me as it relates to local churches and religious systems? Many of us lead communities in contexts that feel (and are) chaotic. In the midst of all of the changes that you have felt and that others and I have described, chaos seems to be a force for destabilization. It's true. When we are a part of systems that begin to experience a measure of disruption, what is our typical response? To immediately try and regain control, right? It's a natural reaction. And many times it is the right one.

But many times we misread what is happening in our environments. We equate chaos with crisis and take immediate and decisive action. But chaos often unfolds in ways that make decisive action dangerous. We don't have enough information. Many times what we experience as a crisis is really the final stages of some complex reality that has been slowly unfolding around us that we have not had the eyes to see. If you are in a developing country that erupts in revolution, that is more than a crisis; it is a dynamic and iterative system that has likely been simmering for a long time. When the chaos of revolution finally comes to a boil, the constantly changing realities of what is happening on the ground require a different kind of response. In such a scenario, you want to be with someone who has the ability to read the environment in a way that allows them (and you) to be adaptive and creative in keeping with what is happening. To react decisively might limit you to a path that once chosen could prove disastrous if you cannot make adjustments.

I remember meeting with my spiritual director and friend, Benedictine monk Father Adam Ryan, at a particularly chaotic time early in the life of Jacob's Well. As I described to him what was happening in my context, all my conversation centered on trying to regain control of what I perceived as a crisis. Father Adam pointed me to the creation account of the Genesis 1 narrative in which we discover the Spirit of God hovering over the chaos and out of the chaos calling forth life. He told me that chaos is often a prerequisite to new creation in Scripture. When we try prematurely to regain control of something chaotic there is a good chance we could undercut the very thing God is doing among us, if only we had the eyes to see the emerging order that, while alien to our sensibilities, is nevertheless present.

With that framework I began to look backward into my story and discovered that often before God began to do something new and creative in or around me, it was preceded by chaos. This discovery helped me to reinterpret and renarrate times in my life and ministry that, in a setting of control, had seemed confusing and frightening. Through this different paradigm I began to see chaos as an opportunity for transformation and hope. With that posture I started to move forward differently as well. I began to retrain myself to ask different kinds of questions in the midst of seeming chaos: Where are the patterns? In the midst of this disruption, where are the opportunities? In crisis, we want control. In chaos, we want discernment and a willingness to surrender controls in order to engage the rapidly changing environment in ways that we can maximize.

This brings us to one particular example of a chaotic system that illustrates what I am trying to describe here. Can you imagine a chaotic system of fluid dynamics that defies mastery in one context but can be engaged powerfully in another? What is it? An ocean wave. You can either battle and be battered by a wave, or you can learn to adapt and surrender to the rapidly evolving complex pattern beneath your surfboard and ride it until it washes out of its own accord. Chaos theory recognizes a kind of order that demands a different posture. Think of a surfer's posture. It is not a posture of control but of balance, awareness, and adjustment. That kind of engagement sounds incredibly rigorous, doesn't it? It also sounds incredibly fun. I get excited just writing about it because of what it implies for leaders and the level at which we must be engaged.

What if leaders and communities resisted the impulse to assert and gain control over their environment when it begins to get a little funky and disruptive? What if leaders sought to stay present in the midst of chaos in order to discern the presence and activity of the Holy Spirit hovering in love and creativity over a new act of creation? What if leaders so postured would actually begin to work in concert with God's Spirit rather than in opposition to it? What if the description that Jesus gave to Nicodemus of the Holy Spirit as an unpredictable wind caused communities to surrender to this Holy Wind the way a ship raises its sail and runs?

A Posture of Cultivation: From Programmer to Environmentalist

If you have been involved in formal church ministry for any length of time, you are familiar with an approach to church life that is largely about administering programs. Many of our churches are filled with programs: children's ministry programs, Bible study programs, discipleship programs, evangelism programs, social justice programs—you name it, there is a program for it. Often programs are curriculums constructed somewhere outside the local community. Individuals with a particular need in their church can find a particular program designed to meet that need in a predetermined way. With such an orientation churches are sometimes less communities than corporate hosts for a variety of programs that people come to access. In this scenario, staff members are those people who run programs. With the focus on the program, staff people are largely interchangeable. Very little imagination is required to run these programs. What is called for is efficacy and efficiency. In fact, imagination can be dangerous because it has a tendency to undermine conventional practice.

My concern about orienting our churches around programs is not so much that they meet felt needs. It is important to address the real needs people bring with them to church. My struggle is that too often programs accept such needs on their own terms. I have found that often those terms must be renegotiated.

Let me give you a practical example of how this might play out in a church. Let's say a person comes into a church wanting to get connected or involved. How do we respond? When we have a program orientation, we suggest they take a membership class or join a group with people in a similar life stage to their own. Programming of this sort pays a certain kind of immediate dividend for the people who participate. The basic underlying assumption in this framework is that anyone who asks ought to have immediate access to relationships in the least possible amount of time with a minimal amount of effort. But can we really expect people to develop relationships of significance and depth when this assumption colors our approach to facilitating them? You know the old adage: "You get what you pay for." It is true. The basic underlying assumption that we try to animate at Jacob's Well is that real relationships and connection *take time and significant investment*. We tell people that in order to begin to connect at Jacob's Well they need to plan on hanging around for at least six months before they can expect to feel like they are a part of the community. More than that, they need to actively invest and reach out, not passively sit back and wait for someone to make something happen for them.

Where else can you enter a complex relational environment and expect to immediately and automatically feel at home? Whether you are new on the job, have recently married into a new family, or have begun to participate in a new sport or a new hobby, there is an expectation that some time will need to pass before you understand what is going on and have a basic lay of the land. Along the way, some structured programs may offer some assistance, but such programming is no substitute for time, effort, and perseverance.

My description may make it sound to you like we are initially almost hostile to people who show up at Jacob's Well. Nothing could be further from the truth. We believe deeply in the real need for people to connect to other human beings and form meaningful and lasting relationships. In fact, we believe in it so much that we refuse to allow people to take shortcuts in an attempt to get there. Our basic approach is not to create, discover, or facilitate a program but rather to cultivate an *environment of hospitality* that animates the whole posture of the community as it relates to its surrounding environment. When we settle for programs, not only does it relieve the people it seeks to serve from stretching and doing the hard work of building relationships, it also lets the rest of the church off the hook as it relates to embodying the Christian virtue of hospitality—a fundamental aspect of discipleship for people who claim to follow Jesus Christ.

Do you see yourself as a leader who is cultivating an environment or as an administrator running programs? How are we cultivating life in our communities? I believe that churches need leaders who are environmentalists. Environmentalists can help to shape relational and spiritual ecologies that generate life as the natural outgrowth of a healthy and dynamic ecosystem.

Over the last couple of years I have run into older pastors who in the later years of their lives and ministries have taken up the practice of gardening. Maybe years of cultivating a community of people in a local church environment has produced leaders who feel at home with their hands buried deeply in the soil of a garden that nurtures the potential for growing life that is both beautiful and nourishing. What if leaders began to see themselves in this light? What if leaders saw themselves less as administrators or programmers and more as environmentalists or ecologists who help to imagine and nurture the space under their influence in order that life might grow from it—not by imposing something from the outside in but rather from the ground up, in the same way that through dependence on the Holy Spirit the manifestation of a godly life is fruit growing naturally from a healthy tree? What if leaders assumed a posture of cultivation, of kneeling and digging in the earth, of planting and watering, of weeding and culling and, ultimately, harvesting?

A Posture of Trust: From Defensiveness to Creativity

In each of the postures I have proposed thus far, there is a common assumption underlying these transitions. In order to be able to make some of these moves, there is a basic assumption of *trust*. Do you see it?

What is required to move as a leader from the position of giving answers to asking questions? Such a move requires that you trust the people with whom you dialogue enough to listen to what they have to say. Similarly, to move from the head to the heart means that you trust there is something in the heart that is worth searching for and discovering. To move from spoken words to living words means that you trust enough of what you are saying to live it out in ways that might involve suffering. To move from preparation to meditation implies that you trust that if you are still and present and attentive there might actually be a *There* there to meet you and shape you in solitude. To allow yourself to transition from control to chaos suggests you are beginning to trust that despite the seeming data flooding your senses to the contrary, there is pattern and chaos and life hidden somewhere in the mess and press of your environment. Finally, to engage your community in a manner similar to that of a gardener cultivating life from soil speaks to a level of trust you have in the hidden processes of life that go on underneath the ground when all surface evidence points to dormancy, if not death. To live and lead in many of the ways I am describing calls for a basic posture of trust. However, this can be hard because the level of trust that is required may be beyond what you might feel in your current context.

I have a strong sense that many Christians and most leaders have a hard time with trust these days. In our culture many

Christians feel embattled and have taken on defensive postures believing their survival is at stake. The tenor of religious dialogue generally, and Christian dialogue specifically, contributes to a sense of being under attack. Everyone is shooting at everyone. Friendly fire is killing more than enemy fire—that is, if we could decide on who our "enemy" is beyond the most recent person who offends us. Balkanization indeed. This toxic lack of trust, and the active posture of suspicion in the broader environment, has invaded many places close to home, including our local church communities. Leaders feel at odds with their congregations and struggle to build meaningful relationships. Parishioners feel at odds with their leaders and struggle to be vulnerable with them. While we would never openly admit this to anyone out loud, many of us do not trust God. It seems we believe God is passive, and the role of leaders and church and theology in the face of God's apparent passivity is to defend him from all challengers. It is as if we believe God cannot defend himself—and after what we have witnessed on the cross of Christ, maybe there is something there that is worth paying attention to, something very sacred and important to be discovered.

People in our culture are asking very important questions right now about God, about Scripture, about the church, and about many other topics and issues they struggle with. Many of them worship in our churches. Questioning basic assumptions about reality is a natural by-product of a culture in transition. However, we cannot ask questions and seek God in the midst of our questions if at the same time we are defending some secured ground that protects the identity of God. The presuppositions and rigidity of such a posture will ultimately render impotent any true seeking.

This issue is vital for a book dealing with the ways leaders engage their communities. If you posture yourself in any of the ways I am suggesting, you are making yourself vulnerable to be misunderstood and potentially attacked. Moving from certainty (or better, the *myth* of certainty) to uncertainty in order to be faithful will be misunderstood and misinterpreted. Jesus confronted a religious system in his day that had grown unresponsive to the God it supposedly worshiped and served. The greatest demonstration of this is that when God actually arrived in the person of Jesus Christ, those in authority did not recognize or acknowledge him. More than that, those who held power actively opposed and persecuted him, resulting in his execution. What was Jesus's response to this? Isaiah says of the Suffering Servant that though

> he was oppressed and afflicted,
>   yet he did not open his mouth;
> he was led like a lamb to the slaughter,
>   and as a sheep before its shearers is silent,
>   so he did not open his mouth.
>
> Isaiah 53:7

In the Gospels Jesus is interrogated by his accusers. Mark records the interaction between the high priest and Jesus during his trial. "Then the high priest stood up before them and asked Jesus, 'Are you not going to answer? What is this testimony that these men are bringing against you?' But Jesus remained silent and gave no answer" (Mark 14:60–61).

What is my point? Am I suggesting that leaders assume a self-proclaimed martyr role when they face opposition? No. What I am saying is that leaders must be wise and realistic about the dynamics of change. We must recognize the reality that when systems and structures are forced to undergo change, it creates enormous tension and insecurity, and often those people who call attention to these realities become the object of people's fears and insecurities. It is easier to shoot the messenger than to be present to the complex realities that are being played out around us.

It seems to me that Jesus trusted his Father and the work that God was doing in and through him to such a radical degree that he did not feel the need to defend himself at every turn. Why should we follow his example? For at least two reasons. First, when people are hostile and in attack mode, engaging them on their terms is rarely profitable, and we often end up behaving or speaking in ways that undermine the work we are called to do. Second, when we feel the need to defend ourselves, it stops us from doing the very thing that we are called to do: embody and create an alternative. Jesus described, manifested, and invited people into his kingdom as he created it on earth as it is in heaven—without concern for his own well-being. He did not construct it carefully and then defend it violently as if he had something to fear from those who wielded power. When we feel the need to defend something, we need to check ourselves. What are we fighting for? What are we fighting against? Are the stakes higher for us in our context than they were for Jesus in his? If not, why do we feel we must do something that Jesus himself refused to do?

In order to be creative *we need to learn to trust God more—or differently*. We must believe that what we are doing is not so much dependent on us as it is on God. In order to see God at work, we have to reposture ourselves. We cannot see God at work in his creation when we are crouched defensively behind a carefully constructed wall. When we trust that God is out ahead of us and seek out his life in and around and outside our walls, we engage with freedom and passion the creative possibilities that arise as God engages his creation for his purposes. But mostly what we do is strive to catch up and join him.

We also recognize that such dynamic work always involves struggle and opposition. We know that Jesus was beyond reproach and blameless, but we cannot be so confident in ourselves. When we face challenges and questions from those around us, we can welcome them as opportunities to engage our perceptions with a posture of humility that allows for the possibility of refinement and correction. Why? Because we are not defending something that we have manufactured but rather experimenting in order to be faithful. Such an approach to struggle bears witness to our trust in God and his purposes—that he would provide people to be foils to our creativity to further refine it for his own glory and not merely foes to be overcome as we try to build our own kingdoms.

Do we trust God? Really? Do we trust the people in our churches? Do we trust God's creative and disruptive work in and around us? When we spend the majority of our energy defending the hallowed grounds of our staked-out territory, something vital is lost. What do we give up in such an arrangement? What if leaders engaged God, our faith, and our communities with a posture of faith and trust—even in the midst of the upheaval we are experiencing? What if leaders refused to try to defend God when God himself refused to take such a posture on his own behalf? What if we quit trying to keep a rather reckless Messiah safe and secure from all challengers and instead followed him out into the generative chaos of creation—the way Peter did when he ventured out of the boat in order to encounter Jesus on the waves? What if we developed a posture of trust that helped us move from defensiveness to creativity?

A Posture of Joy: From Work to Play

Plato once said that you could learn more about people by watching them play for one hour than you could through a lifetime of conversation with them. Think about that. It is a compelling idea. It suggests that something fundamental to human identity is accessible only when people cut loose and enjoy themselves. In theory, I like the idea. But in reality, it frustrates me. Why? I have a hard time playing. I used to be pretty good at it, but as I have gotten older it's not as easy as it used to be. Working I can do. Thinking I can do. Responsibility and obligation I have down cold. But playing? These days I have a hard time playing.

What does it say about a person when they can't play? It means I take myself too seriously. Can you relate? And when we throw faith into the mix it tends to get worse, not better. Churches take themselves very seriously. When this orientation toward life and faith is combined with a posture of defensiveness toward the surrounding environment, a fairly grim, or at least utilitarian, picture of what it means to follow God and be the church emerges. We are about God's "business," so we better get to work and make something happen. It reminds me of the bumper sticker, "Jesus is coming back: look busy!"

But what happens when we start to live in a trust-saturated relationship with God, our church community, and the world around us? One thing that I have experienced as a result of trust is relief and joy. Because we can appreciate what is happening around us without needing to manufacture or control it, the possibility of enjoying what we do and who we are enters into the equations of our lives. Do you know how attractive joy is? We live in a culture that is consumed with happiness and pleasure—two phenomena that rely on circumstances largely beyond our ability to control. Joy is different. Joy flows from an acknowledgment that regardless of our circumstances, we are known and loved. And out of that conviction flows not only joy but peace, presence, and love. From those manifestations of the Spirit's presence come the ability to relax, celebrate, play, and have fun.

I believe this is the idea that is at the heart of the Sabbath. By taking a break from effort and labor to rest, we acknowledge the true source of life: God. As I study the liturgical year of the Hebrew people, I discover a community that knew not only how to work but how to play. Their life had a rhythm, and a regular part of their rhythm was parties. Hebrew liturgical parties (festivals) were community-wide celebrations of God's provision. Of course the people shared the responsibility for the bounty of provision: their labor combined with God's gifts of animals, seed, earth, rain, and sun provided what they needed to live. But the Hebrews seemed to understand something I often think we do not. What value is there to having provision if you never pause to enjoy it and acknowledge the goodness of God, the fruitfulness of the labor, and the resulting bounty? There is another aspect that I think is important to consider as well. By taking time to rest and have fun, we allow our bodies to replenish themselves and be renewed. In fact, in the Torah God *commanded* that the land be allowed to have seasons where no farming was done in order that it too could be restored.

During the second semester of my sophomore year in the college of design, I took a class on color theory. In one of her few lectures to us, our professor took some time to share with us how creativity works. Let me set up her comments by saying that design is largely about solving problems. Graphic design is about solving communication problems through combinations of colors, images, shapes, text, concepts, and the media that will convey it. To study this particular discipline of design is to learn how to solve communication problems graphically. Our professor warned us that when a designer gets involved in this kind of problem solving, he or she can only work creatively and productively for a certain amount of time. Once this limit is reached, the chances of solving the problem diminish exponentially. She said the challenge in this situation is that designers are tempted to think that if only they would work a little bit harder or longer, the problem would be solved. She suggested that *effort* was not the issue. When we got stuck on a certain problem, she recommended that rather than continuing to go at it, we do just the opposite—walk away. In fact, not just walk away, but go and do something completely different. If you have been designing for an hour and you are stuck, play thirty minutes of basketball, watch fifteen minutes of television, or make something to eat, she said. Why? Because disengaging allows our brains to rest and be replenished. Further, engaging in a different kind of activity engages the other hemisphere of the brain to take the stage for a while.

If we students followed her advice, we saw amazing things happen. While we rested, our brains connected the dots and solved the problem. She was right more times than not. I have never forgotten it. I have approached creative work in this way ever since. But creative work is not just the domain of artists. Creativity is the provenance of anyone who wants to engage dynamically with his or her environment in any discipline. Moreover, creative work is not merely the domain of individuals but the vocation of communities as well.

At Jacob's Well we instituted a communal spiritual discipline in an attempt to take this idea (not too) seriously. Once a year we take a communal pilgrimage. Pilgrimage is an ancient communal spiritual practice that fills the pages of our Scriptures. Over a long weekend our community goes on a journey together for no other purpose than to rehearse, reenact, and renarrate God's story of liberation. On the Passover Jews would go on pilgrimage to Jerusalem to celebrate the festival and remember and reidentify with the first liberation from Egypt under the leadership of Moses. Their pilgrimage also anticipated a future exodus when God would finally lead Israel to freedom. That is what he did through the liberation from sin that Jesus instituted in his life, teachings, death, and resurrection. That is a cause for celebration and a story to be remembered, rehearsed, renarrated, reenacted, reidentified with, and any other "re" you can imagine. It has provided a necessary break from the ordinary routines of life to rest and be replenished. In light of God's generosity and trustworthiness we can pause, rest, play, and tell stories about God's faithfulness in our personal and corporate lives. We can put our busyness on hold and do (and be) something different. So that is what we do. We spend a whole weekend, from late Friday afternoon to Sunday night playing, sleeping, worshiping, eating, and laughing. And amazing things happen.

When our churches and leaders cannot stop working long enough to play, we are missing something fundamental about being human beings made in the image of God. We are too focused on what we are doing rather than seeing what God has done and what he promises he will continue to do because of his faithfulness, not our effort. This lack of playfulness tells us something about our lack of trust in God. And it warns us that if we are not careful, our labor will ultimately produce an uninspired rehashing of solutions we have already tried, no matter how sincere we are or how hard we work. What if leaders refused to take themselves so seriously? What if communities learned how to institute times of rest and play with the same vigor that they used to attack capital campaigns, volunteer recruiting, and strategic plans? What if churches gained reputations as communities of people who know how to party in the way of Jesus? What might it look like for our collective posture to manifest joy?

A Posture of Dependence: From Resolution to Tension—and Back Again

It is only when we stay in a posture of engaged dependence—of learning, vulnerability, availability, stillness, surrender, cultivation, trust, and joy—that we will find real life in all its creative and dynamic glory. This new life will cause us to see God, the Scriptures, our churches, the world, and ourselves in new (and old) ways. And the result of these new (and old) ways of seeing will not be maps or visions that let us off the hook by delivering us to freshly secured and resolute terra firma. No, I think the result will be new ways of *being* that cause us to become more brazenly dependent on God and each other and willing to lean into ambiguity, mystery, and creativity so that we might be faithful to God's work in the midst of a dynamic and ever-changing liquid landscape—what Leonard Sweet has called *"terra aqua."*[2]

Tension is a good thing. Tension is created when two seemingly opposed realities are held in a dynamic relationship that demands engagement and interaction. Such tension is a struggle for us, however. Tension is discomfiting. To minimize discomfort, we opt for a resolution that maximizes one half of a complex reality at the expense of the other half. When we do this, something vital is sacrificed.

Throughout the Scriptures such dynamic tension is on display. The theological dynamic of the incarnation of Jesus Christ bears witness to two seemingly opposite characteristics of God's identity: his immanence and his transcendence. It plays out in our understanding of salvation. Paul teaches us that it is by grace through faith and not through works that a person is made righteous. James is quick to remind us, however, that right beliefs are not the true demonstration of God's work in a person but rather that right belief is always manifested through right action—authentic faith manifested in good works. Such a dynamic tension forces us to a posture of engaged dependence because in our own strength we are able to live into one or the other but rarely both simultaneously. Theological systems that refuse to hold in tension the twin realities of God's sovereignty and human freedom relieve us from living into these tensions in a dependent and dynamic posture of faith. Instead, we try to resolve them to our satisfaction.

In the postures that I have proposed there needs to be more tension than I have previously allowed. We must abide in the tension between questions *and* answers, between the head *and* the heart, between spoken words *and* living words. It is not an either/or option. It is both/and. Why? Because there is no long-term life to be found in abandoning and marginalizing one set of competencies or leaders with traditional skill sets for an emerging set of leaders or skills, no matter how life-giving they initially appear to be. When we hold these twin realities in dynamic tension, life emerges as we depend *on God*.

It is true that a person or a system is sometimes so embedded in one way of seeing and behaving in reality that in order to break free it must overcorrect by swinging to the other extreme. But such swings are ultimately reactions and not generative or sustainable over the long term. They are like the plants in

Jesus's parable that sprout up quickly but then wither because they lack any significant root structure. People and systems that are reactive lose steam very quickly. To be merely reactive is to become nothing more than the reversed, mirrored (and distorted) reflection of that which is rejected.

My hope is that what I am proposing is not merely a reaction but rather a testimony and a description of where I, as a leader, and we, as a community, are discovering life in God. To say that our life has come about as the result of ridding ourselves of all of the characteristics from which we have emerged would not be honest. Worse, it would be disingenuous and ungrateful. If we take on a posture of dependence that seeks to move us from resolution to tension, then we must allow there to be tension in our transition. We will learn, I hope, to prepare *and* meditate, work *and* play, cultivate *and* program, as well as a hundred other things. I hope we will discover order in chaos that frees us to resist the urge to control while at the same time acknowledging what Paul said to the church in Corinth: "God is not a God of disorder but of peace" (1 Cor. 14:33). What if leaders learned to live in and lead out of tension? What if leaders learned to discover the kind of dangerous peace that comes from knowing and engaging God in a creative and dynamic way? What if leaders refused resolution, not because resolution is bad but because it too often comes about as a way of escaping the demanding posture of dependence?

Struggle *and* Opportunity

What have you discovered about yourself in considering these nine potential postures? What have you discovered about how you lead your church or your faith system, whatever that may be? What is your posture? And what is the posture of your community or institution? How is your posture affecting what you communicate and what you hear back? Or is your posture keeping you from hearing certain things? If that is the case, and I believe for those of us in leadership we must always assume that it is, you have a challenging but rewarding opportunity ahead of you. What would it look like for you to invite feedback about your leadership posture and the posture of your community?

The postures that we have assumed or inherited create the possibility for struggle *and* opportunity. We must engage and live in this tension, looking honestly at where we are in order to discover where we might go. Rather than trying to leave our struggles behind, we can see them as a clue that will help us find the pathway of opportunity. But such opportunity will only manifest itself to us inasmuch as we are willing to become vulnerable. Such vulnerability is inherently risky because it means we might do things badly for a while as we seek to discover new expressions of life. Yet this is no less risky than maintaining the status quo. We must not delude ourselves into believing that there are easy answers or simple solutions. But neither can we shrink back in fear of what we don't know and haven't mastered. The true nature of the work that is at the heart of all creativity and discovery is like the parable that likens the kingdom of heaven to a treasure hidden in a field. "When a man found it, he hid it again, *and then in his joy* went and sold all he had and bought that field" (Matt. 13:44, emphasis added).

10

Reckoning with Intuition

learning to trust your gut

We must assume an attitude of waiting, accepting the fact that we are creatures and not creator. We must do this because it is not our right to do anything else; the initiative is God's, not man's. Man is able to initiate nothing; he is able only to accept. If God does not call, no calling takes place. If God does not come, there is no history! History is the coming of God to man, and the way in which man replies. . . . In short, He is what creates, and we creatures are in the act of becoming.[1]

Carlo Carretto, *The God Who Comes*

If I were called upon to state in a few words the essence of everything I was trying to say both as a novelist and a preacher, it would be something like this: Listen to your life. See it for the fathomless mystery that it is. In the boredom and pain of it no less than in the excitement and gladness: touch, taste, smell your way to the holy and hidden heart of it because in the last analysis all moments are key moments, and life itself is grace.[2]

Frederick Buechner, *Now and Then*

Listen to Your Life, Redux

If you want to hear God, listen to your life. I first read Buechner's statement over a decade ago, and it has shaped my life in significant ways. For some of us the invitation to listen to life in order to hear God comes as good news. It was good news when I first read it, and it still is. If it resonates with you, perhaps like me you have had a sneaking suspicion that God is at work all around us, even if we have not always had the eyes to see it. To be invited to "touch, taste, and smell" our way into a discovery of God's activity opens up before us vistas of possibility we did not expect to find. The ordinary becomes sacred: the raw materials by which God in Christ works out our salvation, personally and communally. If our whole life is the means by which God engages us, then I must live differently—attentively engaged in a posture of trust and hope toward all that I know and experience.

At the same time, a challenge like the one Buechner issues can be frustrating for a great number of us. Listen to your life? What does *that* mean? The opaque and open-ended nature of what he is inviting us toward can produce anxiety. Just tell us what to do, we say. We'll execute it. We are accustomed to discovering God and his life *out there*. We observe it and go and lay hold of it. Listen to my life? Can you be more specific?

I believe a great many of us have forgotten, or maybe we never knew, what it is like to relate to God, each other, and ourselves in this manner. We have sought answers from experts who promise success rather than postures that would allow us to be integrally engaged in the discovery of life ourselves. Now we are discovering that laying hold of other people's answers no longer provides the promise that we once thought it might. We must reckon with our environment and with God in a different way. The answer lies in God, in us, and in the engagement between God and us. We must listen to our lives and engage. Such a way of engaging with God might strike you as unusual or alien, but I think it says more about our culture and our conditioned way of knowing than it does about how God speaks to, engages, and interacts with his people.

In the tenth chapter of John's Gospel, Jesus tells a group of people that includes Pharisees and his disciples that his purpose is to bring full and abundant life to those under his leadership. To illustrate his point he uses the metaphor of a shepherd caring for his flock.

> The one who enters by the gate is the shepherd of the sheep. The gatekeeper opens the gate for him, and the sheep listen to his voice. He calls his own sheep by name and leads them out. When he has brought out all of his own, he goes on ahead of them, and *his sheep follow him because they know his voice*. But they will never follow a stranger; in fact, they will run away from him because they do not recognize a stranger's voice.
>
> John 10:2–5, emphasis added

I want to draw your attention to the dynamic that exists between the shepherd, his voice, and the sheep. Jesus says in a direct and explicit way that his sheep hear his voice. He doesn't say that if his sheep pray in a certain way, they can discern his leading. He doesn't say that if his sheep hire the right consultant to talk about the nature of shepherds and how their voices have sounded through time, they will hear him now. For Jesus it is simple: his sheep know his voice and when they hear it, they follow.

We do not believe this. We have made hearing the voice of God the rarest and most unusual of experiences—even for people who claim to know and follow God. We talk about hearing the voice of God, of knowing and following the will of God, as if it is the most difficult and challenging thing in the world. According to Jesus it is not. Oswald Chambers describes the accessibility of God's will:

> At first we want the consciousness of being guided by God, then as we go on we live so much in the consciousness of God that

we do not need to ask what His will is, because the thought of choosing any other will never occurs to us. If we are saved and sanctified God guides us by our ordinary choices, and if we are going to choose what He does not want, He will check, and we must heed. Whenever there is doubt, stop at once. Never reason it out and say—"I wonder why I shouldn't?" God instructs us in what we choose, that is, He guides our common sense, and we no longer hinder His Spirit by continually saying—"Now, Lord, what is Thy will?"[3]

The words of Jesus and Chambers call to mind God's words to the Israelites in Deuteronomy. God tells them that what he commands is neither too hard nor too far away, whether high or low: "The word is very near you; it is in your mouth and in your heart so you may obey it" (Deut. 30:14). God is determined to reveal himself and his purposes to us. We can anticipate and rely upon God generously giving himself to us. We seek to know and follow God because God first knows, loves, and pursues his people and wants us to have life. Carlo Carretto writes,

And his coming and his presence are not only the result of our waiting or a prize for our efforts: they are his decision, based on his love freely poured out. His coming is bound to his promise, not our works or virtue. We have not earned the meeting with God because we have served him faithfully in our brethren, or because we have heaped up such a pile of virtue as to shine before Heaven. God is thrust onward by his love, not attracted by our beauty. He comes even in moments when we have done everything wrong, when we have done nothing, . . . when we have sinned.[4]

This is good news indeed. God is a Shepherd who speaks out of the overflow of his love. His people, his sheep, know and respond to his voice. Why then has it become so complicated, hard, and unusual for people and churches to have a sense of what God's purposes are for them?

Naming My Frustration

We must relearn what it means for us to seek God as a people. This is the vocation of leadership in the church—creating environments that allow us to seek and respond to God in faithfulness as a people. Ministry as an end in itself? Destructive. Ministry as a by-product of everything else in the environment being in harmony? Creative, generative, chaotic, and beautiful.

When I have the opportunity to share such ideas with leaders and people in the church, what I hear back comes only after a long, hard stare. Then they often say this: "I knew it. I have carried this around inside forever! I knew something was off. This makes sense of so much." Or this: "You have given words to what I have known but could not articulate. I have not been able to really get onboard with such and such program, and now I know why." When people say such things, I react in a couple of ways. First, I am encouraged that in our conversation they have found language to help them bring to the surface internal struggles they have felt and yet have been unable to legitimize for lack of language. However, my second reaction is one of frustration, sometimes mild and sometimes profound, depending on the circumstances. The reason I get frustrated is because people have learned to ignore or betray what the Spirit of God in them has been saying for who knows how long—and the reason they have marginalized what I believe is the voice of the Spirit of God in them is because in many cases their leaders told them to do so. Maybe not explicitly, but the message has come across loud and clear: You cannot trust your heart or the voice you hear speaking inside you. You cannot listen to your life. Seeking God for God's sake is not enough.

How tragic. How untrue. And it is no surprise that such people have come to view themselves as outsiders and malcontents, to believe something is wrong with them. But maybe something is right with them, and there is something wrong with their leaders. Remember that Jesus says of his sheep, "They will never follow a stranger; in fact, they will run from him because they do not recognize a stranger's voice" (John 10:5).

Intuitive Knowing

I use the word *intuition* to describe an inner way of knowing, believing, and living. There might be better words, but I like *intuition* because it calls to mind a hidden reality that can be either engaged or ignored—much like God himself. The Oxford American Dictionary defines *intuition* as "the ability to understand something immediately, without the need for conscious reasoning." Intuition is a gut-level reckoning. It is an inner voice that speaks to us in a way with which our conscious, reason-oriented minds are often at odds. This voice I am describing, this intuitive way of reckoning from the gut is, I believe, the Spirit of God alive and at work in human beings and human communities born of that same Spirit. But I would go further. I would argue that in many cases God's Spirit is far out ahead of God's people, alive, at work, and speaking in people and communities that do not yet consciously know God in Christ but who are yet responsive to him in many of the ways I am describing. Why?

Often Christians reared on the domesticated faith of Western, scientific, materialistic rationalism are the very people who are least responsive to the voice of the Spirit of God manifested through intuitive, gut-level reckonings. Ironically, my experience is that many people who are well practiced in responding to the promptings of the Spirit do not know that this is what they are doing. The principle of this observation is reinforced by Paul's words in Romans:

> When outsiders who have never heard of God's law follow it more or less by instinct, they confirm its truth by their obedience. They show that God's law is not something alien, imposed on us from without, but woven into the very fabric of our creation.

There is something deep within them that echoes God's yes and no, right and wrong. Their response to God's yes and no will become public knowledge on the day God makes his final decision about every man and woman.

Romans 2:14–15 Message

Have you experienced this dynamic?

Gavin de Becker is a personal security consultant. His expertise relates to violent behavior and learning how to recognize signs of violence to prevent yourself or others from becoming victims of it. He has written a bestselling book on this topic called *The Gift of Fear*. De Becker states that we live in a society that looks to the government, technology, or experts for solutions to our problems, including violence. Can you guess what the number one resource is for protecting oneself against violence according to Gavin de Becker? The best solution for protecting oneself against potential violence comes from a "grander resource that was there all the while, within you. That resource is intuition." He continues:

> It may be hard to accept its importance, because intuition is usually looked upon by us thoughtful Western beings with contempt. It is often described as emotional, unreasonable, or inexplicable. Husbands chide their wives about "feminine intuition" and don't take it seriously. If intuition is used by a woman to explain some choice she made or a concern she can't let go of, men roll their eyes and write it off. We much prefer logic, the grounded, explainable, unemotional thought process that ends in a supportable conclusion. In fact, Americans worship logic, even when it's wrong, and deny intuition, even when it's right.[5]

De Becker's book details, in a fascinating way, how people do in fact *know* certain things but subsequently ignore such knowledge because they have been trained to pay no heed to this means of reckoning. In de Becker's context, the result is often tragic: he describes how people often disregard the intuitive warning signs that tell them they are in danger, that something is *off* or wrong in the environment, and as a result they often end up suffering some form of violence that results in pain and suffering—or even death. He goes on to say that men have these intuitive reckonings as well, but they more often describe them as *gut feelings*. Such intuition or gut feelings are really the body's way of responding to the environment in a highly engaged and complex way. De Becker elaborates: "It isn't just a feeling. It is a process more extraordinary and ultimately more logical in the natural order than the most fantastic computer calculation. It is our most complex cognitive process and at the same time the simplest. Intuition connects us to the natural world and to our nature. Freed from the bonds of judgment, married only to perception, it carries us to predictions we will later marvel at."[6] Truly we are, in the words of the psalmist, "fearfully and wonderfully made" (Ps. 139:14). If God made humans to intuit danger in order to survive, wouldn't it follow that such capabilities would be present for discerning the voice of the Creator so that we might survive not just as animals protecting our territory but also as spiritual beings thriving in communities?

A marketing consultant and former business and science reporter at the *Washington Post*, bestselling author Malcolm Gladwell has discovered a similar phenomenon at work and describes it in his book *Blink: The Power of Thinking Without Thinking*. This book is an amazing tour through the way we reckon subconsciously and intuitively with the world beyond ourselves. Like de Becker, Gladwell notes how difficult it is for us, and particularly for institutions, to take seriously this intuitive way of knowing.

> Our world requires that decisions be sourced and footnoted, and if we say *how* we feel, we must also be prepared to elaborate on *why* we feel that way. . . . It is a lot easier to listen to scientists and lawyers because the scientists and lawyers provide pages and pages of documentation supporting their conclusions. I think that approach is a mistake, and if we are to learn to improve the

quality of the decisions we make, we need to accept the mysterious nature of our snap judgments. We need to respect the fact that it is possible to know without knowing why we know and accept that—sometimes—we're better off that way.[7]

Gladwell says that we need to respect the fact that "it is possible to know without knowing why we know." Do such intuitive ways of reckoning and engaging with God, ourselves, our community, and the environment have to be so unusual and hard-fought?

It is also important to acknowledge that just as all facts and statistics are open to interpretation and manipulation, not all intuitive reckonings are created equal. If we are to give greater credence to our hearts and our spirits, we must also increase our ability to know when we are in error or are being unfaithful to what God is saying. Discernment, accountability, and wisdom are integral aspects of listening personally and collectively for the voice of God revealed in the Scriptures, through history, and within ourselves. Further, my suggestion that we have given away or surrendered a vital aspect of our birthright as followers of Jesus when we stop listening for the voice of God within does not mean that previous understandings of revelation and ways of knowing truth are now passé or irrelevant. These twin ways of knowing must not be pitted against one another in a fight for supremacy. They must instead be held in dynamic tension. Reason is as much a gift of the Spirit as the intuitive ways of knowing that I have described throughout this book. To place them against one another is foolish. In fact, for the church to thrive we must access and unleash *every* resource available to us.

Emerging Leaders, Emerging Communities

More than thirty years ago, Henri Nouwen wrote a book called *The Wounded Healer* about the need for a new kind of leader. In this book he describes one of the roles of wounded healers as *the articulator of interior events*, a person who truly leads people *spiritually* from the inside out. In his description of this integral leader, he calls attention to how little prepared or able many leaders are at directing others in the ways he describes and calls for.

> The first and most basic task required of the minister of tomorrow therefore is to clarify the immense confusion which can arise when people enter this new internal world. It is a painful fact indeed to realize how poorly prepared most Christian leaders prove to be when they are invited to be spiritual leaders in the true sense. Most of them are used to thinking in terms of large-scale organization, getting people together in churches, schools and hospitals, and running the show as a circus director. They have become unfamiliar with, and even somewhat afraid of, the deep and significant movements of the spirit. I am afraid that in a few decades the Church will be accused of having failed in its most basic task: to offer men and women creative ways to communicate with the source of human life.[8]

It has now been a few decades since Nouwen wrote this. What do you think? Has the church failed in its most basic task? I, for one, still have hope. But I also know that for many his prophetic words have come true.

I love the church. I hope you feel that and understand how it drives what I do, how I live, and what I write. I believe the church, the *local* church, is the means by which God generously incarnates and demonstrates his way and his purposes for his creation. I believe that God is still speaking with the voice of a shepherd and that we who are his sheep can hear his voice and respond. I have experienced this alongside others, and these experiences have filled my life with hope—a hope born of trust and the basic conviction that the church is what Paul says it is in Ephesians: "Christ's body, in which he speaks and acts, by which he fills everything with his presence" (Eph.

1:20 Message). It seems to a great many people that the voice of the Shepherd has been silent for a while. Maybe for many of us God is silent in the same way that his voice was still in the time of Eli—right before Hannah and Samuel emerged onto the scene.

Perhaps we are entering a time when God is raising up from the margins women and children and men and communities who hear something that hasn't been heard in a while. Maybe the margins are responding, "Here am I, Lord." Sitting before rigid Pharisees and clueless disciples, perhaps Jesus had the child Samuel and others like him in mind when he said, "Truly I tell you, unless you change and become like little children, you will never enter the kingdom of heaven" (Matt. 18:3). If so, perhaps more than just hearing, such women and children and men and communities are *experiencing* what comes in the wake of foolishly responding to that voice—full and abundant life.

In order for us and our communities to access this life, we will have to trust—like children trust. We have to trust God, yes. But I want to push even further. In order for each of us and our communities to access this life that is offered and promised by Christ, we will have to trust God *in us*—personally and corporately. For it is *Christ in us* that is the hope of glory. Can we trust *that*? What do you think?

What does your gut tell you?

Benediction

Each week at Jacob's Well we conclude our time of corporate worship with two benedictions: one that is sung and one that is read from the Scripture. The words of these two benedictions are spoken and sung in the hope that as we disperse God would quicken in our hearts and in our lives that which we have encountered in our space together. In the same way, my hope and prayer is that what you have encountered in these pages will be like what we experience in our community's worship gatherings—some kind of meeting and connection with God, yourself, others, and the world.

So at this point I would like to offer a benediction, but not one of my own making. *The Wisdom of the Desert*, translated by Thomas Merton, contains the collected sayings of holy men who went to seek God in the desert early in the history of the church. At a time when the church was being subsumed in empire, many people of faith went seeking after God at the margins of their world. To conclude this chapter, and the book, I offer this bit of wisdom from the wilderness of fourth-century Egypt and Israel as a blessing and a benediction for our vocation as disciples and leaders seeking to be faithful to God.

> A brother asked one of the elders: What good thing shall I do, and have life thereby? The old man replied: God alone knows what is good. However I have heard it said that someone inquired of Father Abbot Nisteros the great, the friend of Abbot Anthony, asking: What good work shall I do? and that he replied: Not all works are alike. For Scripture says that Abraham was hospitable and God was with him. Elijah loved solitary prayer, and God was with him. And David was humble, and God was with him. Therefore, whatever you see your soul desire according to God, do that thing, and you shall keep your heart safe.[9]

For each of us, our communities, and for the sake of the world, may it be that you grow in your love of God . . . and learn to trust your gut.

Notes

Chapter 1 In the Beginning

1. Henri Nouwen, *Sabbatical Journey* (New York: Crossroad, 1998), 10–11.
2. Stanley Hauerwas, "Why We Are Afraid to Die in America" (Emergent Theological Gathering, Chapel Hill Bible Church, Chapel Hill, NC, January 20–22, 2003).
3. Miroslav Volf, *Exclusion and Embrace* (Nashville: Abingdon, 1996), 199.
4. Peter Rollins, *How (Not) to Speak of God* (Brewster, MA: Paraclete, 2006), 12.

Chapter 2 A Way in the Wilderness

1. T. S. Eliot, "Little Gidding," no. 4 of *Four Quartets* (New York: Harcourt, Brace and Company, 1943), 59.
2. John Howard Yoder, "Armaments and Eschatology," *Studies in Christian Ethics* 1 (1888): 58.
3. J. R. R. Tolkien, *The Fellowship of the Ring*, The Lord of the Rings (1965; Boston; Houghton Mifflin, 1993), 83.
4. Whole volumes could be devoted to this problem. Subsequent conversations I have had with seminary presidents, professors, and students reinforce to me almost ten years since I graduated from seminary that this dynamic is still on the minds of many people who care deeply about theological training. And why shouldn't it be? Seminaries are no less products and potential victims of their environments than people, churches, denominations, or businesses. Any cursory scan of certain Christian magazines demonstrates one aspect of this dynamic. Pages are filled and subdivided with advertisements from institutions of Christian higher learning seeking to differentiate themselves from all other such institutions with similar aims while at the same time assuring students that all the basics will be covered. In their uniformity of aim, they have become virtually indistinguishable.

Chapter 3 Making Sense of My Story

1. Richard Rohr, "Holy Fools: Ushers of the Next Generation of the Church," *Sojourners*, July 1994, http://www.sojo.net/index.cfm?action=magazine.article&issue=soj9407&article=940711.

2. Thomas Merton, *The Seven Storey Mountain* (New York: Harcourt Brace, 1976), 129–30.

3. Parker Palmer, *Let Your Life Speak* (San Francisco: Jossey Bass, 2000), 4.

4. Stanley J. Grenz and John R. Franke, *Beyond Foundationalism: Shaping Theology in a Postmodern Context* (Louisville: Westminster John Knox, 2001).

Chapter 4 A Cautionary Leadership Parable

1. Margaret J. Wheatley, *Finding Our Way: Leadership for an Uncertain Time* (San Francisco: Berrett Koehler, 2005), 28.

Chapter 5 Being There

1. Marshall McLuhan and Quentin Fiore, *The Medium Is the Massage* (Corte Madera, CA: Gingko, 2001), 68.

2. Walter Truett Anderson, *The Truth about the Truth* (New York: Tarcher Putnam, 1995), 7–8.

3. N. T. Wright, *The Challenge of Jesus* (Downers Grove, IL: InterVarsity, 1999), 152.

4. Richard Foster, *Celebration of Discipline: The Path to Spiritual Growth* (San Francisco: Harper & Row, 1978). Also, Richard Foster and James Bryan Smith, eds., *Devotional Classics: Selected Readings for Individuals and Groups* (San Francisco: HarperSanFrancisco, 1993).

5. Wade Bradshaw, "Reaching the Postmodern Generation," *Covenant Theological Seminary Online Resources*, 2003, http://www.covenantseminary.edu/resource/Bradshaw_ReachingThe.pdf.

6. Ibid.

7. Shane Hipps, *The Hidden Power of Electronic Culture* (Grand Rapids: Zondervan, 2005), 48.

8. Ibid., 49.

9. Ibid.

10. Ibid., 51.

11. Stanley Hauerwas, *Unleashing the Scripture: Freeing the Bible from Captivity to America* (Nashville: Abingdon, 1993), 15.

12. A. W. Tozer, *The Pursuit of God* (Camp Hill: Christian Publications, 1982), 9 (emphasis added).

13. Neil Postman, *Amusing Ourselves to Death: Public Discourse in the Age of Show Business* (New York: Penguin, 1985), 8.

14. Ibid., 9–10.

15. Hipps, *Hidden Power of Electronic Culture*, 72.

16. Josh McDowell, *Evidence That Demands a Verdict: Historical Evidences for the Christian Faith* (Nashville: Thomas Nelson, 1993).

17. Daniel Pink, "Revenge of the Right Brain," *Wired*, February 2005, http://www.wired.com/wired/archive/13.02/brain.html, an article adapted from Daniel H. Pink, *A Whole New Mind: Moving from the Information Age to the Conceptual Age* (New York: Riverhead Books, 2005). The revised subtitle for the 2006 edition aptly reads *Why Right-Brainers Will Rule the Future*.

18. Ibid.

19. Daniel Pink, *A Whole New Mind*, 18.

20. Ibid., 21.

21. Shel Silverstein, *The Giving Tree* (New York: Harper & Row, 1964).

22. Louis Markos, "Myth Matters," *Christianity Today*, April 23, 2001, http://www.ctlibrary.com/ct/2001/april23/1.32.html.

23. Esther de Waal, *Every Earthly Blessing: Celebrating a Spirituality of Creation* (Ann Arbor, MI: Servant, 1991), 13, emphasis added.

24. George G. Hunter III, *The Celtic Way of Evangelism: How Christianity Can Reach the West . . . Again* (Nashville: Abingdon, 2000), 72.

25. Stanley Hauerwas and William H. Willimon, *Resident Aliens* (Nashville: Abingdon, 1989), 18.

26. Ibid., 17–18.

27. Ibid., 44–45.

28. Ibid., 45.

29. Ibid.

30. Tim Stafford, "God's Missionary to Us," *Christianity Today*, December 9, 1996, http://www.ctlibrary.com/ct/1996/december9/6te24a.html.

31. Stanley Hauerwas, quoted in Peter Steinfels, obituary for Notre Dame theologian John H. Yoder, *New York Times*, January 7, 1998, accessed from http://theology.nd.edu/people/research/yoder-john/index.shtml.

Chapter 6 Being Here and There

1. Blaise Pascal, *Pensées* (New York: Penguin, 1995), 54–55.

2. Rudolf Otto, *The Idea of the Holy* (London: Oxford, 1958), 26.

3. C. S. Lewis, *Mere Christianity* (New York: Touchstone, 1980), 136.

4. Hauerwas and Willimon, *Resident Aliens*, 72.

5. Dietrich Bonhoeffer, *Life Together* (San Francisco: Harper, 1954), 26–27.

6. Hauerwas and Willimon, *Resident Aliens*, 21 (emphasis added).

7. Brian J. Walsh and Sylvia C. Keesmaat, *Colossians Remixed* (Downers Grove, IL: InterVarsity, 2004), 133–34.

8. Adapted from Tim Keel, "Naked in the Pulpit," *Leadership* (Winter 2005): 79. This article first appeared in the Winter 2005 issue of *Leadership*.

9. Ibid., 80.

10. Otto, *The Idea of the Holy*, 6 (emphasis added).

11. Ibid.

12. Ibid., 31.

13. Chris Carter, "The X-Files Undercover: Chris Carter," http://www.foxhome.com/trustno1/low/behind/b2main.html.

14. Chaim Potok, *The Book of Lights* (New York: Fawcett Crest, 1981), 25, 27.

15. Daniel B. Clendenin, *Eastern Orthodox Christianity: A Western Perspective* (Grand Rapids: Baker, 2003), 55–56.

16. Ibid., 77–78.

Chapter 7 Being Here, There, and Everywhere

1. H. L. Mencken, "The Divine Afflatus," *New York Evening Mail*, November 16, 1917.

2. Wendell Berry, *Life Is a Miracle* (Washington, DC: Counterpoint, 2000), 53–55.

3. Richard Florida, *The Rise of the Creative Class* (New York: Basic, 2002), 59.

4. Ibid., 60.

5. Ibid., 62–65.

6. Ibid., 65.

7. Ibid., 22.

8. James Surowiecki, *The Wisdom of Crowds* (New York: Anchor, 2005), xiv–xv.

9. Steven Johnson, *Emergence* (New York: Touchstone, 2001), 74.

10. Florida, *The Rise of the Creative Class*, 30.

11. Ibid., 33.

12. Ibid., 35.

13. Alan Roxburgh, *The Sky Is Falling!?! Leaders Lost in Transition* (Eagle, ID: ACI, 2005), 145.

Chapter 8 A Modest Proposal

1. Miroslav Volf and Dorothy C. Bass, eds., *Practicing Theology* (Grand Rapids: Eerdmans, 2002), 247.

2. Peter M. Senge, *The Fifth Discipline* (New York: Currency Doubleday, 1990), 11.

3. Jason Byassee, "RE: Emergent," June 2006, personal email.

4. Thomas Merton, *The Sign of Jonas* (New York: Harcourt Brace Jovanovich, 1981), 86–87.

5. Ibid.

Chapter 9 Opening Up and Leaning Forward

1. Walter Brueggemann, *Prophetic Imagination* (Minneapolis: Fortress, 2001), 14.

2. Leonard Sweet, *SoulTsunami: Sink or Swim in New Millennium Culture* (Grand Rapids: Zondervan, 1999), quote accessed at http://www.leonardsweet.com/includes/ShowSweetenedReviews.asp?articleID=98.

Chapter 10 Reckoning with Intuition

1. Carlo Carretto, *The God Who Comes* (New York: Orbis, 1976), 46–48.

2. Frederick Buechner, *Now and Then* (San Francisco: Harper, 1983), 87.

3. Oswald Chambers, *My Utmost for His Highest* (Westwood: Barbour, 1963), 155.

4. Carretto, *The God Who Comes*, 15.

5. Gavin de Becker, *The Gift of Fear* (New York: Dell, 1997), 12.

6. Ibid., 13.

7. Malcolm Gladwell, *Blink: The Power of Thinking Without Thinking* (New York: Little, Brown, 2005), 52.

8. Henri Nouwen, *The Wounded Healer* (New York: Image, 1972), 37–38.

9. Thomas Merton, *The Wisdom of the Desert* (Boston: Shambhala, 1960), 33.

Tim Keel is the founding pastor of Jacob's Well, a growing church in Kansas City, Missouri. He is married to Mimi, and together they have three children: Mabry, Annelise, and Blaise. Tim received a BFA in design from the University of Kansas and an MDiv from Denver Seminary. An avid learner, Tim loves reading, exploring, writing, and teaching. He is passionate about creating spaces for people to connect to God, themselves, others, and the surrounding world. Tim also serves on the board of directors for Emergent Village.

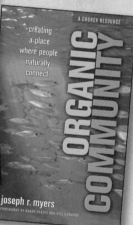